Additional Praise for *Running with Scissors*

"Burroughs has memorialized his bizarre childhood, showing off a dark wit that often rivals that of David Sedaris—while telling a true story that would make even Sedaris cringe."

—*New York*

"Screamingly funny . . . In the end, the book celebrates Burroughs's resilient, upbeat spirit, which helps him surmount one of the weirder childhoods on record."

—Deirdre Donahue, *USA Today*

"[*Running with Scissors*] will transport you."

—*Vogue*

"Irreverent, scurrilous, profane, licentious, horrific, and vile. It'll warp your mind, upset the neighbors, and lower your standing in the community. In other words, it's funny as hell."

—*Elle* (Nonfiction Book of the Year)

"Written with humor and clear affection for its oddball characters, *Running with Scissors* is a story of shocking discovery and unlikely survival."

—*The Onion*

"*Running with Scissors* is Dave Peltzer with a whoopee cushion attached. . . . You're just thankful to read a memoir that's genuinely memorable, not mawkish."

—*The Observer* (London)

"*Running with Scissors* is a story so strange it could never be fiction. . . . A huge critical and commercial success . . . deftly written, smart, and funny."

—*GQ* (U.K.)

"A lasting treasure, a gorgeously written true-life story destined to be cherished and quoted long after its last page is read. . . . Bravely stands as a life-affirming survival guide for all the misfits of the world."

—*The Tampa Tribune*

"It's gross, it's shocking, and its humor is blacker than a thousand midnights. . . . But this hilarious, provocative, and oddly touching book draws you into a bizarre world and keeps you rooting for its unusual narrator to survive, thrive, and break free."

—*The Hartford Courant*

"Brutal, disturbing, and often wildly funny . . . a stirring and stunning testament to a boy's strength in an environment of unfathomable heartache and dysfunction."

—*Minneapolis Star-Tribune*

"A surreal and entertaining trip through a young life most readers will thank God wasn't theirs . . . Burroughs never lets his readers forget that stuck in the middle of all the madness is a confused boy."

—*The Plain Dealer* (Cleveland)

"Bound to please fans of dark humor . . . Burroughs's account, full of frightening and hilarious images, is an entertaining, moving tale of an unconventional 1980s coming-of-age. It could be the one book you remember reading this summer."

—*Fort Worth Star-Telegram*

"The most enthralling memoir since A *Heartbreaking Work of Staggering Genius*."

—BN.com (Barnes & Noble)

Also by Augusten Burroughs

Sellevision

Dry

Magical Thinking

Possible Side Effects

RUNNING WITH SCISSORS

A MEMOIR

Augusten Burroughs

Picador
St. Martin's Press
New York

For
Dennis Pilsits

www.picadorusa.com

Picador® is a U.S. registered trademark and is used by St. Martin's Press under license from Pan Books Limited.

For information on Picador Reading Group Guides,
as well as ordering, please contact Picador.
Phone: 646-307-5629
Fax: 212-253-9627
E-mail: readinggroupguides@picadorusa.com

Library of Congress Cataloging-in-Publication Data

Burroughs, Augusten.
    Running with scissors : a memoir / Augusten Burroughs.
        p. cm.
    ISBN-13: 978-0-312-42541-8
    ISBN-10: 0-312-42541-4
    1. Burroughs, Augusten—Childhood and youth. 2. Burroughs, Augusten—
Homes and haunts—Massachusetts—Amherst. 3. Novelists, American—20th
century—Biography. 4. Amherst (Mass.)—Social life and customs. I.Title.

PS3552.U745 Z477 2002
813'.6—dc21
                                                                    2001058857

First published in the United States by St. Martin's Press

First Picador Edition: June 2003

Second Picador Edition: September 2006

10 9 8 7 6 5 4 3 2 1

AUTHOR'S NOTE

ACKNOWLEDGMENTS

GRATITUDE DOESN'T BEGIN TO DESCRIBE IT: JENNIFER EN-
derlin, Christopher Schelling, John Murphy, Gregg Sullivan,
Kim Cardascia, Michael Storrings, and everyone at St. Martin's Press. Thank you: Lawrence David, Suzanne Finnamore,
Robert Rodi, Bret Easton Ellis, Jon Pepoon, Lee Lodes, Jeff
Soares, Kevin Weidenbacher, Lynda Pearson, Lona Walburn,
Lori Greenberg, John DePretis, and Sheila Cobb. I would also
like to express my appreciation to my mother and father for,
no matter how inadvertently, giving me such a memorable
childhood. Additionally, I would like to thank each and every
member of a certain family for taking me into their home and
accepting me as one of their own. Most of all, I would like to
thank my brother for demonstrating, by example, the impor-
tance of being wholly unique.

Look for the ridiculous in everything
and you will find it.

—Jules Renard, 1890

RUNNING WITH SCISSORS

SOMETHING ISN'T RIGHT

MY MOTHER IS STANDING IN FRONT OF THE BATHROOM MIR-
ror smelling polished and ready; like Jean Naté, Dippity Do
and the waxy sweetness of lipstick. Her white, handgun-
shaped blow-dryer is lying on top of the wicker clothes hamper, ticking as it cools. She stands back and smoothes her
hands down the front of her swirling, psychedelic Pucci dress,
biting the inside of her cheek.

"Damn it," she says, "something isn't right."

Yesterday she went to the fancy Chopping Block salon in
Amherst with its bubble skylights and ficus trees in chrome
planters. Sebastian gave her a shag.

"That hateful Jane Fonda," she says, fluffing her dark brown
hair at the crown. "She makes it look so easy." She pinches
her sideburns into points that accentuate her cheekbones.

People have always said she looks like a young Lauren Bacall, especially in the eyes.

I can't stop staring at her feet, which she has slipped into treacherously tall red patent-leather pumps. Because she normally lives in sandals, it's like she's borrowed some other lady's feet. Maybe her friend Lydia's feet. Lydia has teased black hair, boyfriends and an above-ground pool. She wears high heels all the time, even when she's just sitting out back by the pool in her white bikini, smoking menthol cigarettes and talking on her olive-green Princess telephone. My mother only wears fancy shoes when she's going out, so I've come to associate them with a feeling of abandonment and dread.

I don't want her to go. My umbilical cord is still attached and she's pulling at it. I feel panicky.

I'm standing in the bathroom next to her because I need to be with her for as long as I can. Maybe she is going to Hartford, Connecticut. Or Bradley Field International Airport. I love the airport, the smell of jet fuel, flying south to visit my grandparents.

I love to fly.

When I grow up, I want to be the one who opens those cabinets above the seats, who gets to go into the small kitchen where everything fits together like a shiny silver puzzle. Plus, I like uniforms and I would get to wear one, along with a white shirt and a tie, even a tie-tack in the shape of airplane wings. I would get to serve peanuts in small foil packets and offer people small plastic cups of soda. "Would you like the whole can?" I would say. I love flying south to visit my grandparents and I've already memorized almost everything these flight attendants say. "Please make sure that you have extinguished all smoking materials and that your tray table is in its upright and locked position." I wish I had a tray table in my bedroom and I wish I smoked, just so I could extinguish my smoking materials.

"Okay, I see what's the matter," my mother says. She turns to me and smiles. "Augusten, hand me that box, would you?"

Her long, frosted beige nail points to the box of Kotex maxi pads on the floor next to the toilet bowl. I grab the box and hand it to her.

She takes two pads from the box and sets it on the floor at her feet. I notice that the box is reflected in the side of her shoe, like a small TV. Carefully, she peels the paper strip off the back of one of the pads and slides it through the neck of her dress, placing it on top of her left shoulder. She smoothes the silk over the pad and puts another one on the right side. She stands back.

"What do you think of that!" she says. She is delighted with herself. It's as if she has drawn a picture and placed it on her own internal refrigerator door.

"Neat," I say.

"You have a very creative mother," she says. "Instant shoulder pads."

The blow-dryer continues to tick like a clock, counting down the seconds. Hot things do that. Sometimes when my father or mother comes home, I will go down and stand near the hood of the car to listen to it tick, moving my face in close to feel the heat.

"Are you coming upstairs with me?" she says. She takes her cigarette from the clamshell ashtray on the back of the toilet. My mother loves frozen baked stuffed clams, and she saves the shells to use as ashtrays, stashing them around the house.

I am fixated on the dryer. The vent holes on the side have

hairs stuck in them, small hairs and white lint. What is lint? How does it find hair dryers and navels? "I'm coming."

"Turn off the light," she says as she walks away, creating a small *whoosh* that smells sweet and chemical. It makes me sad because it's the smell she makes when she's leaving.

"Okay," I say. The orange light from the dehumidifier that sits next to the wicker laundry hamper is looking at me, and I look back at it. Normally it would terrify me, but because my mother is here, it is okay. Except she is walking fast, has already walked halfway across the family room floor, is almost at the fireplace, will be turning around the corner and heading up the stairs and then I will be alone in the dark bathroom with the dehumidifier eye, so I run. I run after her, certain that something is following me, chasing me, just about to catch me. I run past my mother, running up the stairs, using my legs and my hands, charging ahead on all fours. I make it to the top and look down at her.

She climbs the stairs slowly, deliberately, reminding me of an actress on the way to the stage to accept her Academy Award. Her eyes are trained on me, her smile all mine. "You run up those stairs just like Cream."

Cream is our dog and we both love her. She is not my father's dog or my older brother's. She's most of all not my older brother's since he's sixteen, seven years older than I, and he lives with roommates in Sunderland, a few miles away. He dropped out of high school because he said he was too smart to go and he hates our parents and he says he can't stand to be here and they say they can't control him, that he's "out of control" and so I almost never see him. So Cream doesn't belong to him *at all*. She is mine and my mother's. She loves us most and we love her. We share her. I am just like Cream, the golden retriever my mother loves.

I smile back at her.

I don't want her to leave.

Cream is sleeping by the door. She knows my mother is leaving and she doesn't want her to go, either. Sometimes, I wrap aluminum foil around Cream's middle, around her legs and her tail and then I walk her through the house on a leash. I like it when she's shiny, like a star, like a guest on the *Donnie and Marie Show*.

Cream opens her eyes and watches my mother, her ears twitching, then she closes her eyes again and exhales heavily. She's seven, but in dog years that makes her forty-nine. Cream is an old lady dog, so she's tired and just wants to sleep.

In the kitchen my mother takes her keys off the table and throws them into her leather bag. I love her bag. Inside are papers and her wallet and cigarettes and at the bottom, where she never looks, there is loose change, loose mints, specs of tobacco from her cigarettes. Sometimes I bring the bag to my face, open it and inhale as deeply as I can.

"You'll be long asleep by the time I come home," she tells me. "So good night and I'll see you in the morning."

"Where are you going?" I ask her for the zillionth time.

"I'm going to give a reading in Northampton," she tells me. "It's a poetry reading at the Broadside Bookstore."

My mother is a star. She is just like that lady on TV, Maude. She yells like Maude, she wears wildly colored gowns and long crocheted vests like Maude. She is just like Maude except my mother doesn't have all those chins under her chins, all those loose expressions hanging off her face. My mother cackles when Maude is on. "I love Maude," she says. My mother is a star like Maude.

"Will you sign autographs?"

She laughs. "I may sign some books."

My mother is from Cairo, Georgia. This makes everything she says sound like it went through a curling iron. Other people sound flat to my ear; their words just hang in the air. But when my mother says something, the ends curl.

Where is my father?

"Where is your father?" my mother says, checking her watch. It's a Timex, silver with a black leather strap. The face is small and round. There is no date. It ticks so loud that if the house is quiet, you can hear it.

The house is quiet. I can hear the ticking of my mother's watch.

Outside, the trees are dark and tall, they lean in toward the house, I imagine because the house is bright inside and the trees crave the light, like bugs.

We live in the woods, in a glass house surrounded by trees; tall pine trees, birch trees, ironwoods.

The deck extends from the house into the trees. You can stand on it and reach and you might be able to pull a leaf off a tree, or a sprig of pine.

My mother is pacing. She is walking through the living room, behind the sofa to look out the large sliding glass door down to the driveway; she is walking around the dining-room table. She straightens the cubed glass salt and pepper shakers. She is walking through the kitchen and out the other door of the kitchen. Our house is very open. The ceilings are very high. There is plenty of room here. "I need high ceilings," my

mother always says. She says this now. "I need high ceilings."
She looks up.

There is the sound of gravel crackling beneath tires. Then,
lights on the wall, spreading to the ceiling, sliding through
the room like a living thing.

"Finally," my mother says.

My father is home.

He will come inside the house, pour himself a drink and
then go downstairs and watch TV in the dark.

I will have the upstairs to myself. All the windows and the
walls and the entire fireplace which cuts straight through the
center of the house, both floors; I will have the ice maker in
the freezer, the hexagonal espresso pot my mother uses for
guests, the black deck, the stereo speakers; all of this contained in so much tall space. I will have it all.

I will walk around and turn lights on and off, on and off.
There is a panel of switches on the wall before the hall opens
up into two huge, tall rooms. I will switch the spotlights on
in the living room, illuminating the fireplace, the sofa. I will
switch the light off and turn on the spotlights in the hallway;
over the front of the door. I will run from the wall and stand
in the spotlight. I will bathe in the light like a star and I will
say, "Thank you for coming tonight to my poetry reading."

I will be wearing the dress my mother didn't wear. It is
long, black and 100 percent polyester, my favorite fabric because it flows. I will wear her dress and her shoes and I will
be her.

With the spotlights aimed right at me, I will clear my
throat and read a poem from her book. I will read it with her
distinctive and refined Southern inflection.

I will turn off all the lights in the house and go into my bedroom, close the door. My bedroom is deep blue. Bookshelves are attached to the wall with brackets on either side of my window; the shelves themselves are lined with aluminum foil. I like things shiny.

My shiny bookshelves are lined with treasures. Empty cans, their labels removed, their ribbed steel skins polished with silver polish. I wish they were gold. I have rings there, rings from our trip to Mexico when I was five. Also on the shelves: pictures of jewelry cut from magazines, glued to cardboard and propped upright; one of the good spoons from the sterling silver my grandmother sent my parents when they were married; silver my mother hates ("God-awful tacky") and a small collection of nickels, dimes and quarters, each of which has been boiled and polished with silver polish while watching *Donnie and Marie* or *Tony Orlando and Dawn*.

I love shiny things, I love stars. Someday, I want to be a star, like my mother, like Maude.

The sliding doors to my closet are covered with mirror squares I bought with my allowance. The mirrors have veins of gold streaking through them. I stuck them to the doors myself.

I will aim my desk lamp into the center of the room and stand in its light, looking at myself in the mirror. "Hand me that box," I will say to my reflection. "Something isn't right here."

LITTLE BOY BLUE NAVY BLAZER

My FONDNESS FOR FORMAL WEAR CAN BE TRACED TO THE womb. While pregnant with me, my mother blasted opera on her record player while she sat at the kitchen table addressing SASEs to *The New Yorker*. Somehow, on the deepest, most base genetic level, I understood that the massively intense music I heard through her flesh was being sung by fat people dressed in cummerbunds and enormous sequined gowns.

When I was ten, my favorite outfit was a navy blazer, a white shirt and a red clip-on tie. I felt I looked important. Like a young king who had ascended the throne because his mother had been beheaded.

I flatly refused to go to school if my hair was not perfect, if the light didn't fall across it in a smooth, blond sheet. I wanted my hair to look exactly like the mannequin boys' at

Ann August, where my mother shopped. One stray flyaway was enough to send the hairbrush into the mirror and me running for my room in tears.

And if there was lint on my outfit that my mother couldn't remove with masking tape, that was a better reason to stay home than strep throat. In fact, the only day of the year I actually liked going to school was the day the school photo was taken. I loved that the photographer gave us combs as parting gifts, like on a game show.

Throughout my childhood, while all the other kids were starting fights, playing ball and getting dirty, I was in my bedroom polishing the gold-tone mood rings I made my mother buy me at Kmart and listening to Barry Manilow, Tony Orlando and Dawn and, inexplicably, Odetta. I preferred *albums* to the more modern *eight tracks*. Albums came with sleeves which reminded me of clean underwear. Plus, the pictures were bigger, making it easier to see each follicle of Tony Orlando's shiny arm hair.

I would have been an excellent member of the Brady Bunch. I would have been Shaun, the well-behaved blond boy who caused no trouble and helped Alice in the kitchen, then trimmed the split ends off Marcia's hair. I would have not only washed Tiger, but then conditioned his fur. And I would have cautioned Jan against that tacky bracelet that caused the girls to lose the house-of-cards-building contest.

My mother chain-smoked and wrote confessional poetry around the clock, taking breaks during the day to call her friends and read drafts of her latest poem. Occasionally she would ask for my opinion.

"Augusten, I've been working on what I believe could be the poem that finally makes it into *The New Yorker*. I believe it could make me a very famous woman. Would you like to hear it?"

I turned away from the mirror on my closet door and set the hairbrush on my desk. I loved *The New Yorker* because it featured cartoons and ads. Maybe my mother would get her poem published right next to an ad for a Mercury Grand Marquis! "Read it, read it, read it," I bounced.

She led me into her study, took a seat at her desk and turned off her white Olympia typewriter. Then she quickly checked the cap on her bottle of Wite-Out before clearing her throat and lighting a More cigarette. I sat on the twin bed she had converted into a sofa with throw pillows and an Indian bedspread.

"Ready?" she asked

"Okay."

She crossed her legs, resting the side of her wrist on her knee as she leaned forward and read from the page. "Childhood is over. My youth. And bonds with people I have loved are broken now. My grief ascends into the clouds. And those tears that fall from the sky build the land anew, even the dead climb from their graves to walk with me and sing. And I . . ."

She read for many pages, her voice perfectly modulated. She practiced reading her poems out loud into a microphone that she kept in the corner of the room on a stand. Sometimes, when she was visiting her friend Lydia or in the living room trimming her spider plants, I would borrow the microphone and stuff it down the front of my pants, examining myself from every angle in the mirror.

When she was finished reading her poem, she looked up

at me and said, "Okay, now I need your honest reaction. Did it feel powerful to you? Emotionally charged?"

I knew that the only correct answer to this question was, "Wow. That really does seem like something you'd read in *The New Yorker*."

She laughed, pleased. "Really? Do you really think so? *The New Yorker* is very selective. They don't publish just anyone." She stood and began to pace in front of her desk.

"No, I really think they would publish this. All the stuff about your mother pushing you backwards into the heart-shaped goldfish pond in the backyard, the thing with your paralyzed sister, that was great."

She lit another cigarette and inhaled deeply. "Well, we'll see. I just got a rejection letter from *The Virginia Quarterly*. So that worries me. Of course, if *The New Yorker* did accept this poem, your grandmother would see it. I can't imagine what she would say. But I can't let her reaction stop me from publishing." Then she stopped pacing, placed one hand on her hip and brought the other one holding the cigarette to her lips. "You know, Augusten. Your mother was meant to be a *very* famous woman."

"I know," I said. The idea that someday we might have our own stretch limousine parked in the driveway instead of that awful brown Dodge Aspen station wagon was so thrilling that I almost couldn't stop myself from screaming. "You *will* be famous," I told her. "I just know it." I also knew I wanted tinted windows and a mini-bar in the back.

My father was otherwise occupied in his role of highly functional alcoholic professor of mathematics at the University of

Massachusetts. He had psoriasis that covered his entire body and gave him the appearance of a dried mackerel that could stand upright and wear tweed. And he had the loving, affectionate and outgoing personality of petrified wood.

"Can we play checkers," I whined, while he sat at the kitchen table grading papers and drinking vodka from a tumbler.

"No, son. I've got too much work to do."

"Later can we play checkers?"

My father continued to scan the page with his red pen, making a note in the margin. "No, son. I told you, I've got a lot of work to do and later I'll be tired. You go out and play with the dog."

"But I'm sick of the dog. All she wants to do is sleep. Can't you play *one game?*"

Finally he looked at me. "No, son, I can't. I've got a lot of work to do, I'm tired, and my knee is acting up."

My father had a bad knee. Arthritis caused it to swell, so he would have to go to his doctor and have it drained with a needle. He limped and wore a constant pained expression on his face. "I wish I could just sit in a wheelchair," he used to say. "It would be so much easier to get around."

The one activity my father and I *did* do together was take the garbage to the dump. "Augusten," he called from downstairs in the basement. "If you load the car up, I'll take you for a ride to the dump."

I slipped on a mood ring and ran downstairs to the basement. He was wearing a red-and-black checkered field coat, hoisting two green plastic bags over his shoulders as he winced in pain. "Make sure the top is closed," he warned. "You don't want that bag breaking open and spilling garbage all over the floor. That would just be a nightmare to clean up."

I dragged one of the bags across the floor toward the door.

"Jesus, son. Now, don't drag that bag. You'll tear the bottom and we'll have garbage all over the place. I just warned you about that."

"You said check the tops," I said.

"Yes, but it should go without saying that you can't drag a garbage bag across the floor."

He was wrong. I'd seen the commercials for Hefty garbage bags on TV. "They won't break," I corrected him, dragging.

"Now, Augusten. You've got to *carry* that bag. If you can't behave and carry that bag, I won't let you come to the dump."

I sighed deeply and carried the bag outside to the Aspen, then returned to the basement for another. We tended to let garbage collect for weeks, so there were always at least twenty bags.

When the car was filled, I squeezed into the front seat between my father and one of the trash bags. The sour smell of old milk cartons, egg shells and emptied ashtrays filled me with pleasure. My father, too, enjoyed the aroma. "I rather like that smell," he commented as we made the six-mile trip to the public dump. "I wouldn't mind living next to a landfill one bit."

At the dump, my father and I opened the rear hatch of the station wagon and all of the doors. Perched on the ledge overlooking the pit where we threw the bags, the car looked poised for flight. Its doors were like wings and the grille in front seemed to be smiling. Here, I was free to pull out a bag, drag it across the ground and then hurl it out.

Afterward, we drove past the gray cinder block recycling building where people left the remains of their broken baby strollers, rusty stoves and unwanted dollhouses.

"Please, can I take it home?" I whined upon seeing a chrome coffee table with a chipped, smoked-glass top.

"No, we're not taking any of that stuff home. You don't know where any of this garbage has been."

"But it's still good." I knew I could hide the chip by fanning a display of magazines on the surface, like in a doctor's office. And it certainly wouldn't be dirty after I polished it with Windex for three hours.

"No, son. Now stop touching that filthy thing and get back in the car. And don't touch your face now that you've got those coffee table germs all over your fingers."

My mood ring went black. "Why can't I have it? *Why?*"

My father sighed, exasperated. "I told you," he said through clenched teeth, "we don't know who that dirty thing belonged to. We just finished taking trash *out* of the house. We don't need to be bringing more trash *in*."

I sat pressed against the unlocked door, miserable. It was my secret hope that the door would fly open on the highway and I would tumble from the car, rolling onto the highway where I would be crushed beneath the tires of the Barstow onion truck behind us. Then my father would be sorry he wouldn't let me have the coffee table.

Unfortunately, my parents loathed each other and the life they had built together. Because I was the product of their genetic fusion, well, it's not surprising I liked to boil my change on the stove and then shine it with metal polish.

"You infantile tyrant," my mother shouted from her position on the sofa, legs folded up beneath her. "You goddamn bastard. You'd like nothing more than to see me slit my wrists." She absently twisted the tassel on her long crocheted vest.

This was Cream's cue and she tucked her tail between her legs and slipped from the room, heading downstairs to sleep next to the boiler.

My father's face grew red as he added a splash of tonic water to his glass. "Deirdre, will you just settle down. You're hysterical, just hysterical." Because he was a professor, he was in the habit of repeating himself.

She stood up from the sofa and walked slowly across the white shag carpeting, as if finding her mark on a soundstage. "I'm hysterical?" she asked in a smooth, low voice. "You think *this* is hysterical?" She laughed theatrically, throwing her head back. "Oh, you poor bastard. You lousy excuse for a man." She stood next to him, leaning her back against the teak bookcase. "You're so repressed you mistake creative passion for hysterics. And don't you see? This is how you're killing me." She closed her eyes and made her Edith Piaf face.

My father moved away from her. He brought the glass to his lips and took a deep swallow from his drink. Because he'd been drinking all evening, his words were slightly blurry. "Nobody's trying to kill you, Deirdre. You're killing yourself."

"I wish you'd rot in hell," she spat. "I regret the day I ever married you."

While they were fighting, I was sitting at the dining-room table fastening and unfastening the lobster claw clasp on the gold chain my mother had bought me in Amherst. I worried constantly that it would fall from my neck. And the only thing that reassured me was to test its dependability over and over again. I glanced up and said, "Can't you two *stop* fighting? You always fight and I hate it."

"This is between me and your father," my mother said coldly.

"*No it's not,*" I shouted with surprising volume. "It's not just between you because I'm here too. And I can't stand it. All you ever do is scream at each other. Can't you just leave each other alone? Can't you try?"

My mother replied, "Your father is the one who is making things difficult for us."

Eventually, the fight moved next door to the kitchen, providing them with better lighting as well as potential weapons.

"Look at your damn face," my mother said. "You've got the face of a man twice your age. Thirty-seven years old going on eighty."

My father was very drunk by now and the only way he could imagine restoring silence to the house was to stop my mother from breathing.

"Get your damn hands *off* of me," my mother screamed, struggling against my father's hands, which had found their way around her neck.

"Shut the hell up, you bitch." His teeth were clenched.

I had followed them into the kitchen, and was standing in the doorway in my Snoopy pajamas. "Stop!" I screamed. "Stop this!"

In one motion, my mother shoved my drunk father, sending him reeling backward against the kitchen counter. His head hit the dishwasher on the way down and when he made contact with the kitchen floor, he didn't move. A small pool of blood began to form under his ear and I was sure he was dead.

"He's not moving," I said, moving closer.

"This spineless bastard is only playing another one of his pitiful games." She nudged his bad knee with her red toe. "Get up, Norman. You're frightening Augusten. Enough of your pranks."

My father eventually sat up, leaning his head back against the dishwasher.

With disgust, my mother tore a Bounty paper towel from the roll and handed it to him. "I should just let you bleed to death for terrifying our son like that."

He pressed it against the side of his face to absorb the blood.

Seeing that my father was still alive, I was now worried about my mother. "*Please* don't hurt her," I said. "*Please* don't kill her." The problem was, my father's unemotional nature scared me. There was a difference between the calm expression of the man on a jar of Taster's Choice coffee and the blank expression my father wore. I was afraid he was, like my mother said, Bottled with rage, ready to snap.

Again, I leaned forward. "*Please don't kill her.*"

"Your father isn't going to kill me," my mother said, switching on the front burner of the stove, pulling a More from her pack, and leaning over to light it on the heating coil. "He'd rather suffocate me with his horribly oppressive manipulation and then wait for me to cut my own throat."

"Will you please just shut the hell up, Deirdre?" my father said, weary and drunk.

My mother smiled down at him, blowing smoke through her nostrils. "I will *please shut the hell up* the day you *please drop the hell dead.*"

I was seized with panic. "Are you going to cut your own throat?" I asked her.

She smiled and held out her arms. "No, of course not. That's just a figure of speech." She kissed the top of my head and scratched my back. "Now, it's nearly one in the morning; way past your bedtime. You need to go to sleep so you can be ready for school in the morning."

I walked off to my room, where I selected an outfit for school and carefully arranged it on hangers at the front of the closet. I would wear my favorite polyester tan pants and a blue shirt with the vest cleverly sewn on. If only I had a pair of platform shoes the outfit would be complete.

Still, knowing my clothes were ready gave me a sense of calm. I could *control* the sharpness of the crease in my double-knit slacks, even if I couldn't stop my mother from hurling the Christmas tree off the porch like she did one winter. I could polish my 14k gold-plated signet ring with a Q-tip until the gold plating wore off even if I couldn't stop my parents from throwing John Updike novels at each other's heads.

So I became consumed with making sure my jewelry was just as reflective as Donnie Osmond's and my hair was perfectly smooth, like plastic.

Besides clothing and jewelry, there were two other things I valued in life: medical doctors and celebrities. I valued them for their white jackets and stretch limousines. I knew for sure that I wanted to be either a doctor or a celebrity when I grew up. The ideal would have been to play a doctor on a TV show.

And this is where the fact that we lived in the woods surrounded by pine trees came in handy. Because in desperation, pine trees can become Panavision cameras. Their broken branches, boom mics. This allowed me to walk through the woods or down the dirt road we lived on, imagining that there was always a camera trained on my every move, zooming in close to capture my facial expression.

When I looked up at a bird in the sky, I wondered how the light was falling on my face and if that branch was catching it just right.

Mine was a delusional world filled with tall trees that held long lenses and followed me on dollies. A fallen branch in the woods was not a fallen branch; it was "my mark."

When I wasn't "on the set" throwing branches around with my bionic arm or doing a toothpaste commercial in front of a boulder, I was trying to trick my mother into taking me to the doctor.

By the time I was ten, I was having weekly allergy shots— eleven in each arm. I had persistent warts on my fingers that needed to be burned off and my throat was constantly sore due to the dust that I cupped into my hands and inhaled.

A visit to the doctor meant exposure to those crisp, clean white jackets and the glint of a silver stethoscope around the neck. I was also aware that doctors got to park where they wanted and speed without getting tickets, both of which seemed the height of privilege when President Carter had made us all drive forty miles an hour and live in the dark.

I had two doctors that I saw regularly. Dr. Lotier, who had long hairs sprouting from his nose and the backs of his hands, and a dignified Indian allergist named Dr. Nupal. Dr. Nupal drove a white Mercedes (I asked him) and smelled like freshly washed hands with subtle undertones of Aqua Velva.

Just thinking of my doctors filled me with soothing images of overhead fluorescent lighting, shiny new needles and shoes so polished they inspired in me a sense of awe unequalled by anything except the dazzling sets of the Academy Award shows.

And then there was Dr. Finch.

As the mood in my home changed from one of mere hatred to one of potential double homicide, my parents sought help from a psychiatrist. Dr. Finch looked exactly like Santa Claus. He had a shock of thick white hair, a full white beard and eyebrows that resembled toothbrush bristles. Instead of wearing a red suit trimmed with white fur, he wore brown polyester slacks and a short-sleeved button-down white shirt. He did, however, sometimes wear a Santa hat.

The first time I ever saw him he appeared at our house in the middle of the night, following an especially bad fight between my parents. As my mother hyperventilated on the sofa, smoking cigarette after cigarette, the doorbell rang. "Oh, thank God," she said, quickly getting up from the couch to answer the door.

He was carrying a balloon and there was a button on his jacket lapel that read, "World Father's Organization." He peered over my mother's shoulder and looked directly at me. "Hello there."

I moved back, unsure.

"Please, come in," my mother said, motioning him inside. "I've just been a frantic wreck waiting for you to get here."

The doctor said, "It's okay now, Deirdre." Then he reached in his pocket and handed me a button, identical to the one on his lapel. "Would you like one of these? As a gift?"

"Thanks," I said, taking the button and inspecting it.

Then he reached in his pocket again and withdrew a handful of balloons. "And these," he said.

"Okay," I said again. The colorful balloons seemed out of context, given my mother's mood, but I liked them anyway. I could blow them up, tie them into a bunch and then attach them to Cream's collar or tail.

The doctor turned to my mother. "Where's Norman?"

She bit the nail of her thumb, her brow creased with worry. She'd gnawed off all the polish and the nail itself was chewed down to the quick. "He's downstairs. Drunk."

"I see," he said, removing his heavy black coat and draping it over the chair in the front hall.

"I was afraid for my life tonight," she said. "I thought for sure he was going to kill me. That this would finally be the night."

Earlier in the evening, my parents had been screaming at each other. The screaming escalated until my father was chasing my mother through the house with a Danish fondue pot held high above his head.

My mother began to calm down now that the doctor was here. "Would you like a Sanka?" she offered.

He asked for a bologna sandwich with horseradish.

And then he looked at me and winked. "Don't worry about your parents, buckaroo. We'll get this all sorted out."

"I just pray to God that Norman doesn't snap. One of these days he's going to snap and kill us all," my mother said as she busied herself in the kitchen making a sandwich for the doctor.

"Enough," Finch said loudly. "That's not the way to talk around your son. You need to comfort him, not frighten him."

My mother said, "That's right, I know. I'm sorry. Augusten, I'm just very upset right now. The doctor and I need to speak." Then she turned to him and lowered her voice. "But I am worried, Doctor. I do believe our lives are in danger."

"May I have one of those?" he asked, pointing to a hot dog he glimpsed as my mother opened the refrigerator door to put away the lettuce.

She look puzzled. "Oh. Would you like a hot dog instead of the sandwich I just made?"

He reached into the refrigerator, sliding the raw Oscar Mayer wiener from the pack. He took a bite. "No, just like this. As an appetizer." He smiled, causing the white whiskers of his mustache to twitch as he chewed.

I liked him. And with his jolly, red-faced cheeks and his easy smile, he really did seem like Santa. Although it was difficult to imagine him being able to fit down a chimney, it was just as hard to imagine him wearing a white jacket. He certainly didn't seem like a real doctor, the kind of doctor I worshiped. He seemed like he should be in a department store letting kids pee on his lap and whisper brand-name bicycles in his ear.

As my mother saw more and more of Dr. Finch over the year, I needed to be reminded constantly that he was a real doctor. "An M.D. doctor?" I would ask my mother.

"*Yes*," she would say with exasperation, "*an M.D. doctor*. And as I've told you a hundred times, he earned his M.D. at Yale."

I'd even asked her how she found him, imagining her riffling through our outdated Yellow Pages or reading restroom stall walls. "Your own doctor, Dr. Lotier, referred me," was her tidy reply.

But still I was suspicious. Instead of being gloriously clinical and sanitized, his office was a hodgepodge of rooms on the top floor of an office building in Northampton. The waiting room had pale yellow paint on the walls that was peeling off in sheets, cracked rattan furniture, and an old gray metal file cabinet on top of which was a Mr. Coffee. There were posters of rainbows and balloons on the wall. A thick blanket of dust covered everything. Then there was a middle room that was used for storage of boxes and decade-old magazines. And then an even more inner room where the doctor saw his patients. You had to go through two doors, one right after the other, to get to that inner room. I liked these double doors and wished I had them in my room at home.

Like Santa, Dr. Finch gave me presents. It wasn't uncommon for him to hand me a glass paperweight etched with the name and logo of a prescription drug. Or a five-dollar bill that I could spend downstairs at the drugstore, which still had a soda fountain. And there was a certain glint in his eye that seemed to promise more, later. It was always as if he had one hand behind his back, something hidden up his sleeve.

Every Saturday, I rode in the brown Dodge Aspen with my parents to Northampton. We would sit in complete silence and my parents would chain-smoke the whole way. Occasionally my mother would comment that there was a smell like manure emanating from my father's ears. And sometimes he would tell her that she was a fucking bitch. Other than that, not a word was spoken.

They took turns with the doctor. First my father would go in. Then my mother. Then the two of them together. The entire process took all of Saturday and we would usually drive through McDonald's on the way home, my parents ordering nothing and me ordering two of everything and the two of them watching me eat and saying, "Don't choke, you're eating much too fast."

While they were in with Dr. Finch, I would sit on the rattan love seat and talk to the doctor's receptionist, Hope. She had high cheekbones that made her look like an Indian princess and incredibly thick, long, straight black hair that she sometimes wore pulled into a ponytail and secured with a leather butterfly barrette. She favored trim black wool slacks and knit tops, even in the summer. She always had on some interesting piece of jewelry—an elephant pin, ladybug earrings, a silver bracelet made of two dogs chasing each other's tails.

"Do you have a white cap?" I asked her.

She smiled. "What do you mean, a white cap? You mean like a sailor's cap?"

"No," I said. "I mean like a regular doctor's office receptionist. At the hospital I go to in Springfield for shots, they all wear white caps like the nurses."

Hope laughed. "Oh, God. I'm not that kind of receptionist. We're a lot more casual here, can't you tell?" She reached across her desk and straightened the snow globe.

"Do you like working for him?" I asked. Maybe I could pry her for details.

"I love working for Dad."

"He's your father?"

"Didn't you know that?"

"No."

Hope got up from behind her desk and came to sit next to

me on the sofa. "Yeah, Dr. Finch is my father. That's why I work here. I wouldn't work for just any doctor."

I couldn't imagine working for my father. We could barely take care of the garbage together. "Do you have any brothers or sisters?"

Hope laughed again. "You could say that." Then she looked up, stuck out her left hand and began counting them off. "There's Kate, me, Anne, Jeff, Vickie and Natalie. We're Dad and Agnes's *biological* children. Plus Dad's adopted son, Neil Bookman. So that's seven of us."

Instantly, I was consumed with envy. "And you all live together?"

"Not quite. My sister Kate lives around the corner with her daughter and so does my sister Anne and her son. Jeff lives in Boston. Vickie lives with some friends. But Natalie is there a lot. I live there. Plus, we have a dog and a cat. And of course Mom and Dad. There's always someone over at Sixty-seven."

"What's Sixty-seven?"

"Sixty-seven Perry Street. That's where we live. You should come by sometime with your parents. You'd have a lot of fun there."

I had to admit, the idea of seeing a real doctor's house was nothing less than thrilling. I imagined walls hung with exotic and expensive tapestries, polished marble floors, columns that stretched for hundreds of feet. I saw water fountains out front with hedges trimmed into the shapes of zoo animals.

"Hey, do you want a Coke?" Hope asked.

"Okay."

Hope got her pocketbook from under her desk. She pulled out her wallet and handed me a five-dollar bill. "I'll buy them if you run downstairs and down the street to O'Brian's drug-store to get them. You can even get yourself a candy bar."

When I returned, Hope was sitting behind her desk, typing on a page she'd inserted into her black manual typewriter. "We've got to stay on top of these insurance forms," she said, "if we ever want to get paid. It's a lot of work running a doctor's office."

I felt guilty that I'd taken so much of her time, that I had been keeping her from doing her job. "I'm sorry," I said. "I didn't mean to bother you so much, asking you all these questions." I set the paper bag with the Cokes on her desk and handed her the change.

"Don't be crazy," she said. "You're not a bother. Jeepers, I'd much rather talk to you than fill out those dumb insurance forms." Then she pulled the paper from the carriage and set it on her desk. She reached into the bag for one of the Cokes and popped the top. "I can always do that stuff later."

The phone rang and Hope answered, using a voice so smooth and professional, you'd think she was wearing a white nurse's cap. "Dr. Finch's office," she said. She listened for a moment. "I'm sorry, the doctor is in with a patient right now. Shall I have him return your call?" She winked at me.

As we sat on the sofa drinking the Cokes, Hope asked me about my own family. "What's it like living at your house?"

"I don't know," I said. "I like to hang out in my room and do stuff there."

"I like your ring," she said, pointing to my pinkie.

"Thanks. It's from Mexico. It's real silver."

"It's very nice."

"Thanks."

"I have one almost just like that."

"You do?"

"Mmm hmm," she said. Then she showed me the ring on her left hand. "See?"

It was almost exactly like mine, except not very shiny. "You want me to polish it for you?"

"You could do that?"

"Sure."

She slid the ring off her finger and handed it to me. "Here you go then. You can bring it to me next time your parents come to see Dad."

I had only meant that I could polish it with my shirt. "You mean you want me to take it and polish it?"

"Well, sure."

"Okay." I slipped the ring into my front pocket.

Hope smiled at me. "I can't wait for it to be as new and shiny looking as yours."

As time went on, my parents' relationship became worse, not better. My father grew more hostile and remote, taking a particular liking to metallic objects with serrated edges. And my mother began to go crazy.

Not crazy in a *let's paint the kitchen bright red!* sort of way. But crazy in a *gas oven, toothpaste sandwich, I am God* sort of way. Gone were the days when she would stand on the deck lighting lemon-scented candles without then having to eat the wax.

Gone, too, were the once-a-week therapy sessions. My mother began seeing Dr. Finch nearly every day.

My parents' divorce was explosive. But as with all things that explode, a clean, flattened area was created. I could see the horizon now. The fights between my parents would be over because they weren't speaking; the tension in the house would be eased because there was no house. The canvas was now clean.

Now, my mother and I would be on our own, like in the movie *Alice Doesn't Live Here Anymore* or my favorite show, *One Day at a Time*.

She would get better in our new Amherst apartment. I would go to my new elementary school, then junior high, then high school, then Princeton and become a doctor or the star of my own highly rated variety show.

And our dog, Cream? She refused to move. We took her to Amherst with us, but she ran all the way back to Leverett to the old house. The new people who lived there said they'd take care of her. So even she would get a new life.

Life would be fabric-softener, tuna-salad-on-white, PTA-meeting normal.

THE MASTURBATORIUM

D R. FINCH LEANED BACK IN HIS RATTAN SWIVEL CHAIR AND folded his arms behind his head. My mother sat across from him on the floral love seat and I sat in the armchair between them. My mother's razor-stubbled legs were tightly crossed. She wore leather sandals with thin straps and tapped her foot in the air nervously. She lit her third More.

I was twelve but felt *at least* fourteen, my parents had been divorced for over a year and my mother was seeing Dr. Finch constantly. Not just every day, but for *hours* every day. And if not in person, certainly on the phone. Sometimes, like now, I would get sucked into one of their sessions. My mother felt it was important that the doctor and I get to know each other. She felt that maybe he could help me with my school troubles. The trouble being that I refused to go and she felt powerless to force me. I think it may have also distantly bothered her that I didn't have any friends my age. Or any age, really.

The two friends I had when we lived in the country weren't my friends anymore. My mother had angered *their* mothers. So they weren't allowed to hang around with me. I was never quite sure what my mother did to piss those mothers off. But knowing my mother, it could have been anything. As a result, I was isolated and spent all my time gazing out the window of our rented apartment and dreaming of the day when I turned thirty. Except when I was sitting in Dr. F's office.

"As spiritually evolved as I may indeed be," Dr. Finch said, eyes twinkling with playfulness, "I'm still a human being. A male human being. I am still very much a man."

My mother blew a cloud of smoke over her head. "You are a goddamn sonofabitch," she said. She used her teasing voice, as opposed to her disturbing *let's go to the mall in blackface* voice.

Finch laughed, his face reddening.

"That may be," he continued. "Men are sons of bitches. That would make you a sonofabitch, Augusten." He looked over at me.

"And you a bitch," he said to my mother.

"I'm the biggest bitch in the world," my mother said, crushing her cigarette out in the soil of the potted jade plant on the coffee table.

"That's very healthy," Finch said. "You need to be a bitch."

My mother's face tightened with pride and she raised her chin slightly. "Doctor, if being a bitch is healthy, then I am the healthiest damn woman on the face of the earth."

Finch exploded in laughter, slapping his thighs.

I failed to see the humor in the situation. As far as I was

concerned, my mother was a bitch, period. She was a rare psychotic-confessional-poet strain of salmonella.

"Do you actually use it?" I said, changing the subject from my mother and back to what we were talking about, namely the room in the rear of the office.

Finch turned to me. "Absolutely. As I was saying, I am a man and I have needs."

I tried to understand. "Do you use it, when? Between patients?"

Finch laughed again. "Between patients. After patients. Sometimes if a patient is particularly tedious, I will excuse myself to the Masturbatorium." He picked up a copy of *The New York Times* from the low glass-topped rattan table in front of his chair. "This morning I have been reading about Golda Meier. An incredible woman. Highly evolved. Spiritually, she is the woman who should be my wife." His face flushed slightly and he adjusted his belt buckle. "So reading about her, well, it always has a powerful effect on my libido. Just five minutes before you came in here I was admiring her picture in the paper. As a result, I will need to relieve myself after the two of you leave."

I looked at the closed door, could picture the ratty couch in the room behind it; the bookcases filled with drug samples; the ancient copies of *The New England Journal of Medicine*. I could picture the *Penthouse* magazines, columns of them, next to the sofa. The thought of fat Dr. Finch ditching a patient to go jerk off in the back room while he looked at pictures of airbrushed vaginas—or worse, Golda Meier—was disturbing.

"Would you like a tour?" he asked.

"Of what?" I said.

My mother coughed.

"Of the Masturbatorium, of course," he roared.

I rolled my eyes. I did sort of want a tour, but it seemed sick to actually be excited. I looked at the poster of Einstein on the wall behind his head. It read: *Boredom is an affliction of youth.* "No, I'm bored. I have to go."

"Well, alright. But it's your loss," he said. "You don't know what you're missing."

Actually, I did know because Hope had already shown me the room months ago. Although it seemed like I probably shouldn't let him know I'd seen it already. "Okay, let's go on a tour."

With great effort, he rose from his chair.

"May I bring my cigarette into your Masturbatorium, or do I need to put it out?" my mother asked.

"Smoking is a great privilege in my sanctuary. But for you, Deirdre, I will allow it."

My mother bowed. "Thank you."

But opening the door to the Masturbatorium revealed a surprise. Hope had left her post as receptionist and was napping on the seedy couch.

"What is this?" Finch bellowed. "Hope!" he boomed.

Hope startled awake. "Jesus, Dad. You scared the shit out of me." She blinked against the light. "Oh my God, what's the matter with you?"

Finch was furious. "Hope, you have no business being in here. This is my Masturbatorium and you're using my blanket." He pointed at the colorful crocheted throw Hope had wrapped around herself.

The tassels along the edge were stuck together.

"Dad, I was just taking a nap."

"This is not the place for naps," he bellowed.

My mother turned around to leave. "I think I'll get a fresh cup of Sanka."

"Wait a minute, Deirdre," Finch said.

My mother froze. "Yes?"

"Do you see how Hope's behavior is wrong?" he asked.

My mother brought her cigarette to her mouth. "Well, I really don't know."

Hope sat up on the couch.

"Deirdre, answer me," Finch demanded. "Do you see how Hope's sneaking in here and invading my private space is wrong?"

After a moment of thinking about it, my mother said, "Well, I can understand not liking one's space invaded. I can understand how it would be upsetting to have somebody messing with your things without asking."

"Then confront her!" Finch directed.

I stood back, not wanting to get sucked in.

"Well, I . . ."

"Deirdre, speak up! Tell Hope what you feel."

My mother looked at Hope as if to say, What can I do? Then she said, "Hope, I don't think it's right for you to disturb your father's space without asking."

"This is none of your business, Deirdre," Hope said. Her eyes were squinty with anger.

My mother took another drag from her cigarette and tried to leave again. "I really think I'll just get another cup of Sanka."

Finch grabbed her arm. "Just a minute there, Deirdre. Are you going to let Hope walk all over you like that? Jesus Christ, Deirdre. Are you going to be Hope's doormat?"

My mother turned sharply to Finch. "I'm not Hope's goddamned doormat, Finch. This just isn't any of my business; she's right. It's between you and your daughter."

"Bullshit!" Finch shouted. "That's just pure evasive bullshit."

"It most certainly is not," my mother said. She tossed her cigarette on the floor and mashed it out with the toe of her sandal. "I am not getting in the middle of this." She brushed imaginary lint off the front of her black turtleneck.

Hope said, "Dad, you're overreacting. Leave Deirdre out of this. It's between you and me."

"You," he said, pointing at her, "stay the hell out of this."

Hope shrunk against the back of the sofa.

"What do you think, young man?" he said, looking to me.

"I think you're all crazy," I said.

"That's the spirit!" he said, with a chuckle. Then he turned to Hope. "Go back and mind the telephones, make fresh coffee. Do your job like a responsible woman. Just because you're my daughter doesn't mean you can take advantage of me, sleeping all day long."

Hope got up off the sofa. "Come on, Augusten," she said, leading me out into the front room.

"What was *that* all about?" I said, once Hope was sitting behind her receptionist's desk. I leaned against the window ledge and looked out at the traffic eight stories below.

"Dad's just trying to help your mom," she said. "He's not really angry with me."

"It seemed like he was pretty angry with you."

"Nah. He's just trying to help your mother get in touch with her anger. Your mother represses her anger and it makes her very sick."

The office was stuffy, hot. There was a fan in the window

that was blowing out. I wanted to turn it so it blew into the room, but Hope insisted that it was better to blow the hot air out of the room, as opposed to sucking the warm air in. "I hate my life," I said.

"No you don't," Hope said, absently stacking a pile of insurance forms on her desk. She reached for the Wite-Out.

"I do. It's so stupid and pathetic."

"You're a teenager. You're supposed to feel your life is stupid and pathetic."

I walked over to the small table next to the sofa and made myself a cup of hot water with Cremora. My mother would be in there for hours. "Why aren't you married?"

Hope gently brushed Wite-Out onto one of the forms. She answered without looking up. "Because I haven't met a guy that's as great as my dad."

"What do you mean by that?" I said.

Hope held the page up to the light and checked her work. "I mean that most guys are jerks. I haven't met one yet that's as emotionally and spiritually evolved as my father. I'm holding out."

"How old are you?" I asked her. Hope and I were becoming friends. I thought that even if her father wasn't a psychiatrist and even if my mother wasn't seeing him constantly, we'd still be friends.

"I'm twenty-eight," she answered. She blew on the page.

"Oh."

For a while, we just sat in silence; me drinking my Cremora and Hope painting insurance forms with Wite-Out. Then I said, "He doesn't really use that room for . . ."

"Hmmm?" she said, glancing up.

"Your father. That room of his. He doesn't really . . . it's not his Masturbatorium, is it?"

Hope shrugged. "Probably, yeah."

"That's so disgusting," I said.

"What's disgusting about it? Don't you masturbate?"

"Huh?"

"I said, don't you masturbate?" She looked at me with her head tilted slightly to the side, waiting for my answer. As if she'd merely asked me the time.

"Well, it's different. It's not . . . I don't know."

"How is it different?" She was strangely intense.

"I'm not a *doctor*."

"What? You don't think doctors masturbate?"

"That's not what I mean. I just mean, it's weird to have a room. You know, a Masturbatorium or whatever."

"I don't think it's so weird," Hope shrugged.

"So you're not married because you're waiting for a guy with a Masturbatorium?" I asked.

"Very funny."

I tried to recall if I shook his hand when I saw him. I couldn't remember so I said, "Nature calls," and excused my-self to the bathroom to scrub my hands in scalding hot water.

IMAGINE MY SHOCK

As we made a left turn on Perry Street, my excitement peaked. "Look at *that* house," I said, pointing out the window. It was a pristine white Victorian with a slate roof and widow's walk on top. "I bet it's just like that one. I bet it's even nicer." I pictured a silver Mercedes 450 SL parked sideways in the crushed clamshell driveway, roof down, M.D. plates glinting in the sun.

My mother was having an emergency session with Dr. Finch, a session at his home. Now I would finally get to see it. Hope had told me all about how much fun it was. "There's always someone around, always something fun to do," she'd said. I couldn't believe it had taken so long for me to finally see where he lived. Visiting the personal residence of John Ritter would not be more exciting than this.

A doctor's house.

I had dressed up in pressed gray slacks, a crisp white shirt and a navy blazer for the occasion. At the last minute, I added a gold-tone ID bracelet.

"It's just down here," my mother said. "On the right."

The street was lined with immaculate homes, each more stately than the next. Perfectly trimmed hedges, double fire-place chimneys, tall front doors painted glossy black, porches fronted with latticework. It was a protracted-jaw, New England money street. "This is nice," I remarked. "I'd love to be a doctor."

"I imagine a lot of the Smith professors live on this street," my mother said. Smith College was just past the center of town.

And then up on the right, I saw one house that did not belong. Instead of being white and pristine like all the others, this house was pink and seemed to sag. From a distance, it looked abandoned. In a neighborhood of whispers, it was a shriek. "That's not it, is it?" I said warily.

My mother hit the blinker and slid the car over to the side of the road. "That's it," she said.

"It can't be." Utter disbelief.

"That's *it*, Augusten," she said. She killed the engine and tossed the keys in her bag.

"Wait," I said, feeling panic. "That can't be it."

"That's Dr. Finch's house," she said, finally.

We got out of the car and I shielded my eyes from the sun as I scanned the house. The pink paint was peeling off, ex-posing veins and patches of bare wood. All the windows lacked shutters and were covered with thick plastic, making it impossible to see inside. And the lawn—at least what was *once* a lawn—was nothing more than firmly packed earth that had the look of heavy foot traffic. Parked crooked in the driveway with the nose touching the corner of the house was an old, gray Buick Skylark. It was missing all its hubcaps.

My mother walked across the dirt to the front porch and I followed. She rang the doorbell, which generated a strange and very loud electric buzz. I pictured wires deep inside the wall crossing, then sparking to make this sound, which was reminiscent of a chain saw in the distance.

Nobody answered the door, but I could make out the distinct sound of running from inside, a tinkle of piano keys and then a crash.

She hit the buzzer again, holding it.

A moment later, the door opened and a hunchback appeared. It was a lady hunchback with kinky, grayish, almost purple hair. She was holding an electric can opener, the cord dangling to the floor.

"Hello, Deirdre," the hunchback said. "Come in." She stood back and waved the can opener in the air, indicating our welcome. She resembled a candy cane without the red stripes. She leaned forward, head down, as if trying to assume the crash position in an airplane while standing.

My mother said, "Thank you, Agnes," and she stepped inside.

I followed. The lady reminded me of Edith Bunker from *All in the Family*, except with *really* bad posture.

"Hello," the hunchback said to me. "You must be Augusten. Am I pronouncing your name right? Uh Gus Ten, isn't that right?"

"Yes," I answered with practiced courtesy. "It's nice to meet you."

"I'm Agnes, Dr. Finch's wife. You two make yourself at home and I'll go get the doctor." She turned and walked down the narrow, creaky hallway that was next to the stairs.

My mother turned to me. "Stop making that face," she whispered.

The house smelled like wet dog and something else. Fried eggs? And it was such a mess. The runner I was standing on was so threadbare that it appeared to have melted into the wood floor beneath it. I stepped around my mother and peered into the room on my right. It had tall windows and a large fireplace. But the sofa was turned over on its back. I stepped around to look into the opposite room. It was also a mess, strewn with clothes, newspapers and a colorful plastic Big Wheel.

"No doctor lives here," I whispered to my mother.

"Shhhhh," she whispered, gripping my arm firmly. "Behave."

I glanced down at my pressed polyester slacks and saw they had already collected lint. I plucked the strange animal hair off my knee and let it go, watching it float to the floor. And then looking at the floor, I saw more fur. There was fur everywhere, streaking across the carpet, gathered in thick balls in the corners against the wall.

I'd never seen such squalor. That people lived here was shocking enough; that a *doctor* lived here was just unthinkable.

"I'll wait in the car," I said.

"You will *not* wait in the car. It'll be hours. And it's rude. You'll stay here and get along with the Finch children."

A moment later, two ratty girls came running down the hallway, side by side. They both had long, greasy, stringy hair

and dirty clothes. They were Vickie and Natalie; I'd met them
before at the doctor's office. Natalie was a year older than me,
thirteen. Vickie was fourteen. Natalie was okay, but Vickie
was weird. She didn't even live at home. Natalie told me she
lived with a bunch of hippies.

"Hi, Augusten," Natalie said sweetly.

Immediately, I didn't trust her. "Hi," I said back.

"You're all dressed up," Vickie smirked. "Going to church?"
She giggled.

I hated her already. She wore shredded jeans that seemed
to be held together by embroidery thread in all the colors of
the rainbow. There was a patch of a pot leaf stitched onto the
knee.

"Deirdre?" The doctor called from somewhere within the
house.

"Yes, Dr. Finch," my mother shouted back. "I'm near the
front door."

"Come on," Vickie said. "We're supposed to keep you occupied."

And with that, they led me away.

We were young. We were bored. And the old electroshock
therapy machine was just under the stairs in a box next to
the Hoover.

"C'mon you guys, it'll be fun," Vickie said, pulling at the
stuffing that was leaking from a hole in the sofa's arm.

Natalie reached into the tube, then wedged a quarter-inch
of Pringles into her mouth. She chewed noisily, spilling
crumbs down the front of her striped halter-top. She wiped

her hands on her bare knees. "I hate Charles Nelson Reilly. Who the fuck is he, anyway?" she asked.

"You *guys*," Vickie whined.

I brought my hand to my head. I liked how smooth my hair felt under my palm. It comforted me. I also liked *Match Game*. "Let's just watch this," I said.

Vickie pulled a long clump of stuffing out of the arm and flicked it onto the floor. "Barf. This show sucks." Their cat, Freud, immediately leapt off the bookcase and pounced on the stuffing.

Natalie raised the tube up to her lips and tipped it, sliding the last of the crumbs into her mouth. She tapped the bottom and it sounded like a small drum. Then she threw the tube at the cat.

He bolted, the stuffing caught in his hind claw.

Vickie snickered.

I exhaled and accepted the fact that my pants might lose their crease. I said, "Did your father really use that thing anyway?"

Vickie jumped up out of her chair. "Yeah, he used to shock people and everything. C'mon, it'll be a wicked blast."

Natalie rolled her eyes and turned to me. "We might as well, there's nothing better to do."

It was hopeless to protest. Although I hadn't known Vickie and Natalie for very long, I had already learned that I had no control over anything that happened when I was around them. Once, at the doctor's office, they opened the window and threw sardines down at people on the street. They would have thrown the coffeemaker out the window too, if Hope hadn't stopped them just in time.

Gene Rayburn placed his hand on the contestant's shoulder in a consoling fashion and I got up off the sofa and followed Vickie and Natalie into the hallway.

Vickie turned on the light. It was a bare bulb, attached to a gilt bronze fixture bolted to the wall. The walls in the hallway were covered with brown burlap. I found the burlap a fascinating and original wall treatment, and I didn't mind at all that it was ancient, peeling and dusty.

"Whoa, look at this motherfucking thing," Vickie said as she dragged the box out from under the stairs.

Natalie kicked it gently as if to check for signs of life.

I leaned forward and peered into the box. It resembled my father's shortwave radio, except it had wires coming out of it. And two large dials. "It's weird," I said, intrigued.

"Help me carry it," Vickie ordered, bending over.

Natalie and I both leaned over and took the other end. Although Natalie could easily have done it herself, I felt I had to help her, to be useful. We carried it back into the TV room and set it on the floor in front of the couch.

"Now what?" Natalie said.

I absently brushed at the front of my dress slacks.

"Okay now, you guys. We gotta set it up. So Augusten, you're the patient and Natalie, you're the nurse."

"I'm not gonna be any cunt-licking nurse," Natalie snapped.

"Well you sure-as-shit are *not* gonna be the doctor."

"I'll be the patient. *He'll* be the nurse," Natalie said.

I felt my face flush, both horrified and certain that I would be the nurse. "I'll be the nurse," I said, just wanting to get on with it. "I don't care. Let's just start."

"Nursy," Natalie teased.

"Should I take this off?" I said, meaning my navy blazer that I had worn because I was visiting a doctor's house.

Vickie scowled. "That thing is so queer. You should just chuck it."

"Why are you always so dressed up anyway?" Natalie said.

"I don't know," I said. I was instantly mortified and slipped the blazer off, tossing it carelessly onto the wing chair.

Natalie dove onto the sofa, stomach-first, then turned on her back. Her arm hung off the couch and the back of her hand touched the floor. "What's wrong with me then?"

"Here," Vickie said, lifting up the machine.

I picked up the other end and we hoisted it out of the box. *"What's wrong with me?"* Natalie cried louder.

We set the machine on the floor and Vickie kicked the box out of the way. It knocked against the TV. "You're psychotic," she said.

Natalie grinned. "Okay, I can be psychotic. I'm a paranoid schizophrenic." She fluttered her eyelashes. "Just like Dottie Schmitt.

Vickie made a face. "Oh, God. She's disgusting. Did you know she's so filthy that Agnes has to peel her bra off for her?"

Natalie gasped. "Where did you hear that?"

"It's true, Agnes told me herself."

"Who's Dottie?" I said.

"And then Agnes has to scrub under her tits with a sponge to get rid of all the scum." Vickie shrieked, grossing herself out.

They laughed.

"Who is she?" I said again.

"She's one of Dad's crazy patients," Natalie said. "You'll meet her."

I will? I thought. *Why?*

This is when Poo Bear ran into the room, naked and shrieking. Poo was about six years old, the son of Vickie and Natalie's older sister Anne. His small penis jiggled and his laughing mouth was ringed with purple jam.

"Hey, Poo," Vickie cooed at her little nephew.

"Poo Bear," Natalie said, sitting up. "What's a doin', pooin'?"

He paused in front of the TV and slapped his arms against his side. "I'm a can opener," he said.

I could smell his feet from across the room.

"You're a can opener?" Natalie said tenderly. "That is sooooooo cute."

"What's that?" he said, pointing to the machine.

Vickie said, "That's Dad's old shock therapy machine. We're fooling around with it. Wanna play?"

He smiled shyly and grabbed his little penis with his hand. "I dunno."

"C'mon, Poo. You'll have fun. You won't get hurt, I promise," Natalie said.

"Yeah, you watch us first, then you can play. Okay? Just watch," Vickie said.

Natalie lay back on the sofa and closed her eyes. "Ready," she said.

Vickie then kneeled in front of the sofa. Gently, she picked up a wire and arranged it around Natalie's head. She placed the end of the wire against Natalie's ear. She tucked another wire under Natalie's neck. Then she pretended to plug the machine in by stuffing the cord under the sofa. Next she placed her hand on the dial. "Nurse," she called.

"Okay," I said.

"Come here,"

I kneeled down next to her. "What should I do?"

"The patient may scream, so you'll need to place the bite guard in her mouth."

"Okay, where's that?"

"Just use a pencil," Natalie said, looking up.

"Shhhhh," Vickie scolded. "You can't talk."

Natalie closed her eyes again and opened her mouth.

I reached over to the table beside the sofa and grabbed a pen. "Will this work?"

"Yeah," Vickie said.

I placed it in Natalie's mouth and she clamped down on it.

"Okay, Nurse. Are we ready?"

"Yes, Doctor," I said.

Vickie turned the dial on the machine. "I'm now giving you one million volts."

Natalie convulsed, her whole body trembling. She opened her eyes and rolled them back in her head. She screamed over the pen.

Vickie laughed. "That's good, that's good." The wire under Natalie's neck slipped out and Vickie tucked it back in. "Nurse, increase the voltage," she said.

I reached over and turned the dial. "Okay, it's all the way up," I said.

Natalie shook violently.

"She's repressing a memory," Vickie said. "We need to go deep into her subconscious mind."

Natalie screamed louder and the pen flew out. She was

shaking with such force that I was worried she'd really hurt herself.

Poo Bear burst into tears and ran from the room.

Natalie stopped.

Vickie laughed.

Poo Bear disappeared down the hall, his cries of terror growing fainter as he ran deeper into the house.

"Woops," Natalie said. She was sweating and red-faced.

"We better get him," Vickie said.

They ran out of the room, chasing after Poo.

I glanced at the TV, a commercial for Herbal Essence. And then I ran after them.

Poo Bear was squatting beneath the grand piano in the living room. His eyes were squeezed closed. He was shitting.

I froze.

Vickie and Natalie sat on the sofa across from the piano. They sat side by side, hands in their laps, like they were watching him do scales.

"Oh," I said. "Sorry."

Poo Bear pinched a turd out on the bright blue wall-to-wall carpeting and Vickie and Natalie clapped.

"Way to go, Poo," Vickie cheered.

Natalie giggled. She slapped her knees.

Poo Bear opened his eyes and looked at me. He grinned with his grape jelly mouth. "Poo can poo," he said.

I looked at Vickie and Natalie. "Have you seen my mother?"

"She's in the kitchen," Natalie said. I started to leave, but she added warningly, "*With my dad.*"

"Well, I just have to ask her one thing, really quick."

She watched as Poo brought his finger to his nose and sniffed.

I backed out of the room and walked down the hall. The old Victorian had many rooms and many hallways; two stairways and so many doors that it was easy to get lost. But the kitchen was easy—just straight back at the end of the house.

My mother was sitting at the kitchen table, which was piled high with dirty dishes caked with food. She was smoking a cigarette.

"Mom?"

She turned to me, opening her arms. "Augusten."

I hugged her. I loved her smell, Chanel No. 5 and nicotine. "How much longer are we gonna stay? I wanna go home."

She hugged me closer and stroked the back of my head with her hand.

I pulled away. "Are we gonna go soon?"

She picked her cigarette from the rim of a plate on the table and sucked the smoke into her lungs. When she spoke, her words came out smoking. "Dr. Finch is saving our lives, Augusten. It's important that we be here now."

In the distance, I heard Poo Bear laugh.

She took another drag from her cigarette, then plopped it into what was left of a glass of milk. "I know this is all new for you and it's very confusing. But this is a safe place. This is where we need to be. Right here in the doctor's own home, with his family."

Her eyes looked different. Wider, somehow. Not her own. They scared me. So did the roaches scrambling across the table, over the dishes, up the arm of a spatula.

"Have you been playing with the doctor's daughters? With Natalie and Vickie?"

"I guess."

"And have you been having a good time?"

"No, I wanna leave." The doctor's house was not at all what I had expected. It was weird and awful and fascinating and confusing and I wanted to go home to the country and play with a tree.

A toilet flushed down the narrow hallway that led from the kitchen. There was a deep clearing of a throat, a rumble. Followed by the unlocking of a door.

"Augusten, Dr. Finch and I are talking now. You go back and play with the girls."

My heart pounded. I was seized with panic. I desperately needed to check my hair in a mirror. "Please, can we go? I don't want to be here anymore. It's too weird here."

I looked up and there he was. "Well, well, well," he boomed, approaching me with his hand extended.

I grabbed it, wondering if he'd hidden something in it. A joy buzzer, maybe, or more balloons.

His eyes widened along with his smile. "What a firm hand-shake. That is an excellent handshake. A ten-plus on the Great Scale of Handshake Ratings."

He was short, but seemed much larger. He occupied a lot of space in the room.

"How are you doing, young man?" He smacked me on the shoulder, like a father on TV; like Mike Brady or Ward Cleaver.

"Okay." I could feel the bottoms of my feet sweat. I couldn't tell *him* that his own freaky kids and his own filthy house were the source of my distress.

"Take a seat here," he said, gesturing at a chair.

I moved the roasting pan to the table and sat. He took the chair between my mother and me. I looked back and forth between them and for awhile nobody said anything. My mother lit another cigarette and Dr. Finch scratched the back of his head.

"Your mother is in a state of crisis," he said finally.

She blew a plume of smoke into the air. "That's an understatement," she said under her breath.

"Do you know what that means?" he asked me.

In the distance, somebody began to pound on the piano keys. "I don't know," I said.

"What that means is that your mother is in trouble with your father. Your father is very angry with your mother right now." He elbowed a plate out of the way and placed his hands on the table, clasping his fingers. "Your father may want to hurt your mother."

I swallowed. *Hurt her?*

"Your father is a very sick man, Augusten. And I believe he is homicidal. Do you know what homicidal means?"

I looked at my mother and she turned away. "It means he wants to kill her?"

"Yes. That's what it means. Some people, when they get angry, become depressed. That's what depression is, it's anger turned inward. Other times, they project that anger outside of themselves. And that's healthier for the person. But you have to be very careful dealing with somebody who is that angry."

Freud pressed up against my leg, raising his tail. I leaned over and stroked his back. It was sticky. "Oh."

"So your mother is not safe from your father right now. She needs to be protected. Do you understand?"

I was terrified but also excited. Dr. Finch left every single light in the house on, as opposed to my father who never let us turn any lights on, always saying something about the Middle East being the reason we had to live in the dark. "What do we do?"

"Well." He leaned back in the chair, folding his arms behind his head. "I'm going to take your mother to a motel. And you're going to stay here at my house."

I'm what?

"There's plenty of room here for you. You'll be very safe." He smiled warmly.

Again I looked at my mother, but she still wouldn't look at me. She was focused on the table. I followed her line of vision and I think she was looking at this one spoon that had a reflection of the ceiling light in it. Almost like you could eat the light if you wanted to, like it was cereal. "I have to stay here?"

He rose from the table. "Deirdre, talk to your son. When you're finished, I'll be in the car."

He patted me on the head firmly, then turned and left.

My mother mashed her cigarette out in the plate. "There's not much room on this table, is there?" she said.

"What's going on? Why is my father trying to kill us?"

My mother sighed. As she exhaled she seemed to shrink into the chair. Even her perfume seemed to fade. She looked at her hands, turning them over in front of her face like they were misplaced artifacts she had pulled from the earth. Then she looked at me. She leaned forward and whispered, "Without Dr. Finch, your father will kill us. Dr. Finch is the only person in the world who can save us."

I glanced at the window, half expecting to see my father clutching a meat cleaver and half expecting to see an elf wearing a stocking cap with a bell on the end waving at me. "Why?"

She turned away. "He has a lot of anger at his mother and he's projecting it all onto me. Years and years of rage that he's denied."

My father had always seemed cold to me. He wasn't affectionate or loving. He never played with me or touched me on the head like Dr. Finch. Which is maybe why I flinched so much when anybody touched me. But I didn't realize he was a monster. But maybe that made sense. Maybe that explained why he was so cold.

Then my mother reached out and took my hand. She held it tightly. "God is working through Dr. Finch. The doctor is very spiritually evolved. I believe we'll be safe with him, and only him."

How long do I have to stay here? One night? Two? Where will I practice my Barry Manilow lip-syncing? "Can't I come to the motel, too?" I loved motels, especially the little soap bars and the paper strip across the toilet bowl.

"No," she said, quickly. "You stay here."

"But why?"

"Because the doctor thinks that's best."

"*But why?*"

"Augusten, don't argue with me now. You'll stay here and be safe."

I had the sensation of falling, even though I was sitting. I looked up at the clock on the wall, but it had no hands. Somebody had taken the clear plastic cover off the front and taken the hands away. Seeing this caused my eyes to itch, so I pulled at my eyelids.

"For how long? You have to tell me," I pressed.

My mother stood, looping her bag over her shoulder. She clutched her cigarettes and lighter in the other hand. "Not long. Two days. Maybe a week."

"A week?!" I said as loud as I could without screaming, even though I wanted to. "I can't stay here in this house for a week." I slammed my hand on the table and roaches scattered like a splash of water. "What about school?"

"You hardly go to school as it is," she said flatly. "A week won't make any difference."

She was right about that. From kindergarten I'd been a very poor student, steering clear of the kids and clinging to the teachers, waiting to go home. The only friend I had was Ellen, who peed standing up like a boy, and I only liked her when it was the two of us alone. The rest of the kids hated me, calling me names like *freak* and *faggot*. So in truth, a week away from school wasn't such a bad thing. Unless it meant staying here in this weird house. My heart started beating really fast as I tried to think of something to say to make my mother change her mind. But I felt too confused to think of anything.

She placed the back of her hand against my cheek. "I'll visit you in your dreams. Did you know I can do that?"

"Do what?" I said, hating her.

"I can travel in my dreams. Once, I dreamt I went to Mexico. And when I woke up, there were pesos in my hand."

Her eyes scared me. They looked radioactive.

I folded my arms across my chest and watched Freud jump onto the stove, stepping around the burners, settling in the center.

"We'll be okay," she said.

Then she was gone.

I stood alone in the kitchen, listening to the dim electric buzz of the clock as it secretly counted the seconds, the minutes, the hours. Briefly, I fantasized about slicing my mother's fingers off with the electric knife that was hanging by its cord from the curtain rod.

THE CLEANING LADY

T HE NEXT AFTERNOON I WAS SITTING IN THE TV ROOM
when I heard a strange sound. At first I thought it was a wolf.
The doctor's wife, Agnes, had fallen asleep in the wing chair
with her head rolled back and her glasses perched on top of
her head, tangled in her violet perm. She was snoring. The
television was blaring and rolling its screen like it was frus-
trated that nobody would watch it. And I was sitting on the
sofa alone because Hope had gone into the kitchen. I was
sitting there watching Agnes snore when all of a sudden I
heard the sound coming from somewhere upstairs.

When I was ten, I had an after-school job helping two local
dog trainers teach their black labs to retrieve. One of them
also had a wolf hybrid. The whine I heard from upstairs
sounded like that dog, only younger.

Did the Finches keep a wolf in the house?

It would make sense, I thought. They seemed to be sort of crazy. They were up at all hours of the night, they didn't care if you used a coaster on the table under your glass. They didn't even care if you used a glass.

The wolf moaned again, but this time it also called out a name. "Agnes."

The sound was coming from the top of the stairs. But it was muffled, like it was behind a door.

"Agnes!" Now it sounded like an old lady. Frail, but insistent.

I was wondering if I should poke Agnes on the shoulder or maybe just slap the coffee table really hard to wake her up, but just then her eyes fluttered and she mumbled. Automatically she reached for her black vinyl purse, an air conditioner–sized accessory that was never more than a foot from her body.

"*Agnes!*" It was almost a howl. I could picture a ghoulish old lady, hands mangled by arthritis, crawling along the floor upstairs.

"Uh, oh. Okay, yes, okay, I'm coming," Agnes muttered. Somehow she'd heard the old lady in her sleep and now she was standing up and heading for the stairs, as if programmed at birth to do so. "I'm on my way," she called. Agnes looked weary and fatigued. Her body was like a bag of sand that she was forced to drag around.

"Where'd Agnes go?" Hope asked brightly when she walked back in the room. She was carrying a box of croutons and offered me one.

"Oh, no thanks."

"You sure? They're good when they get a little stale." She shook the box.

"That's okay, I'm not hungry." The box looked old and worn, like it had been filled and refilled for many years.

She shrugged and sat on the sofa. "Okay."

"Who is that lady?" I asked. "The one who was calling for Agnes?"

Hope smiled and then she chuckled, popping a crouton into her mouth. "Oh," she said, rolling her eyes, "so you heard Joranne."

"Who?"

"*Joranne*," Hope said. "She's one of Dad's patients. She's wonderful."

I waited for more.

"Is that where Agnes went, upstairs?"

I nodded.

"Yeah, so okay. Joranne is really special. She's one of Dad's patients and she's staying in the middle room upstairs."

I would be living in the same house with a crazy woman? And then I realized I already was living in a house with a crazy woman—my mother.

"She's a very sick lady," Hope added, crunching a handful of croutons. Then, "Ouch," and she spit one into her hand. She smiled up at me. "That one was a little *too* stale." She brushed it onto the floor.

"What's wrong with her?"

Hope sighed and set the box of croutons on the coffee table. "Joranne is a very brilliant lady. She's incredibly well-read and very interesting. She loves Blake."

"Who?"

"He was a painter," Hope smiled at me. Her face said, *Oh,*

I forgot you're only twelve. You're so mature for your age.

"Oh," I said. I still didn't get why she was here.

"She's an obsessive compulsive neurotic," Hope stated.

"A what?"

She turned sideways on the sofa to face me. "Obsessive compulsive neurotic. That's the technical term for her condition."

This sounded impossibly exotic and I immediately wished I was one too, whatever it was.

Hope then explained that this meant Joranne could not leave the room upstairs for any reason. In fact, she had not left the room once since she was brought to the house two years ago during a personal crisis in a nor'easter.

"She's been here for two years?" All I could think was, *wow*.

"A little over, yeah."

What kind of doctor lets a patient live in his house for *two years*? And did she really never come downstairs?

"She's never been downstairs once. Agnes brings all her meals up to her. And everything has to be wrapped in aluminum foil. She's afraid of dirt. So nobody can even step into her room. When Agnes brings her a food tray, she has to stand in the doorway. Nobody is ever allowed inside. Her room is really spotless by the way. Too bad the rest of the house doesn't look like that," Hope laughed.

If Joranne had never been downstairs, she'd never seen the overturned sofa in the living room, the dog shit under the grand piano or the moving blanket of roaches that covered all the dishes and pots and pans that were piled in the sink and on the kitchen table. She'd never seen the scrappy old burlap that hung from the walls instead of wallpaper. If Joranne had never come downstairs, she didn't realize that the stairs themselves were tearing away from the wall and that every time somebody climbed them, they looked like they might come crashing down. I said to Hope, "If Joranne saw the downstairs, what would she do?"

Hope howled. "Oh, she'd absolutely die. It would just kill her. Can you imagine?"

I liked that I hadn't offended Hope about the house. Somehow the fact that she knew it was kind of gross made it okay that she lived here.

Hope told me that Joranne only left her room to walk into the back bathroom and that nobody else in the house was allowed to use it.

"Really?" What an exclusive, mysterious disease. I wanted it.

Hope began to laugh. When I asked her what was so funny, she laughed harder. Her eyes filled with tears.

"What is it?" I had to know. I loved Hope. Even though she was so old—twenty-eight—she was so much fun. She was the only reason I could stand sitting in Dr. Finch's waiting room for five hours at a time.

Hope's laughter wound down and she said, "She eats the sink caulking."

"The what?" The more I heard, the more incredible this creature became. I liked her very much.

"The sink caulking. You know, that stuff around the sink and between the tiles? She peels it away and then just pops it in her mouth." Hope broke into laughter again.

All I knew was, I had to see this lady. Now. "Can . . . I mean, is there any way . . ." I wasn't sure how to ask.

"Would you like to meet her?"

"Yes." I reached for the box of old croutons and took one out.

"We can try. But she usually doesn't meet new people."

A door was slammed. Then Agnes came walking down the creaky stairs. "Oh Joranne, Joranne, Joranne," she was saying under her breath. She came into the TV room where Hope and I were sitting. "That Joranne is going to drive me insane."

"What is it now?" Hope said.

"She didn't like her spoon."

"What's the matter with her spoon?"

"She said there was a spot on the spoon I brought her for her soup. I took that spoon and I didn't see any spot. So I wiped it off on my shirt and handed it back to her and she just closed the door in my face." She wound her index finger around next to her ear; sign language for *crazy*.

But I believed Joranne. Unlike her, I'd seen the kitchen. And I was sure that any spoon that came from that mess would have at least one stain. If she only knew. This made me want to meet her even more.

"We'll go talk to her," Hope said. She got up from the couch.

"Oh, I wouldn't do that," Agnes warned before walking away. "She's in rare form tonight. Got every light in the room burning."

"Never mind that," Hope said. "Come on, Augusten. Let's go see her."

I followed Hope up the stairs but I didn't like the idea that we were both on the stairs at once. I let her stay three steps ahead.

At the top of the stairs, I stood back in the hallway and Hope knocked on the tall white door.

Nothing.

Hope knocked again.

Nothing.

She glanced over at me like, *see?* Then she knocked again and said, "Joranne, come on, open up. It's me, Hope. And I've got a friend here I want you to meet. His name is Augusten. He's twelve and his mother is a poet and you'll really love him."

A moment later, the door opened very slowly.

Hope stood up straighter.

A frail old lady peered out into the hall, squinting against the bare lightbulb that was attached to a fixture on the wall. "Who?" she said, sounding exactly like an owl. It came out more like *hoooooooo.*

"Augusten," Hope said. Then she turned to me. "Augusten, this is Joranne."

I moved forward and stuck out my hand for her to shake but she recoiled. So I quickly tucked my hand back at my side and said, "Hi."

She said "Hello" with great dignity. There was an elegance about her, a certain sophistication. Like she could be the queen of some Danish country or a professor of literature at Smith.

For a moment, we just stared at each other. I was looking at a real, live crazy person. She was so crazy that she had to live in the psychiatrist's house. And her room was so bright that it looked like a stage. She was dressed all in white, even a white shawl. And she looked very clean and glowy, like a ghost except not transparent.

"It's nice to meet you," she said.

She didn't seem crazy.

Then she turned to Hope and her voice changed from one of formality back into the wolfish whine. "Agnes brought me a dirty spoon. *She's soiled me!*"

Then Joranne burst into tears. She sobbed and pulled a Kleenex out from the cuff of her gown. Her thin veneer of composure began to crack and crumble down all around her. Now she was a crazy lady.

"Oh, Joranne. It's okay. Agnes didn't mean it. I'll get you another spoon."

"What am I going to do?" she sobbed. I could have sworn that she briefly eyed the white rubber piping along my sneaker bottoms.

When she brought her hands to her face to blot her nose, I noticed her hands were bright red, and etched with cracks. They were raw.

"It's okay, Joranne. I'll go downstairs and get you a brand new spoon."

Joranne continued to cry but she nodded. Then she backed into her room and closed the door.

Hope looked at me and smiled. She headed downstairs and I followed.

In the kitchen, Hope grabbed a spoon from the pile in the sink and then reached under the cabinet for the Ajax. There was no room to wash the spoon in the sink, so I followed her into the bathroom.

"Did you see her hands?" Hope asked, taking a pair of Agnes's tattered white underpants out of the standing water in the sink and slinging them over the curtain rod.

"Yeah," I said. "Why were they so red?"

"They were red," Hope said as she scoured the spoon under hot water, "because she's been washing her hands. She gets into this thing—hand me that towel."

I grabbed the towel off the back of the toilet bowl and handed it to her.

"Anyway, she gets into these, like, mental traps. She can't stop washing her hands. She'll do it for hours and hours until Dad makes her stop. He's the only one who can stop her."

In some strange way, I understood this concept. When I was a little kid, I would have to bathe with a towel next to the tub to wipe stray drops of water from the insides of the tub. I liked the water to be at one level with no splatters, anywhere, ever.

"The spoon must have set her off."

I wondered how any doctor could fix a person who could go crazy just because of a spoon. I decided that my mother must be right. Dr. Finch must be a very special doctor, different and better than all the others. A thin layer of trust had formed in my mind, like a scab.

"I'm gonna bring this upstairs to her. You better just wait down here. I'll meet you back in the TV room in a few minutes." She paused and lowered her voice. "Dad's trying to wean her off all of us because he feels she's nearly ready to live on her own. He's already found her a nice apartment in the center of town and in a month, she'll be living there. So it's good that she met you, she needs to get used to meeting new people." We left the bathroom with the newly cleaned spoon and headed to the front of the house. Hope smiled at me, mouthing the words, *wish me luck.* Then she headed up the stairs.

I backed into the hall slowly, listening to see if Joranne screamed when Hope brought her the spoon. I didn't hear anything. So I walked into the TV room and it was empty. I sat back down on the sofa and glanced at my watch. Five-and-a-half days until my mother came to pick me up. Assuming she hadn't lied about me only staying here for a week. Before she left with Dr. F she told me that I'd be "spending a lot of time with the Finches in their home." So I knew it was going to be more than just this one week. It would be a day here, another day there. Maybe even weeks at a time. I could sense that it was getting more and more difficult for her to have me for even a day. And my father didn't want me at all. He had found himself an apartment in the bottom of a house deep in the woods. I'd only been there once since the divorce.

For a second, I felt a bottomless sadness. So completely alone. Like one of my stuffed animals at home that I was too old for now, that sat on the shelf in my closet, mashed against the back wall.

And then a thought entered my mind that was too terrifying to contemplate: had Joranne only planned to stay here for a week?

I stopped biting the inside of my mouth and stared straight ahead, my eyes unfocused. What if I was being tricked? What if I ended up staying here not for a week but a *year? Or more?*

No, that could never happen, I told myself. Don't freak out, it's just a week.

And then I heard something crash down the hall in the kitchen and this made me smile and wonder what new mess had just happened. In a way there was enough confusion and distraction here to keep my mind off the fact that my parents didn't seem to want me. If I let myself think about that too much, I wasn't sure I'd be able to climb out. So I held my breath and listened for more sounds. There was nothing.

I glanced down at my slacks and noticed an unsightly stain. It was some sort of grease. It would never come out. I shrugged, got up and ran for the kitchen to see what small disaster had happened.

One day late my mother picked me up from the Finch house. There was no excited knocking on the door, no opening of arms, no smothering with kisses. She simply slid the brown station wagon up alongside the house and sat there waiting. I don't know how long she'd been sitting there when I finally caught a glimpse of a car parked out front, noticed it was her and ran outside.

"You're back!" I cried, running barefoot out of the house, over the dirt path to the street, to her window which was rolled all the way up.

She continued to stare straight ahead, even as I banged on the glass.

Exhaust spilled out against the curb, and the car itself seemed weary, the engine sounding ready to fall out onto the street.

I knocked again on the window, and finally she blinked, turned and saw me. She slowly rolled down her window and leaned her head out. "Are you ready to go to Amherst? Do you have your things?" she asked flatly.

I turned back to the house, noticed I'd left the door wide open. Then I realized it didn't matter, somebody would close it. And I had more shoes in Amherst, anyway. I walked around the front of the car to the passenger side and climbed in.

"Where'd you go? How was it? What happened?" I fired my questions at her as she pulled away from the house and headed for Amherst.

She answered none of my questions. She simply looked straight ahead, though not quite at the road, never checking her rearview mirror, not lighting a single More.

She had come back for me, just like she said she would.

Only, where was she?

JUST ADD WATER

As I SPENT MORE AND MORE TIME WITH THE FINCHES DUR-
ing that year, I could feel myself changing in profound ways,
with stunning speed. I was like a packet of powdered Sea
Monkeys and they were like water.

My double-knit slacks were replaced by an old pair of
Vickie's jeans that Natalie found in a pile next to the clothes
dryer. "These will look excellent on you." When I expressed
apprehension at wearing the virtually crotchless Levi's, she
said, "Oh, get over it. It's just a little ventilation." I stopped
trying to force my hair into a smooth, glossy sheet and instead
let it run its unruly, curly course. "You look so much better,"
Natalie said. "Like you could be a drummer with Blondie."
Inside, I felt I'd aged two years in the space of a few months.

I loved it. And there was so much freedom in the house, everyone was so easy-going. They didn't treat me like a little kid.

But as free and accepting as the Finches were, I worried about their reaction to my deep, dark secret. The fact that I was gay had never been a big deal to me—I'd known all my life. And because I seldom interacted with other kids, I hadn't really been programmed to believe it was wrong. Anita Bryant on TV talked about how sick and evil gay people were. But I thought she was tacky and classless and this made me have no respect for her. But I wasn't sure what the Finches would think, partly because they were Catholic and to me Catholic people seemed very white-knuckled and tight-fisted about life in general. I was worried my being gay would push the Finches' acceptance of me past the breaking point.

"Big deal," Hope said when I told her.

We were taking a walk around the neighborhood at night and it had taken me twenty minutes to confess. "I figured it out on my own anyway," she said, glancing at me sideways and smiling.

"You did?" I asked, alarmed. Did I emit a certain gay odor? Or maybe it was my unnatural obsession with cleanliness that clued her in. It was one thing to *be* gay. But it was something else altogether to *seem* gay.

"My adopted brother Neil is gay, too," she said, stopping to pet a cat.

"He is?" There was a gay Finch?

"Yeah, Neil Bookman. He used to be a patient of Dad's, but now he's Dad's adopted son."

"How old is he?" I wondered. Was he my age? A year older?

"Thirty-three," Hope said.

That seemed pretty old to be adopted. "Where does he live?"

"Well," Hope began as we continued walking, "he used to live out back in the barn. But then he got mad that Dad wouldn't give him a room inside, so a few months ago he moved to Easthampton, into some house with a divorced woman. But he still keeps his room in the barn. Kinda like a pied-a-terre."

My timing couldn't have been worse. Here I was, just starting to basically live with the Finches, and the only gay one had just moved out.

"He visits a lot. I can call him if you like. You two should get together. I think you'd really like each other."

I'd never seen a real, live gay man in person before; only on the *Donahue* show. I wondered what it would be like to see one without the title "Admitted Homosexual" floating in blocky type beneath his head.

A week later, Hope called me in Amherst to tell me that Bookman would be over that afternoon. I was on the next bus.

Agnes was on the sofa in the TV room, eating out of a bag of Purina Dog Chow. When she saw me walk into the room, she laughed. "It's not as bad as it looks. It's actually quite good. Would you like to try some?"

"Uh, no thanks," I said.

She said, "You don't know what you're missing," and popped another brown nugget into her mouth.

"She's right. They actually are pretty good," said a low voice behind me.

I turned around and saw a tall, thin man with short black hair and a black mustache. He had friendly brown eyes. "Hi, Augusten. Remember me? Bookman? God, the last time I saw you, you were like this tall." He lowered his hand to waist height.

"Hi," I said trying not to sound electrified with excitement. "I sort of remember you. A little. I think you came over to our house sometimes when I was a kid."

"Yeah, that's right. I visited your mom."

"So," I said, stuffing my hands in my pockets, trying to look casual.

"So Hope said you wanted to meet me. I'm flattered. I feel famous." He smiled.

"Yeah, well. You know, now that I'm staying here all the time, I wanted to get to know everybody."

His eyes flashed and his warm smile vanished. "You're staying here? You have a room here?"

I remembered about the barn, how the doctor made him stay in a barn and not a room. I backtracked. "Well, not exactly. I mean, I'm hanging around here a lot. I don't have a room or anything."

He seemed relieved. "Oh," he said. "Okay."

Hope walked into the hallway and put her arm around Bookman. "Hey big brother," she said. "I see you two found each other."

"That we did," Bookman said. "Not so tight, Hope, Jesus. I'm not a dog."

"Oh, poor baby," Hope said, releasing her arm. "I forget how fragile you are."

"Is that Hope?" Agnes called out from the TV room. "Tell her she owes me four dollars."

"I'm right here Agnes, you can tell me yourself."

"Oh, uh, okay," she stammered, "that was you. I thought I heard you. You owe me four dollars."

Hope leaned her head into the room. "I know I do and I'll get it to—holy cow, Agnes. Are you eating dog food?"

"Why does everybody make such a fuss? It's just a little kibble."

"*Oh, Mom,*" Hope said, grimacing. "That stuff's not clean, it's made for dogs."

"It's pretty good," Bookman said, playfully licking his lips.

She spun around. "Don't tell me you're eating it, too."

"Just a little. You should try it."

"No way am I eating dog food."

Agnes said, "Oh, you're such a fussbudget. Always afraid to try something new. Ever since you were a little girl you've been afraid of new things."

"I'm not afraid to try new things," Hope said. "But I draw the line at dog food."

"I don't want to try it either," I said.

Bookman placed his hand on my shoulder and it was like my entire body warmed five degrees, instantly. "Try a little."

I had to now. "I'll try it if Hope does."

Hope looked at me and rolled her eyes. "Gee, thanks a lot. That means I'm the coward. Okay, fine. Gimme that bag."

Agnes held the bag up and Hope and I reached in and removed one nugget each. Then we looked at each other and popped them into our mouths.

It was surprisingly tasty. Nutty, slightly sweet with a satisfying crunch. I could immediately see how the little pellets could become quite addictive. "They're not awful," I said.

"See?" Bookman said.

"I told you. What did you think? I wouldn't eat them if they didn't taste good," Agnes said, bringing a whole handful to her mouth and tossing them back. She crunched loudly and turned her attention back to a soap opera.

"Well, I gotta go," Hope said. "Dad needs me at the office. We're behind on the insurance forms. See you guys later?"

"Yup. Catch you later," Bookman said.

Hope opened the front door to leave. "Bye, Augusten. Have fun."

"Okay, see ya."

After she left, Bookman said, "So. Do you want to take a walk?"

We walked into the center of town, up to the Smith College campus, then beyond all the way to Cooley Dickinson Hospital. The whole way I was dying to tell him about me. I felt like we had so much in common—being gay, being stuck at this house, being without our own parents. And in a house full of girls, we were two guys. But still I couldn't tell him. I told him everything else—about how my parents' fights had gotten really bad, about their divorce, about how my mother had started to get a little weird, about how she was seeing Dr. Finch all the time now and I was basically living there because she couldn't handle me.

"It's tough to have a sick mom," he said. "My mom couldn't handle me either. Neither could my dad."

"Yeah, mine too. He never wants to see me. And my mother, she's just so caught up in her own stuff. I guess she's been through some really bad things and she needs to focus on herself right now."

"And where does that leave you?" he said.

"Yeah."

"Yeah," Neil said. "Exactly. Here at the crazy house of the even crazier Dr. Finch."

"Do you think he's crazy?"

"In a good way. I think he's a genius. I know he saved my life." And then out of the blue he said, "He was the first person I told I was gay."

"Really?" I said. He'd finally said it. All this time I was beginning to wonder if Hope had been wrong. He seemed so normal, like a regular guy. He didn't have an earring or talk with a lisp and judging by his brown shoes and pale blue polyester slacks, he certainly wasn't gifted with color.

"Me too," I said.

"What?" asked Bookman, pausing on the sidewalk.

"I'm gay."

Somehow, this took him completely by surprise. He gasped, inhaling sharply and his eyes widened. "What? Are you serious?"

"Yeah," I said, feeling embarrassed. "I thought you knew, I thought Hope told you."

"Holy Mary mother of God," he said. "So that's what this was about."

"What?"

"Nothing. So you're gay?" he asked again.

"Yeah," I said.

We continued walking but then he stopped again. "Are you sure you're gay? I mean, how long have you felt like this?"

I told him all my life.

"That's pretty sure." He chuckled.

*   *   *

As we walked down Main Street past the closed stores, Neil said to me, "I just want you to know, I'm here for you whenever you need to talk. I mean, night or day. You can talk to me about anything, this or anything else."

I glanced at him and thought he looked so handsome, bathed in the artificial yellow glow of the street lamp. "Thanks," I said.

"And don't ever worry," he said firmly. "I will never take advantage of you."

"Okay," I said, reaching in my pocket for a Marlboro Light. "You smoke?"

"Yeah," I admitted. It was a habit I'd picked up from Natalie. At first, I was worried that Agnes or the doctor would be furious and not allow it. But they didn't mind as long as "you don't burn down the house."

Neil pulled a lighter from his pocket and lit my cigarette.

"Thanks," I said. Smoking had become my favorite thing in the world to do. It was like having instant comfort, no matter where or when. No wonder my parents smoked, I thought. The part of me that used to polish my jewelry for hours and comb my hair until my scalp was deeply scratched was now lighting cigarettes every other minute and then carefully stomping them out. It turned out I had always been a smoker. I just hadn't had any cigarettes.

"It was great talking with you," Bookman told me when we were back at the house.

"Thanks for everything," I said.

"Thank *you*," he said and smiled warmly, eyes moist.

He left, climbing into his wreck of a car and I sank into the TV-room sofa. I felt mildly intoxicated, like I'd just taken a big swallow of Vicks 44. Then I saw a stray Purina Dog Chow Agnes had dropped on the seat cushion. Without hesitation, I picked it up and popped it into my mouth. No longer would I be afraid of trying new things.

"Hi, Augusten," Hope said, when she came home an hour later.

I was still sitting on the sofa in a daze. "Hi," I said vaguely.

"What are you doing?"

I'd been staring at the radiator. "Nothing. Just got back from walking around with Bookman."

She looked around. "Oh yeah? Good. I need to ask him something. Where is he?"

"Oh, he left," I said.

"Shoot. Do you think if I run down the street I can still catch him?"

"No," I said. "He left like an hour ago."

Hope took a seat on the sofa. "Shucks," she said. "I wanted to ask him if he can fill in for me at the office this Friday. I wanted to visit my friend Vivian in Amherst." Then Hope reached into her canvas rainbow bag and pulled out a small white bible.

"Would you mind doing a bible-dip with me?"

"Sure," I said.

All the Finches did bible-dips. It was like asking a Magic Eight Ball a question, only you were asking God. The way it worked was, one person held the bible while another person thought of a question to ask God, like, "Should I get my hair cut short?" Then the person holding the bible opened it at random, and the person asking the question dropped his or her finger on the page. Whatever word your finger landed on, this was your answer. The doctor was so enthusiastic about bible-dips as a direct form of communication with God that most of his patients performed them. Although nobody did as many dips as Hope.

I held the bible and Hope closed her eyes. "Ready?" I said. She opened her eyes. "Okay."

I opened the bible.

Her finger landed on the word "awakened."

"Oh my God," Hope said. "That's just incredible."

"What'd you ask?"

"I asked if the fact that I missed Bookman means that I shouldn't visit my friend Viv on Friday, if that was a sign."

"So?"

"Well, *so*," Hope said. "I got *awakened*. And to me, that means that I would be disturbing Vivian if I visited her. She did have a cold last month and she's seventy-four. So she probably needs her sleep. If I showed up on Friday, I might wake her up."

I nodded my head and Hope looked up at the ceiling. "Thanks, God," she said.

Hope and God were buddies. Theirs was not a formal relationship steeped in ritual and tradition. It was more of a close yet casual friendship.

Last week, Hope and I were driving around the center of town looking for a parking space. When a red Vega pulled out of a handicap spot in front of Thorne's Market, Hope shrieked. "Okay!"

"You shouldn't park here," I told her. The car smelled

sweet, like wet dog and armpits, and I was sick of sitting in it. But I still didn't feel she should take a handicap spot.

"This space was meant for me," she said.

We climbed out of the car and Hope set her rainbow bag on the hood. In addition to the rainbow bag, Hope always carried a canvas PBS bag and usually a plastic shopping bag. "Lock it," she called.

I locked it, but didn't see the point. As if there was anything to steal: a World Father's Day button, a bag of balloons, a blue plastic Goody hairbrush on the dashboard. Then again, there *was* a box of Valium in the trunk.

Hope reached into her PBS bag and pulled out an electric alarm clock. "Have you got a dime?"

I dug into my pocket, feeling my hip bones, feeling too skinny, and pulled out a dime. "Here," I said, handing it to her.

Then I noticed there was no parking meter. "Hope, there's no meter."

"I know," she said, as she bent over and placed the dime on the sidewalk in front of the car. "It's a tithe. I like to thank God when he does something nice for me."

In Thorne's Market Hope couldn't decide between a tuna sandwich or a turkey sandwich so, even though there was a line behind her, she pulled out her white bible. She did the dip herself, because she was in a hurry. "Harvest," she said. "I landed on the word *harvest*." She thought for a moment and then said, "Aren't turkeys grain-fed? They are, I think. So that's pretty close to a harvest." Then she smiled at the perplexed girl who was standing behind the counter looking mortified and she said, "I'll take the turkey. But on multigrain just to make sure."

At first, I, too, was mortified by all the bible-dipping that went on in this house. But like everything else, I quickly got used to it.

And then I started to do them myself. It was surprising how addictive they could become. When I asked, "Will I like the new Supertramp album?" and landed on the word "starvation," I knew that the album was a dud and I should save my money. It was like being able to turn to the back of the book and look at the answers.

Or it was like asking a parent.

THE BURNING BUSH

Fᴇʀɴ Sᴛᴇᴡᴀʀᴛ ᴡᴀs ᴀ ᴍɪɴɪsᴛᴇʀ's ᴡɪғᴇ. Aɴᴅ ᴀ ᴄʟᴏsᴇ ғʀɪᴇɴᴅ of my mother's. She had a white smile that was usually located just a few inches above a plate of Rocky Road brownies she had baked from scratch just for me. She lived with her family in Amherst, in a warm and comfortable house that sat at the top of a small grassy hill. A clutch of tall white birch trees stood next to the house, their branches just grazing the slate-shingled roof.

Fern was a *perfect* minister's wife who shopped for teak napkin rings with my mother and enjoyed discussing contemporary poetry and visiting the local galleries. She wore her prematurely gray hair in a blunt-cut bob, held back away from her face with a black velvet hairband. And she spoke with a slight British accent, although it was my understanding she had been raised in Vacaville, California. Fern and her family took ski trips to Stowe. They shopped mail-order from J. Peterman and L. L. Bean. She wore nubuck leather kiltie flats from Talbots and a small gold cross around her neck.

And instead of *fuck*, Fern Stewart said *fiddlesticks*.

When my parents divorced, my mother and I had nowhere to live. The house was to be sold; the profits split. But until then, we were homeless.

Fern took us in.

She arranged for us to live in a house just down the street from hers. There was a basement apartment in that house and I was fascinated by the leaded glass windows, the copper plumbing and the wide oak floors. For a few months, I spent part of the time in this small apartment and the other part at the Finch house, in a room near the back bathroom that Hope had cleared out for me.

Many nights, my mother and I had dinner at Fern's. Her family was genuinely warm and always made me feel like they'd been waiting impatiently all day long for me to show up.

Her four children each had perfectly white, straight smiles. Like Chiclets. Even the girls had clefts in their chins. And they always appeared to have just stepped from a hot shower.

As Fern set a pottery bowl of steaming broccoli with homemade cheese sauce on the table, her son would reach for it and offer me the first serving. "Even if you don't like vegetables, you'll love my mom's Gruyère broccoli," he would wink.

His older sister would playfully sock him on the shoulder of his Izod. "Heck, Daniel. Mom could even make us love lima beans!"

Everyone at the table would laugh. Then join hands and say grace.

To me, these people were as exotic as animals in a zoo. I'd never seen anything like them. I wasn't sure whether I wanted to be one of them or simply live among them taking notes and photographs.

I was certain that Fern, unlike my mother, had never hurled the Christmas tree off the deck or baked one of her kids a cornstarch birthday cake. Furthermore, there was no doubt in my mind that Fern never craved a cigarette-butt-and-canned-smoked-oyster sandwich.

In some part of my lower brain stem, I recognized these people for what they were—*normal*. I also recognized that I was more like a Finch and less like one of them.

It was difficult to imagine handsome, preppy Daniel sitting in the TV room at the Finches', pointing at the family dog and laughing because little Poo was lying on the floor in a fit of giggles with his pants pulled down and the dog licking his erect penis. It was hard to imagine Daniel seeing this and then shrugging and turning back to the TV. *Because he'd gotten used to it.*

My mother eventually found us our own place to live. It was one half of a large old house on Dickinson Street, just a few miles up the road from Fern. My mother liked the fact that it was across the street from where Emily Dickinson once lived. "I'm as brilliant a poet as she was, you know. It just feels right for me to be here at this point in my life." And I liked the fact that it was a lot closer to Northampton and the Finches'. Now, instead of my mother having to drive me over there, I could take the PVTA bus. The fact that my "room" was really just a nook without a door told me that I wouldn't be spending much time with Mom.

Dr. Finch had already told me to consider *his* house *my* house. He said I could just show up anytime I wanted to. "Just pound on the door and Agnes will get out of bed and let you in." And I knew Hope really liked having me there. So did Natalie. Even though she was living in Pittsfield with her legal guardian, she came to Northampton a lot. And she said if I was there, she'd come all the time.

At first I'd thought it was weird that Natalie had a legal guardian, considering she already had a father. But Dr. Finch believed a person should choose his or her own parents. So at thirteen, Natalie had chosen one of her father's patients, Terrance Maxwell, who was forty-two and rich. So now she lived with him and attended a private prep school that he paid for. Just like Vickie lived with a pack of hippies that traveled from barn to barn all across America. Every six months or so, Vickie would make a pit stop back home in Northampton.

So I was learning that living arrangements needed to remain fluid. And that I shouldn't get too attached to anything. In a way, I felt like an adventurer. And this appealed to my deep need for a sense of freedom.

The only problem was school. I had just turned thirteen, a seventh-grader at Amherst Regional Junior High. Elementary school had been a disaster, with me repeating the third grade twice. Then after the divorce and the move to Amherst, I transferred to a new elementary school and that hadn't worked either. Now, I was heading for something much worse.

From the first day when I walked in the door and was

assaulted by the smell of chlorine, I knew I wouldn't be attending this school for very long. Chlorine meant a pool. And a pool meant mandatory swimming, and this meant not only *wearing* a bathing suit in front of other kids, but being cold and wet and then stripping it off when my dick was at its smallest.

Another problem was the esthetics. To me, the large gray one-level building looked like some sort of factory that might churn out ground meat products or just the plastic eyes for stuffed animals. It was certainly not the sort of place I would want to spend any real time. The Amherst Cinema, on the other hand, was exactly the sort of place I wanted to hang out. It even had a smoking section. I also liked the Chess King at the Hampshire Mall. They sold reflective shirts and fantastic white dress pants with permanent creases.

But these paled in comparison to the real problem: I was surrounded by normal American kids. Hundreds of them, teeming through the halls like the roaches in the Finches' kitchen. Except I didn't mind those nearly as much.

I had nothing in common with these kids. They had moms that nibbled matchstick-thin slices of carrot. And I had a mom that ate matchsticks. They went to bed at ten o'clock and I was discovering that life could go on well past three in the morning.

The more time I spent at the Finches', the more I realized what a waste of my life this school crap was. It was nothing but a holding tank for kids without bigger plans or ideas. Even Natalie said if she had to go to public school instead of private school, she just wouldn't go.

The Finches were showing me that you could make your

own rules. That your life was your own and no adult should be allowed to shape it for you.

So I would go to school for a day. Sometimes two days in a row. The other twenty-eight days I would do my own thing, which basically meant write in my journal, see movies and read Stephen King novels. I was careful not to be absent for thirty days in a row because this would cause the school board to issue a "core evaluation" which could result, I feared, in reform school.

The trick was to show up for homeroom. And then leave. This created confusion within the school's records. Allowing me to slip through the cracks. And the fact that I had absolutely no friends, knew not one person's name, made my invisibility even easier.

One afternoon I came home early from school. I made my appearance to be counted at homeroom and then I casually walked out of The Factory. It was a beautiful day and I had seven dollars. I was thinking I could go to the Amherst Cinema and see the German film that was playing there. So I decided to stop by Dickinson Street to get another five dollars from my mother.

And when I opened the front door, there was Fern with her face buried between my mother's legs.

My mother was sprawled back on the sofa with her eyes squeezed tightly shut. Fern's head was moving from side to side like a dog gnawing on a rawhide bone. They were both naked; my mother's blue nightgown draped over the arm of the sofa; Fern's blouse and skirt in a heap on the floor.

My mother didn't notice me at first, but Fern opened her eyes and turned her head toward the doorway, keeping her mouth on my mother. She looked right at me and for just a split second, I saw real terror.

Grossed out and disturbed on a deep level, I turned to leave. As I walked out the door I heard Fern howling like an animal, screaming from somewhere down inside her chest.

My mother was shrieking, "Fern, Fern, it's okay."

I went outside onto the porch and just stood there. I felt like, *ick.* But also like laughing. The street was quiet; two-story homes, trimmed hedges, driveways, a cat. *The things people do behind closed doors.* Looking at the yellow house with its green shutters and the brown Dodge Aspen in the driveway, you'd just never imagine it.

It seemed like only a few seconds passed before I heard the door open, felt hands on my shoulders turning me around. Fern was standing there, dressed but untucked, her hair dented. She was crying, her cheeks all shiny, and she was pulling me toward her, trying to hug me, kissing my cheek, my forehead, saying, "I'm sorry, I'm sorry, I'm sorry."

I tried to pull away. I didn't want her mouth on me.

The next thing I knew, Fern was running down the steps, then cutting across the lawn toward her car, her head bowed down in shame like she was ducking rain, her handbag clutched against her breasts.

I thought of her dry-cleaned son, Daniel. I thought of him passing me a basket of rolls at dinner. "My mom's rolls are magic. Here, have one."

When I walked back inside, my mother was sitting naked and cross-legged on the couch, smoking a More. Her breasts were large and sacklike, resting in her lap. She exhaled loudly, then brought her cigarette to her lips and sucked on it like a baby. I could not comprehend how anybody would want to do the things to her that Fern was doing. At that moment, it would have been easier for me to spontaneously grasp quantum string theory.

"I wish you enjoyed school more," she said. "Although I guess it must be very dull compared to your life with me. Would you please hand me my nightgown?"

Her breezy attitude made me mad. She thought of nobody except herself. I yanked her nightgown off the arm of the couch and threw it at her, just missing her cigarette.

"Watch it, Augusten! I've got a lit cigarette in my hand." She glared at me. "Don't act out in anger. If you're upset by this, talk to me about it."

"I just don't understand you. I mean, why? How could I not know? What?" I stammered. "How long have you and Fern been . . . together?"

My mother slipped the nightgown over her head, then stood to pull it down over her body. "Oh, I've loved Fern for a very long time. Our relationship became physical a number of months ago."

"When we were living next door?"

"Augusten, those are private details from my personal life." She held her cigarette between her first two fingers and poised her thumb on her temple. "It's between Fern and I." My mother always spoke like she was being interviewed by *Ladies' Home Journal*. Like she was a celebrity.

So Fern and my mother had been lovers for months. My mother was a lesbian. I'd heard somewhere that being gay might be genetic. Maybe I'd inherited this from her. I worried, what else have I inherited? Would I also be crazy by the time I was thirty-five?

She walked into the kitchen and I followed. I watched her spoon Sanka into a coffee mug and then add hot tap water.

"I worry about you so," she said, blowing into her cup before taking a loud sip. "I worry about you and school."

"I can't stand that place," I said. "And Finch is always talking about how you can't make a person do something when they turn thirteen. That when you turn thirteen you're free."

"Yes, I know he is. But the law says you have to go to school."

"Well, fuck that." I lit one of her cigarettes.

"Please don't smoke my cigarettes. You have a pack of your own, although I wish you wouldn't smoke."

"Well, I do."

"I know you do. I just said that I wish you wouldn't."

"Fine," I said, crushing it out.

"No, don't do that. I'll smoke it," she said, reaching for it. Then, "Well, I know I can't force you to go to school. I can't force you to do anything you don't want to do. But I do wish you'd reconsider."

How could she expect me to think about school at a time like this? Furthermore, if I *had* just stayed in school, look what I would have missed. Fern, the minister's wife, was not only a card-carrying lesbian, but my mother's lover.

Fern was a muff-diver. *And she was diving on my mother's muff.*

"Does her family know?"

"No," was my mother's flat answer. She turned to me and

said very seriously, "And it's important that her husband and her children do not know what's going on between us." She said this like I was going to run right over there and say, "Hey, guess what! Guess what your mom is doing while she waits for the bread to rise!"

Then it was as if the lighting changed and a camera slid down a set of rails, zooming into her face. A musical score practically filled the room. She stood in front of the window so that her nightgown filtered the sunlight and her body glowed in silhouette through the fabric.

"All my life, I have been oppressed. And all my life I have worked hard to fight this oppression. When I was a little girl living in Cairo, Georgia, I had a black nanny named Elsa who lived in a shack on the other side of town." She reached into her pocket and brought a cigarette to her lips, lighting it dramatically and exhaling a plume of smoke into the air. "In those days, black people were called niggers. And I knew that the word nigger was a dirty word. And it was a word filled with hatred and anger. And I knew that it was used to describe black people. I also knew that Elsa was no nigger." She paused to look me straight in the eyes. "I knew it was wrong." She walked across the room and faced the wall. "It has taken me all my life to find myself as an artist." She turned to face me. "And to find myself as a woman. I have struggled against the oppression of my mother. And the oppression of your father. And for the first time in my life, I feel I am truly able to claim myself."

Why listen to a teacher talk about how many quarters Nancy needs to buy six apples if they are four and a half cents each when I could listen to this?

"So Augusten, I hope I have your support in my relationship with Fern. Because at this stage in my life, I do not need and will not accept more oppression. I have spent years, my entire life fighting oppression. I hope I don't have to fight you, too." She exhaled, closing her eyes and letting her chin sag down to her chest.

It seemed that I should clap but I didn't.

Instead I said, "Okay, I don't care. Can I have five dollars?"

She smiled. "*May* I have five dollars. And yes, you may, if I have it. Go get my pocketbook and let me take a look."

PURE PROJECTION

IT WAS A BRILLIANT SATURDAY AFTERNOON, WITH THIN, wispy clouds high in the sky; the perfect day for a parade. As Hope and I blew up balloons and tied them to colorful ribbons, the doctor walked around the house in his underpants and wingtip shoes singing off-key, "To dreeeeam the impossible dreeeeeeeam . . ."

"Dad?" Hope called.

"TO FIGHT THE UNBEARABLE—"

"Dad! I need to know if you want us to tie balloons to your hat or just your umbrella."

Finch came into the room. "I want balloons tied onto everything! Today is a day of joy! Balloons everywhere!"

Hope smiled. "Okay."

I blew up a yellow balloon and handed it to Hope. She

tied a red ribbon around it and then looped this through the band that ran around the doctor's gray felt hat.

"We'll need some more pink balloons for his hat," Hope said. "Pink is Dad's favorite color."

In the end, we inflated about sixty balloons, tying them to his hat, his umbrella, looping them through the buttonholes of his long black wool coat that he intended to wear despite the heat. We tied balloons around our own waists and we even attached two balloons to Agnes, one over each breast.

"I'm not going out in public like this," Agnes complained. "Give me more of them, so I can tie some somewhere else. I can't have just these two."

Overhearing Agnes's complaint, the doctor stepped into the room, now dressed in his suit. "No, Agnes," he boomed. "These are the only balloons you should have. You are the matriarch of the family, the Great Breast-Feeder, and that's what these balloons symbolize."

"Oh, phooey," she said. "I don't buy it."

"I said, you will wear only those two balloons! They are your breastloons."

"Breastloons, that's funny, Dad. I like that."

"You do?" he said, his eyebrows twitching. "Then you shall only wear two balloons too."

Half an hour later, Dr. Finch headed out of his house wearing his balloon-covered coat, holding his balloon-covered rainbow umbrella high above his head. Pink balloons on pink ribbon trailed from his hat.

Hope and I followed a few paces behind him carrying a sign that read, UNITE THE FATHERS OF THE WORLD. TODAY IS WORLD FATHER'S DAY!!!!! I was covered with balloons; they were even tied through my belt loops. But Hope had only two balloons, one over each breast.

Hope's younger sister Anne walked behind us with her young son, Poo. Anne was annoyed that she'd been tricked into being in the parade, and refused to wear the breastloons, but she did carry one. And Poo, of course, had six or seven balloons which were tied to his ankles and dragged on the ground.

Next was Natalie. She'd agreed to the breastloons, but also insisted on wearing sunglasses and a large hat so that nobody she knew would recognize her on the street.

My mother was at the tail end of the parade, looking extremely nervous and distracted. She held one small white balloon in her right hand and her More in the other. She kept enough of a distance so that it appeared she'd just been an average woman, out on an average walk, who just happened to come upon a small white balloon which she decided to pick up. I wasn't sure if she was ashamed to be in the parade, or if she just needed to have her meds adjusted.

"I'm not feeling all that well today," she'd told me earlier. "I'm in the middle of a new poem and it's extremely draining."

The parade marched down Perry Street, across Hawley and up Main Street, right through the center of town.

To attract attention, the doctor played songs from *Man of La Mancha* on his red kazoo.

Children shrieked with delight at the sight of him and the doctor always stopped for them saying, "Ho, ho, ho," and handing their parents a mimeographed newsletter that read, "How Emotionally Immature Fathers Are Failing Their Children and Society in General, by B. S. Finch, M.D."

The parents would smile politely, looking slightly worried, and then when we walked by, they would throw the fliers into the trash. I saw more than one mother inspect her child's hand, to make sure nothing had been slipped into their fingers.

To me, the entire parade thing was so far beyond humiliating that it was okay. I suppose I was just comfortable with the concept of excess.

"Help my father educate the fathers of America," Hope cried earnestly to people as we walked by. "Join The World Fathers' Organization and together we can mend society."

Occasionally we would pass a gaggle of five or six Smith freshmen who would back against a building, whispering and giggling as we walked by.

"You young girls, you innocent maidens, how many of you have strong, mature, potent fathers? Which one of you would like to explore my testicles?" the doctor asked, playfully.

Their smiles would instantly vanish and I could see true fear in their eyes. Obviously, they had been warned of many things in life. But not this.

The doctor would then walk on, whistling.

Once or twice, we were stopped by police. But when Dr. Finch presented them with his driver's license showing he was an M.D., we were allowed to continue. It was amazing to me what you could get away with just by being in the medical community.

My mother lagged behind, pausing to browse in bookstore windows, stopping once to run into a shoe store and try on a pair of sandals.

"What's the matter with you?" I asked her.

"I'm having a difficult time with Fern," she said. "I love

her very much, but her sanctimonious crap just really gets on my nerves. Fern is a very controlling woman."

"I'm sorry she's turned out to be such a bitch," I said.

"Well," my mother said heavily, "it's her husband, Ed, too. He's not at all supportive of Fern's relationship with me. And that just creates additional stress. Fern refuses to leave her family. Even though they're all old enough to take care of themselves. I mean, her youngest daughter is almost your age."

"Well, Deirdre, I hope you work it out." My mother had told me not to call her *Mom*, to call her by her first name instead. She liked to think of us more as friends than as mother and son. It was healthier and more mature, she claimed.

"Thank you," she said. "I hope so too." Then she brightened. "Did I tell you that I had a poem accepted by *Yankee Magazine*?"

Life with the Finches wasn't all parades.

I'd been in the spare bedroom listening to Donna Summer and indulging my obsession with my hair by conditioning it with KMS Repair when I'd first become aware of the argument. The shouting was muffled and distant, coming from the other side of the house, but I could clearly make out certain words rising above "Faster and Faster to Nowhere."

"Cunt!" This came from Natalie.

Then, "*Fucking* cunt!" from Hope.

At once, I picked the needle up off the record and headed out of my room. I would need to sneak down the hallway and then lurk. If I'd heard this fight over Donna Summer—it was not to be missed.

Fights were the essence of 67 Perry Street. We were a vine-yard and fights were our special reserve.

"No, Hope. It's not about you. You think every fucking thing is about you because you're so pathetic and have no life of your own."

"Goddamn it, Natalie. Why are you so hostile? What did I do to you? Why do you hate me so much?"

Natalie laughed nastily. "Pure projection. You're the one who hates me but you won't admit it, you repressed bitch."

"I don't hate you, Natalie," Hope screamed with hatred.

"Denial," Natalie snapped back.

My vocabulary had increased dramatically over the past year. *Projection, denial, repression, passive-aggressive, Lithium, Melaril.*

In addition to calling each other standard names like *bitch* and *whore*, the Finches incorporated Freud's stages of psychosexual development into their arsenal of invectives.

"You're so *oral*. You'll never make it to *genital*! The most you can ever hope for is to reach *anal*, you immature, frigid old maid," Natalie yelled.

"Stop antagonizing me," Hope shouted. "Just stop transferring all this anger onto me."

"Your avoidance tactics are *not* going to work, Miss Hope," Natalie warned. "I'm not going to let you just slink away from me. You hate me and you have to confront me."

I glanced over at the grand piano and thought of happier times. Just last week, a chronic schizophrenic patient of the doctor's named Sue had played show tunes while Natalie, Hope and I stood around the piano singing. *"There's no business like show business, like no business I know . . ."* Sue would play for as long as we wanted her to, provided we didn't use her name. She insisted on being called "Dr. F."

"You need to talk to Dad, Natalie. Something's wrong with you. I'm telling you this because I'm your sister and I love you. You've got to see Dad. Please make an appointment."

I heard Natalie stomping and for a moment, I worried she would come into the living room where I was sitting. She would see me and know that I'd been eavesdropping and then somehow pull me into the middle of this thing. But the stomping wasn't because Natalie was coming into this room. It was because Natalie had wrestled her sister onto the sofa.

"Okay, you bitch, say it."

"Get *off* of me," Hope said, and I could hear she was having a hard time breathing. Natalie was a big girl.

"Admit it!"

"Natalie, get up. I can't breathe."

"Then you're gonna die."

There was a thick silence and then a strangled-sounding Hope. "Alright, alright, I hate you. There, are you happy now?"

Natalie let out a belchy, "Fuck it." She stomped out of the room and up the stairs. "This is all such bullshit." From the top of the stairs she shouted, "You will never have any emotional maturity."

Hope screamed back. "I'll get a restraining order placed against you, Natalie. You're out of control and I'll do it."

Natalie slammed her door.

The fight was over.

It had turned out to only be a four. Maybe a four-point-five on a scale of one through ten; ten meaning police involvement or committal to a psychiatric hospital. The problem was, there was nobody else around to join in. I had encountered an interesting principle: the more people, the better the fight.

Usually, they started with just two people bickering over something small. Like what to watch on TV. Then a third person would enter the room and see two people screaming over the TV and they'd decide to moderate, only they'd end up taking a side. Eventually, someone else would get sucked in.

The most excellent fights involved five or more people. Eventually the fight would be resolved the way all disputes were resolved: Dr. Finch. He would be called at the office or the arguing group would travel en masse to his office, a hostile collective gang, and oust whatever patient he was seeing at the time. "Family emergency," someone would say. And the patient, whether a potential suicide or somebody suffering from a multiple personality disorder, would be transferred to the waiting room to drink Sanka with Cremora while Finch solved the dispute.

Finch believed that anger was the crux of mental illness. He believed that anger, unless it was expressed freely, would destroy a person. This explained the constant fighting in the house. Since they were tiny, the Finch children had been encouraged not just to sing, dance and jump rope but also to vent.

Anger was like the ground hamburger of our existence. Its versatility was inspiring. There was Anger Turned Inward, Repressed Anger, Misguided Anger. There were Acts Made in Anger, Things Said in Anger and people who might very well die if they didn't Face Their Anger.

So we screamed at each other constantly. It was like a

competition and the prize was mental health. Every so often Finch would say, "Hope has been expressing a lot of healthy anger lately. I truly believe she's moved up to the next level in the stages of her emotional development. She's leaving the anal and moving into the phallic." So then everybody hated Hope because she walked around being so smug and emotionally mature.

Although his peacockian displays of anger and his high decibel baritone voice prevented most people from directly confronting him, there were times when the doctor himself was the target of someone's "healthy expression." Usually Agnes's.

The doctor and Agnes had been married for what seemed like hundreds of years. When she'd met him, he was a handsome, promising young medical student. She was an attractive and traditional Catholic girl. Surely, she could have had no idea what she was getting herself into.

She reminded me of a scatterbrained old Cadillac that had been driven into the ground but somehow kept on starting, without fuss. Normally, Agnes was just there in the background, wordlessly agreeing, endlessly sweeping, making herself invisible and generally staying on the sidelines.

So it was especially exciting when Agnes flew into a rage. And all her rages were directed at the doctor.

The problem was that the doctor had a mistress. Actually, he had three of them, and he called each his wife. He was fond of saying, "Agnes is only my wife in the legal sense. Emotionally and spiritually we are not married to each other."

Agnes didn't seem to mind this except when the doctor threw it in her face. And when he threw it in her face it was always with his favorite wife, Geraldine Payne.

Geraldine was the female equivalent of a diesel Mercedes sedan. She was, it seemed to me then, well over six feet tall. She was broad-shouldered and broad-faced. When she lumbered into the room, the word *mistress* did not come to mind.

Dr. Finch adored her. She'd been his muse for over a decade, traveling with him from motor-lodge to motor-lodge. Their love was no secret. Often we would joke, "Can you imagine her on top of him? She'd *crush* him."

Geraldine seldom came over to 67 Perry Street, except under the protection of holidays and special occasions. Agnes would be chilly but polite, never forgetting that she was first and foremost *a doctor's wife*.

And when Geraldine was gone, the screaming would begin.

"*I don't care*," she'd bellow from behind the closed bedroom door. Then something might crash against the wall. "I am your *wife*. You cannot do this to me."

Finch would always laugh. He found her fury absolutely hysterical. His face would grow red and his eyes would tear and sometimes he'd call somebody into the room just to watch Agnes in the blind midst of her rage. "Hope!" he might bellow, "your mother is having a fit of hysteria. It's spectacular!"

Agnes continued screaming regardless of who showed up at the door to watch. It was like she was in a scream-trance. And then, for some reason, she always ended up laughing, too. Somebody might point out how insane she looked, holding the nightstand above her head, and then she would catch herself and laugh.

It fascinated me how she tried to maintain her dignity as a Doctor's Wife. She always spoke of him as "the doctor." And she always wore lipstick, even if she was only cleaning turkey off the ceiling—something that needed to be done on a frequent basis.

When it was the doctor's chance to be furious with Agnes, he could bellow and boom all he wanted but she ignored him completely. He stood in front of her in his loose Fruit of the Loom briefs, his black ankle socks and his black wing tips and ranted. But Agnes just hummed as she trimmed the wicks of her Virgin Mary votive candles with a nail clipper.

Sometimes fights took on a festive, holiday feel.

Jeff, the only biological Finch son and a resident of Boston, kept his distance from his more eccentric Western Massachusetts clan. But when he did come to town, all the Finches and many of the patients would gather—Poo's mother, Anne; the oldest Finch daughter, Kate; occasionally Vickie would show up. Hope and Natalie, my mother, and sometimes the doctor's "spiritual brother," Father Kimmel, with his "adopted daughter," Victoria.

If a ham had been baked or a chicken roasted, it wouldn't be long before animal parts were hurling through the air.

"Yeah, that's just because you think you're too fucking good for us," Natalie might shout.

"Calm down, Natalie. I'm busy in Boston. I've got a job out there."

Hope would try and lay a guilt trip on him. "It wouldn't hurt you to visit Dad at least. It's not like you're in California."

"Yeah," Anne would agree. "I'm a single mom with a son. Are you trying to say you're busier than me? Because if you are, you've got . . ."

Long-buried resentments would float to the surface like dead fish. "Well, Mr. Boston Hot Shot, I seem to remember a certain five-year-old boy who *liked* creamed corn."

To those of us who were not blood relations, the effect was something like watching a porn film. It made us want to try it at home.

"Yeah, well, you're a lousy fucking parent," I might scream at my mother later that evening.

"And you're a selfish goddamn son."

If he wasn't physically sitting in the armchair clapping, the doctor was certainly mentally egging it on. "What a glorious expression of anger," he might say, his voice rising above the cacophony. "Get it out, get it out, get it out!"

HE WAS RAISED WITHOUT
A PROPER DIAGNOSIS

My LIFE CAME COMPLETE WITH A FACTORY-INSTALLED BI-ological brother seven years my senior. All my life I suspected that he was missing some essential part. He didn't require a constant diet of movies to stay alive and whenever I tried to explain my desire to own a beauty empire, he suggested I become a plumber instead. My brother, Troy, was like nobody else in the family. He did not share my mother's wild mental imbalance or my father's pitch-black dark side.

And he certainly didn't understand my appreciation for all things unusual and/or reflective.

Some considered my brother to be a genius. And while it's true that he could program computers the size of deep freezers when he was twelve and had read the Encyclopedia Britannica from A–Z the summer he turned fifteen, I did not consider

him to be any kind of a genius. I considered him deeply lack-
ing in the area that mattered most in life. *Star quality.*

"But you'd look so much better if you just shaved your
beard like Lee Majors," I would whine, wielding my clippers.

"Huh," he would grunt. "Who?"

My brother had a unique way of communicating through
grunts and snorts like, one can only assume, our very distant
ancestors.

When presented with a menu at a restaurant, he would
glance up briefly from his technical manual and bark, "Bring
me the meat lump and five iced teas." He would say this the
instant the waitress walked to the table, before she had the
chance to even say, "Hel—"

My mother interpreted my brother's uncommonly abrupt
nature to be the direct result of my father's lousy parenting.
"Poor Troy," she would say. "He's just so heartbroken by that
bastard he can't even talk."

My brother would look at me and grunt. "Huh. Do I seem
sad?"

I would say, "Well, you're not exactly perky."

He didn't seem especially sad to me. He didn't seem to
contain any emotions whatsoever except a sense of mischief
and humor at the expense of others.

Once he phoned our father in the middle of the night to
tell him I'd been arrested for drunken loitering in the town
of Northampton and had to be bailed out of jail. My father
was alarmed, but not surprised. After my father had gotten
dressed and located his checkbook, my brother called him
back and let him in on the ruse. "Troy, don't play tricks like
that." My brother snickered and replied, "Huh. Okay then."

Because he moved out of our home in Leverett when he

was sixteen, my brother was never involved with any of the Finches. He had met them and considered them "freaks." He also considered our parents "freaks" and remained as far away from them as possible. He was designing electric guitars for the rock band KISS at the time, so I viewed him with a remote sense of awe.

Once, he even let me hang out with him and the band like a groupie. They were playing the Nassau Coliseum in New York and my brother not only paid for me to fly all the way out there, but he met me at the airport in a white stretch limo.

I got to sit next to the stage and watch the band rehearse. I got to see them without makeup. I even got to watch Paul Stanley talk on a portable phone that was the size of an assault rifle.

At one point, Gene Simmons came over to me and joked, "Hey, little boy. Wanna see me without my clothes?"

I wanted to tell him, "Yes."

He laughed and stripped off his jeans so he could put on his stage clothes.

I kept watching until he gave me a funny look and stepped behind an amp.

Sometimes my brother would drive by Sixty-seven and pick me up in his brand new Oldsmobile Toronado. I would slide onto the brown velvet corduroy seat and he would say, "This vehicle has quadraphonic sound. Do you know what that means?" When I would shake my head no, he would launch into a lengthy and highly technical explanation of the science behind quadraphonic sound and what, exactly, it meant from an audio engineering point of view. Then he would say, "Now do you understand?" When I again shook my head no, he would shrug and say, "Well, maybe you're retarded."

He wasn't being mean. That's the thing that's important to understand. To him, I would have to be at least borderline retarded not to understand something so easily comprehensible to him.

Dr. Finch tried repeatedly to engage my brother in therapy, all to no avail. My brother would sit politely in the doctor's inner office, his gigantic arms slung over the back of the sofa, and he would grunt, "Huh. I still don't understand why I need to be here. I'm not the one who's eating sand." When Dr. Finch pointed out to my brother that conflict affects everyone in the family, my brother would grunt, "Huh. I feel okay."

It was assumed, then, that my brother was so deeply mentally ill as to be untreatable. Possibly, he had a profound character flaw.

I knew the reality was far worse. My brother was born without taste or the desire to be professionally lit. "You can't go out in public like that," I would say when I saw him in his beige wool slacks riding up nearly to his nipples, his kelly-green polo shirt three sizes too small.

"Huh. What's the matter with what I have on? These are perfectly good clothes."

My brother was hopelessly without style or any sense of what was going on in the world, culturally. Ask him who Debra Winger was and he'd say, "Is she another one of those freakish Finches?" But ask him to explain how a particle accelerator worked and he could talk uninterrupted for hours. He could even draw you a diagram with his mechanical pencil.

It pained me.

"But highlights would bring out your eyes," I would say. "Especially if you'd get rid of those three-inch-thick lenses on your glasses."

"Huh. I like these glasses. I can see through them."

My brother had very specific likes and dislikes. Basically, he liked anything until it harmed him and then he was wary. All creatures in life had an equal chance with my brother, from terrier to psychotherapist. Those that impressed him with an especially keen mental ability, an amusing trick or had a large portion of food to offer would gain his favor. If my brother could find nothing of value to the person, he would dismiss them entirely. As he did with the Finches and our parents.

I envied his lack of emotional ties. I felt pulled by everyone in every direction, while my brother seemed free of annoying human encumbrances.

One thing he was quite fond of was trains. He would follow a train in his car for hours, riding parallel to the tracks, whether or not there was a road. "Hold on tight," he would shout over the rumble of the tires on the gravel, "there's a good chance we'll roll."

He also liked cars. He liked to take them apart and then put them back together. Which would have been perfectly fine, except when we were younger, he liked to do this on the living room rug.

"Jesus, Troy. What do you think you're doing? You can't take that carburetor apart on the living room rug."

"Huh," he would grunt. "Why not?"

To him, a rug was nothing more than a surface area. And

it had the distinct advantage of being white, so the dark greasy engine parts were easier to spot.

I missed my brother and wanted to see him constantly. I often wished he would pick me up and carry me away with him. But when he did pick me up and carry me away, I soon grew tired staring at the red light on the caboose, my stomach growling and my brother having nothing more to say than, "Look, the caboose."

"I just want a big life, you know?" I would say, examining my hair in the illuminated visor mirror.

"What do you mean?"

"You know, I want to get noticed. I don't just want to be a nothing."

"Huh," he would grunt. "Then be a plumber. People notice plumbers all the time."

And while he didn't crave the company of either parent, my brother didn't seem to be tortured by their very existence like I was. "I can pretty much take them or leave them," he would often say.

When I would scream, "My fucking father won't even give me money for food. He won't take my calls. He wants nothing to do with me at all. I want to stab him with a butcher knife," my brother would reply flatly, "Yeah, he is basically worthless."

Throughout my life, my brother had been the one person I could rely on. Even when it seemed we had absolutely nothing in common, I knew that he was as reliable as a mathematical formula.

Many years later, he would be diagnosed with a mild form of autism known as Asperger's syndrome. It explained his fascination with cars, his peculiar way of speaking and his abrupt nature, as well as his mind-numbing and highly specific intelligence. It also explained his lack of desire to discuss *Three's Company* at any length.

Sometimes I wonder if his life would have been easier if my parents had taken him to a doctor instead of just assuming he was cold and emotionally blocked.

But then I remind myself that my parents had very questionable taste when it came to choosing medical professionals.

With this in mind, I like to think that my brother wasn't so much overlooked as he was inadvertently protected.

THE JOY OF SEX (PRETEEN EDITION)

I'M LYING BACK ON NEIL'S BED, THE TOP OF MY HEAD KNOCK-
ing against the headboard because his cock is inexplicably
down my throat. His photographs—the reason I came up to
his room in the first place—are sliding off, falling on the floor.
I can hear them smack against the floor. Flutter-smack. All I
see is a triangle of dark hair coming at me. This, and I feel
an unprecedented sensation of fullness in my throat. It's hard
to breathe. The air comes into my nose in gasps that seem
controlled by the thrusting of Neil's hips. He thrusts; I get air.
The air comes out my mouth, forced around the shaft of his
cock.

"Yes, fuck yes," he spits. "Jesus mother fucking Christ."

The triangle of hair comes at me, away from me, at me,
away from me, at me, away from me, at me, away from me.

My arms are stretched out at my sides, pinned to the mattress by Neil's hands. I must look like Jesus on the cross. This image actually occurs to me. I also think, *I didn't come here for this.*

It goes on. The thrusting, the lucky sucking of air through my nose, the repulsive sound it makes leaving my mouth, the wet exhale.

"You fucker," Bookman says, biting the word out of the air, like he's taking a chunk of something off with his teeth; a chunk of meat.

He smells funny. It's almost like a food, like you could eat the smell. Well, I guess I am eating the smell. But it's not like any food I've had before. Kind of a cheese, maybe? But darker, warmer, sweeter.

My head is killing me. It keeps smack, smack, smacking the headboard. And the headboard is hitting the wall. We're making a lot of noise.

My eyes are watery now.

I've never had my mouth open so wide. It's embarrassing. I wonder what I look like with this big mouth and my eyes all teary. I can feel my own drool running down my neck and I want to wipe it off but I can't move my hands, my arms.

There's a crack in the ceiling that runs from one corner of the wall, straight across but I can't see how far it goes. The paint on the ceiling is so thick that it's peeling. I want to pull on it like sunburn or dried foot skin.

And then the black triangle smashes into my face. I can't breathe through my nose at all. All I can see is black.

There's something else in my throat. It's filling with liquid.

My eyes feel swollen, like they are going to pop. My head is going to pop.

And then there is a profound subtraction. It comes with a sucking sound. The cock is gone, the triangle is gone, his hands are off my wrists. Blood rushes into my hands.

My head stops hitting the headboard.

This is more relief than I have ever known. I could sleep now. In fact, I feel drowsy.

His smile is in my face. We are nose to nose, eyes to eyes. In a small mean voice he says, "There. Still think you're gay?"

I blink.

He pulls me up so that I'm sitting on the bed.

"You okay?" he says.

I watch the corners of his mustache turn up in a smile.

"You swallowed," he says. "That was incredible. Just incredible. You have a hot mouth."

There is a taste in my mouth that makes me think of alfalfa sprouts.

Neil stands up and steps into his underwear. Briefs. White except for a dark brown streak mark running up the middle of the butt.

I wipe the back of my hand across my mouth, soaking it. I open and close my mouth. My jaw feels tight, stuck. My lips are numb. I touch them with my finger. They seem to feel swollen. Like I've been nuzzling wasps. I need a mirror.

There is one light in the room, a bare bulb that hangs by a cord from the ceiling. Now I can see that the crack travels all the way across. I believe I could peel the paint off in one sheet.

Neil bends over and begins collecting his photographs. "Did you see this one?" he says, holding it up. It's a shot of a black kid on a swing, swinging way up, almost out of the picture. But his eyes are looking right at you.

"Where'd you take that?" I say.

"New York City," he says.

Everything is normal again. We're talking about his pictures. He's not angry with me.

I feel confused. He's Neil again, but who was that? What happened? "What happened?" I say.

He sets the photographs on the bed and looks at me, hands on his hips. He smiles. "That was called sex. You think you're gay? That's what gay men do."

His eyes do this little flashing thing. It's like we're kids at school both running for the swing at recess and he gets there first, sits on it and looks at me. It's that kind of look. *Beat ya to it!*

"Get dressed," he says, tossing my jeans at me. "I gotta drive you back."

He goes over to the chest of drawers to get a cigarette. His back is to me. His bumpy spine showing through his skin. If I run, I think, I could dive into him with my hands, aim for that spine, maybe snap it. He would bend in two; snap; break.

I feel like there's sun on my face.

I hate him so much.

He turns. "Smoke?"

"Okay."

"Here." He tosses me the pack.

I take one out and stick it in my lips. He comes over with his lighter and lights it. It seems sweet of him to do and it makes me not hate him as hard.

I take a drag off the cigarette. The smoke stings my lungs but in a good way. I let the smoke pour through my nostrils like a movie star.

I feel like I've walked through some door, into some room,

and I'll never be able to leave. I feel like nothing is the same. Just like that. Nothing will ever be the same again.

I also feel like I can't ever tell anybody about this. I can't tell Natalie, although I really, really want to.

What happened has to be all mine.

I feel crowded by this. Like I need to go home and think about it for a week or maybe the rest of my life. How can I go to school in the morning? It's already after midnight and I have to be up at seven-thirty to make it there by eight-fifteen.

Neil opens the closet door. Inside a tangle of wire coat hangers crowds the far end of the pole. There's nothing inside except a camera hanging from its neck strap by a hook on the back of the door. He takes the camera and aims it at me.

My underwear is on backwards but I don't care.

He shoots me as I button my shirt. I button it up almost to the top.

"I want to taste me in you," he says, tossing the camera on the bed. He comes over to me and takes my face in his hands. He kisses me. His tongue running across my teeth, filling up my mouth, looking.

I look past his head at the wall. I want to pull away. It's time to go. I have to get home.

He presses up against me. Mashing his pelvis into mine. My bladder is full; I've got to piss.

He pulls away. "Let's go."

We go.

Downstairs, his roommate is sitting on the sofa chain-smoking and watching TV. I have a hunch that she is his failed attempt at heterosexuality. "Hi, honey," she says to me. "What are you, like seventeen?"

"Thirteen," I tell her.

She is fat. She is fat in a way that suggests she always has been, always will be, fat. When she raises her cigarette to her lips, I see that her fingernails are dirty and chewed. Her hair is a ravage of tangles, shoulder-length and the color of straw. A tiny gold cross hangs from a dainty chain around her neck. She is too large for this cross.

"Beer?"

I tell her no. She strikes me as somebody who has tasted a lot of semen. I want to ask her if it all tastes like alfalfa sprouts, or if it's just something funky with him.

Neil says, "I'll be back in a while. I gotta take him home."

"Pick me up some more smokes," she says. She coughs. She takes another drag and turns her face back to the TV. *Mannix.*

Neil takes his keys off the kitchen table, crumbs sticking to his fingers as he swipes. He gives them a toss into the air and catches them. "Ready?"

Of course I'm ready, I think.

We walk outside. I can see my breath, so I hold it. I want to keep it inside. I feel exposed. Enough of me has escaped into the air for the evening.

Neil opens the passenger door for me, like I'm a girl. And suddenly, I feel like a girl. I am ashamed. The door isn't locked.

He walks around to his side and slides in. He starts the car.

The seats are freezing. I move my legs together, then I slide my hands beneath them. I look back at the house. The window near the door provides a dull, yellow light, mixed with some blue light from the TV in the other room. All the other windows are dark. The house itself is dark; during the day it's probably gray or brown. At night, it's black. There is no lawn. Just dirt and gravel where a lawn could go.

"You okay with what happened?" Neil asks, pulling onto Route 5.

I say, "Yeah. Sure."

"Good. I hope I didn't hurt you." He turns to me. "Because I didn't want to do that, hurt you."

I nod.

"I just wanted to show you, you know, what you were in for. Being gay and all."

"Yeah," I say. I say it softly. I hardly say it. Or maybe I don't even say it. Maybe I only think it.

We don't speak for the rest of the drive. My window fogs and this makes me feel like there is no world outside of the car.

Again, that feeling that everything has changed. And the sensation, very real, of spinning.

Hope is awake when I walk in the door. She's in the TV room, sitting on the couch, her legs tucked up beneath her. "Hi there," she says.

"Hey, Hope."

"Did you have fun with Neil?"

I make a smile. "Yeah, it was fun. He showed me his photographs."

Hope unfolds her legs and reaches behind her head to scratch. "Oh yeah? That's great. Did you two talk?"

I step further into the room. The TV is flipping. Why doesn't she adjust the vertical hold? How can she watch her show like this? "Um, yeah. I guess. We talked some." My lips feel swollen and I wonder if it shows.

"You look a little funny," she says. "Is everything alright with you?"

Her feet are stretched out in front of her, buried in the plush, matted fur of her dog, Zoo. When she wriggles her toes, it looks like there are animals deep inside Zoo's fur. The sofa fabric is threadbare, so smooth from wear that it's slick.

I sit. I stare at the TV screen and think how much I want a cigarette, but how I'm too uncomfortable to smoke in the house; how it's still my secret that I smoke. Natalie smokes, but she's braver than me. When Agnes or Hope or her father bitch at her about smoking, she just tells them to fuck off. But I feel like a guest, trapped in my own politeness, so I can't do that. Finally, I say, "It was just weird seeing all the pictures Neil took of New York City. Makes me want to live there someday."

"I could see you in New York," Hope says, turning to look at me.

"Yeah?"

"I really can," she says. Then she takes her small bible from the table next to the sofa and places it in her lap. "You want to ask God about it?"

I shrug. "Okay, I guess."

She pats the sofa cushion next to her. "Let's do a bible-dip."

I slide over.

"Close your eyes," she says.

I close my eyes and think of how to phrase my question. "Okay," I say. "Will I end up living in New York City?"

Hope takes the bible in her hands and opens it to a random page. "Okay," she says.

I stab my finger onto the page and open my eyes.

Hope leans in to see what word I hit. "Strength," she reads.

I sit back. "What does that mean?"

Hope reads the surrounding words to try and gather con-text. "I think it means that you will need a lot of strength before you can move there. That you need to be very sure of who you are. I think it's a very positive bible-dip."

"You do?"

"Absolutely. I think it means you're in an enormous period of growth now and that when you come out of it, you'll be strong enough to live where you want to live."

This makes me feel better somehow. I like that Hope speaks fluent God. I like that she can almost predict the fu-ture.

Zoo rolls over on her side and lets out a deep, tired sigh.

Hope yawns. "I'm sleepy, too, Zoo," she says. She sets her bible back on the table under the lamp and then turns the lamp off. "We're going to bed."

"Yeah," I say, "me too."

Hope leads Zoo out of the room and I sit and watch the TV flip. I can still smell Neil; it's like his smell is trapped between my upper lip and my nose. I think I want to wash my face, take a shower.

The TV flips. I close my eyes. When I do, the dark triangle comes at me again. I swallow.

The crack in the ceiling. When I close my eyes, all I can see is the crack in the ceiling.

SCHOOL DAZE

Her desk was in the center of the room and everyone who sat next to her, behind her and in front of her was her best friend in the whole wide world. They would pass her folded notes, which she would unfold, read and then pass to someone else, giggling. I often saw her leaning over and whispering something in someone's ear. I was sure it was something nice. "Let's surprise Heather after school and take her to a movie!" She had a puffy black afro that she adorned with combs and I used to sit there wishing I could touch it. I imagined it would feel woolly, like a sheep. But also lighter like cotton candy. I knew if I actually *did* reach across the two desks between us and touch her afro, she would scream. She was the whitest girl in school, even though she was black.

She was Bill Cosby's daughter and I loathed her for this.

"He's sooooooo cute," she would say when one of her friends handed her a blue Smurf key chain. Or, "Venus was the goddess of *love*," she would correctly answer in Greek mythology class, her bright white smile occupying one-third of her face.

This girl was everything in life that I wasn't. She was smart, articulate, outgoing and popular. She came from the best of families and never wore the same clothes two days in a row. And I was positive she did not have razor burn on her face from kissing a man twice her age. She made me sick.

One of us had to go.

"I just don't know what to do with you, you're making me frantic," my mother said, chewing her thumbnail down to the quick.

"Well, I'm not going back to that school ever again. I don't fit in there and I never will. I have to get out now."

"But you have to stay in school until you're sixteen. It's the law."

"I can't stay there for another three years," I screamed. "God, I wish I were dead. I should just kill myself." I felt like a trapped animal.

My mother said, "Don't even joke about suicide."

"What makes you think I'm joking?" Maybe I *could* just kill myself and get it over with. Maybe that was my only way out.

She stopped typing and reached for her Wite-Out. "I don't have the emotional energy right now to deal with you when you're all wild like this."

I had been chain-smoking all night and pacing around the house, consumed with dread about school the following morning. I had gone over my list of options in my head and the list was short: leave school now forever.

My mother was in the middle of writing what she considered to be an important poem. "It's fifty pages long and I truly do believe it's going to make me a very famous woman," she said out of the corner of her mouth that wasn't wrapped around her More.

"I don't care about that fucking poem. I'm miserable. You have to do something."

She exploded. "Well, I care very much about this *fucking poem* as you call it. I am putting everything I have into this writing. I have worked hard all my life to be able to claim my writing as my own."

"Well, what about me?" I bellowed. I wanted to shove her typewriter on the floor. I hated it and I hated her. I wanted to be a Cosby.

"You are an adult," she said. "You're thirteen years old. You've got a mind and a will of your own. And I have my own needs right now. My writing is very important to me and I should hope that it would be important to you."

Somehow, my mother had managed to turn this all around to her. She had a knack for this.

"I'm not one of your fans," I shouted. I had heard Christina Crawford say this to her mother in *Mommie Dearest* and I knew my mother hadn't seen the movie, so it would seem original.

"Well, at the moment," she said, "I'm not one of your fans, either." She turned away from me and began typing.

I unplugged her typewriter, freezing it.

"Goddamn it, Augusten. What's the matter with you? Why are you doing this to me? I need support right now. Not attacks from you."

I told her to fuck herself and then I stormed out of the

room and went outside to sit on the front porch and fume. A moment later she appeared at the door. "Dr. Finch would like to speak with you on the telephone." Her voice was calm, composed, like a receptionist's.

"Fine," I said. I worried I might be in trouble for terrorizing my mother. He might tell me that I'd pushed her too hard and now she would go psychotic again, unraveling all the hard work he had done on her.

"Hello?"

"Well, hello there, Augusten. What's this I hear about you not wanting to go to school?"

I couldn't believe it. He was talking about me.

I told him about how miserable I was, how I didn't feel that I fit in and how I felt trapped and depressed and just wanted to be left alone so I could go to movies and write in my journal.

He listened to me without interrupting except with the occasional, "Uh huh," and "I see." Then he said, "Well, the compulsory education laws are such that you have to attend school until you're sixteen years old."

"I know but I can't," I said. I was desperate. He had to help me.

"Well," he said with a deep sigh. I could picture him leaning back, massaging his forehead with his free hand. "The only loophole, or way that I can see to get you out of school for any length of time, would be a suicide attempt. If you tried to kill yourself, then I could legally remove you from school."

"What do you mean?"

"Well, if you were to attempt suicide, I could explain to the school board that you were psychologically unfit to attend school, that you needed intensive treatment. I don't know how long they'd buy it for. Maybe a month, two, three."

"Well, how . . ." I was confused. "How does this happen? I mean, what do I have to do? You don't mean, like, I have to slit my wrists or something?"

"No, no, no, that's not what I mean. It would be a staged suicide attempt. A ruse."

"Oh," I said.

"But you would have to be committed to a psychiatric hospital. Basically what would have to happen is that your poor mother would have to find you—" He chuckled under his breath, amused by the scenario. "—and drive you to the hospital. You'd have to remain there for, oh, probably two weeks for observation."

I confessed that I did not find the idea of staying at a psychiatric hospital that much more appealing than school. Only slightly.

"It'll be like a mini vacation," he said. Then, "Where's your spirit for adventure?"

Now *that* sounded better. Even if I wasn't exactly free to go to movies and see Bookman, I wasn't in school. And that was the main thing. He was right, it would be an adventure.

"Okay, let's do it."

"Now let me speak to your mother," he said.

When she hung up she said, "The doctor is on his way over." She looked pleased. And I realized immediately the reason for this was because I would be out of her hair for awhile. She would have nobody in the house to tell her, "Stop listening to that fucking *Auntie Mame*. It's been fifty times already." She would no longer have to defend her need to compulsively sketch the Virgin of Guadeloupe in lip liner over and over for days at a time until she got the eyes right. She would be able to gorge herself on mustard sandwiches with the crusts cut off.

It was the ideal arrangement for both of us, it seemed.

I was upstairs in my rarely occupied room, staring out the window at the street thinking about that little Cosby bitch. She certainly didn't have to choose between a mental hospital or the seventh grade. Why couldn't I be like that? I told myself, *All I want is a normal life.* But was that true? I wasn't so sure. Because there was a part of me that enjoyed hating school, and the drama of not going, the potential consequences whatever they were. I was intrigued by the unknown. I was even slightly thrilled that my mother was such a mess. Had I become addicted to crisis? I traced my finger along the windowsill. *Want something normal, want something normal, want something normal,* I told myself.

But there were things in my life so much more interesting than school. So much more consuming. Bookman didn't have a regular job. He filled in for Hope at the doctor's office as receptionist when she needed to run an errand. Together, they were his secretarial pool. So most of his days were open. Once I was free from school we could be together constantly. The thought made me ache with *want.*

That whole thing at his apartment really brought us closer together. "I realize that was wrong of me. It was almost abusive; I'm sorry," he had cried.

"It's okay," I told him. Secretly I wanted revenge, but I also wanted his companionship, and that won out.

Bookman gave me attention. We would go for long walks and talk about all sorts of things. Like how awful the nuns were in his Catholic school when he was a kid and how you have to roll your lips over your teeth when you give a blowjob. Then we'd go back to the barn behind the house and fool around upstairs on his musty old mattress.

When I was sitting in school, surrounded by all those painfully normal, Cabbage Patch–owning kids, all I could think about was Bookman. Kissing him, touching him, hearing him say to me, "God, you're becoming my whole world."

How could I just sit there obediently pinning a butterfly's wings to a lab tray or memorizing prepositional phrases? When the other boys in the locker room were showering and talking about their weekends playing soccer, what was I supposed to say? "Oh, I had a great time. My thirty-three-year-old boyfriend said he wished they could package my cum like ice cream so he could eat it all day."

Bookman was the only person who gave me attention, besides Natalie and Hope. My mother certainly didn't. Unless I was holding a spare typewriter ribbon or standing next to the record player when she needed the needle moved back to the beginning of a song, she had no use for me.

And my father wouldn't even accept my collect calls.

As I was picking the paint off the windowsill I saw an unfamiliar station wagon pull up in front of our house. The engine was killed but nobody stepped out. I watched for a few minutes until the passenger window opened and a pink helium balloon escaped and rose up into air. I wondered where he got the helium, and if he had any left over.

The doctor had made a house call.

My mother called me downstairs and Dr. F shook my hand.

He said, "You have a fiercely independent spirit, young man."

My mother said, "He certainly does."

"Are you ready?" he asked.

"Ready for what?"

He cleared his throat and rubbed his hands together. "We need to take a little drive. We have to pick up some supplies from a friend in order for this to work. In the car, we can talk about what we're going to do, what the plan is."

My mother kept glancing back at her typewriter, like it was calling her. I knew it was hard for her to be separated from it for even five minutes.

"You'll need to come with us," the doctor said.

My mother looked alarmed, like she'd just been diagnosed with a disease that would prevent her from ever being able to talk about herself again. She hesitated, then she said, "Okay. I just need to get my bag."

Finch drove, my mother sat in the passenger seat and I was in the back, my forehead pressed against the window. I was beginning to worry about what, exactly, I had agreed to. As soon as we were out of Amherst and onto the highway my mother opened her bag and began searching for something. She pulled some typed pages out and arranged them on her lap. She cleared her throat and turned to the doctor. "Would you like to hear some of this new poem I've been working on?"

He nodded. "Certainly, Deirdre. If you'd like to read it."

"May I smoke?" she asked, sticking a More between her lips and poising her lighter.

"By all means."

"Thank you," she replied almost flirtatiously. I half-expected her to stick a dogwood blossom behind her ear.

For the next half hour, I endured a mandatory poetry reading. She read in her melodic, Southern voice, enunciating perfectly, each inflection practiced. I knew she must have wished there were a microphone clipped to her shirt collar or a camera pointed at her profile.

I couldn't help but think, *This car is taking me to a mental hospital and my mother is treating it like open-mic night at a Greenwich Village café.*

We drove to a farmhouse in the country, surrounded by pastures. Dr. F pulled into the half-circle gravel driveway and stopped the car. He looked at me in the rearview mirror. "It's very important," he began, "that you not ever tell anybody about this."

I wiped my sweaty palms on my jeans and agreed even though I didn't know what I was agreeing to.

"I could lose my medical license," he said.

What was he going to do? And why were we at a farmhouse? The mystery was scary. I wanted to know right then what was going on, but I also felt like I couldn't ask, I had to wait and see.

My mother straightened her papers and put them back in her bag. She looked out the window. "This is a lovely house," she said. "What a beautiful old barn."

"I'll be back momentarily," the doctor said. "You both just sit right here."

After he left my mother said, "Well, you certainly have created quite the adventure for yourself." She rolled down her window and inhaled deeply. "The air is so clean out here, so fresh. Reminds me of when I was little girl in Georgia." Then she took a More from her pack and lit it.

The doctor was gone for about half an hour. When he returned he was carrying a small paper sack. He slid into the car and started the ignition. I was expecting him to pull out of the driveway, but instead he turned around and handed me the bag.

I took it. It contained a pint of Jack Daniel's.

He then reached into the inside pocket of his jacket, removed a prescription bottle, opened it and shook a number of pills into his palm. "I want you to take three of these pills," he directed, "and wash them down with some of that bourbon."

I tried to hide my shock. I was getting pills and liquor, for free, from Natalie's dad. Although it sucked that I had to take them with my mother and him in the car. I wanted to save them for later, wait and take them with Natalie and then walk around the Smith campus, gooned out of our minds. Instead I placed the pills in my mouth and washed them down with a few sips of the liquor. At first it was like fire sliding down my throat but then I got this incredible warm, soothing sensation throughout my body. Until then, I'd only had beer and wine. This was much, much better.

Again, Dr. F said, "Now you need to promise that you won't ever tell anybody about this. The story is that you tried to kill yourself and your mother found you and took you to the hospital. Have you got that?"

I nodded my head. "And I don't have to go to school?"

"Not for awhile," he said.

"Okay." I lay my head back on the seat.

*   *   *

When I woke up, it was because a sweaty woman with yellow hair was trying to stick something down my throat. This seemed to be happening to me a lot lately.

She was a nurse. This registered when she said, "I'm a nurse. You're in a hospital. We have to get those pills out of your stomach. You don't really want to die, do you?"

Of course I didn't want to die. I just wanted to go back to sleep. But when I tried, she pinched me on the arm again and continued to shove what could only be described as a hollow plastic penis down my throat. I gagged, my eyes became blurry with tears as she attempted to empty the contents of my stomach.

I fell back asleep.

The next time I woke up, I was in a bed and there was nobody on top of me trying to cause harm. There was a window in the room, but it hurt to open my eyes because the lids felt so heavy. It was like the light itself had weight, and was forcing my eyes closed.

"Hi," said a voice next to the bed. It was close, but not standing over me.

"Are you awake?" It was a man's voice.

I turned my head in the direction of the voice and my eyes focused on a naked figure, sitting cross-legged on a bed and wearing a pointy green party hat. I was impressed with the realism of my dream. I could even see small black hairs sprouting from just above his kneecaps.

"I'm Kevin," he said.

As more of the room came into focus—the fluorescent overhead lights, the gray metal dresser across from me, and bars on the windows—I realized I was not dreaming. I tried to sit up, but it was like there was a lead dental cape on my chest making it impossible for me to move.

The naked man with the pointy hat came over to me and stood next to me. His penis dangled a few inches above my hand and I had the brief temptation to grab it, as some sort of reality test.

"You tried to kill yourself, huh?" he said. He scratched under his balls.

And then I knew. *I must be in the madhouse.* I vaguely remembered having my stomach pumped.

That had happened to me once before when I was six. I had eaten a wax Santa Claus figure from the Christmas tree and had to be rushed to the hospital in Springfield. This was the second time in my life that a Santa-like figure had caused me to enter a hospital for a minor medical procedure.

"You want some water?" he said.

I nodded.

He left my side and walked over to the doorway where he yelled down the hall, "The new kid's awake and he wants some water!"

Within moments, a nurse appeared carrying a tray with a small paper cup on it.

"How are you feeling?" she asked abruptly.

"Tired."

"No wonder," she said. "You can't take half a bottle of Valium and a quart of booze and not feel tired." She seemed hostile. She handed me a small paper cup filled with lukewarm water.

I swallowed the water in one gulp. It tasted like rust. Then I said, "Where am I?"

She said, "For starters, you're alive." She wrapped a blood-pressure cuff around my arm and started pumping. "Of course, that's the bad news, I guess. The good news is you're in Memorial Hospital where you can get some real help." She turned to Kevin. "And you. Take that hat off and put on some clothes."

After she left and after Kevin had put on a hospital gown, he leaned in and said, "The nurses and doctors? They're all crazy here."

He caught me staring at the green party hat that was still on top of his head. He laughed, taking it off. "They had a little birthday party for one of the old wenches here. Something like her million-and-first birthday. Nurse whatever. Who cares."

I was able to sit up though my head was pounding. "What is this place?"

"It's the loony bin," he said making a crazy face.

I wanted to go for a walk to clear my head. I needed fresh air. "How do you get out? Is there anywhere to walk?"

He laughed. "You don't get out. It's a locked ward, kiddo."

At *least*, I thought, *it's not homeroom.*

Kevin told me he was "in" because he'd tried to kill himself, too.

When I said, "Really?" he nodded.

"Why?"

"Because my life sucks," he said. "My parents are pressuring me to go to a school I don't want to go to, to marry someone I don't want to marry. It's like my whole life is already mapped out for me, at nineteen. I'm just so fucking sick of it. Of everything. You know? Fuck it."

"Do you wish you'd died?" I said.

He thought about this. "Not right this minute."

When he said, "What about you?" I felt a pang of guilt because he seemed so open and I couldn't tell him the truth. Even though I wanted to. I said, "School. I hate school."

"What are you, like eighth grade or something?"

"Seventh. I stayed back in third."

"Christ, that's not so bad. That's junior high. It can't be all that bad."

I wanted to tell him about the perfect Cosby girl but suddenly, this didn't seem like enough of a reason to be locked in a mental hospital. I wanted to tell him about Neil Bookman, about how much I love him and want to be with him and school is only in the way. And I wanted to tell him about how my mother is always going crazy and I have to worry about her all the time. I wanted to say, "Well, I'm only here for a sort of vacation." But I couldn't tell him how I got there. It had to be a secret.

For the next few days, I continued to live my lie, protecting my secret. In group therapy when I had to confront my suicidal feelings, I did my best to ad-lib. "I hate my life," I would say. Or, "I just wanted it all to end." I tried to recall lines from every TV movie I'd seen. I tried to picture Martin Hewitt in *Endless Love* after he burned down Brooke Shields's house out of love. Instead of becoming depressed that I was in the locked ward of a mental hospital, I pretended I was playing a role in a movie, possibly on my way to an Emmy.

I missed Bookman. I wasn't allowed to call and this whole thing had happened so suddenly, I was sure he was worried about me.

I imagined him coming to the hospital and standing outside, screaming my name up at the windows.

I missed him so much that I had physical sensations of loss, all over my body. Like one minute I was missing an arm, the next my spleen. It was making me feel sick, like throwing up.

He wasn't rough to me anymore, like he was the first time we "did it." He was nice now, slow. He told me he was falling in love with me. That I was godlike and that he hadn't known that at first. He said I was becoming everything to him, his *reason.*

I'd never mattered to anyone so much before.

When I finally broke down and confessed about my relationship with Bookman to my mother, she couldn't have been happier. "I am very, very fond of that young man," she told me, gazing off into a space beyond my left shoulder. "He's always been very supportive of me and my writing."

"So you're not pissed?" I said, wondering if the fact that I was involved with a man twice my age would be yet another thing she had to worry about.

"Look, Augusten," she began. "I don't want you to suffer from the same sort of oppression that *I* suffered from as a girl. Because I know"—she lit a More—"how difficult it is to reclaim one's self. I'll tell you, sometimes I wish I had been raised by a mother like me. You're very lucky that I've done so much work, emotionally. And it makes me so happy to be able to support you."

I said, "Good. I'm glad it doesn't bother you. Because it's a serious thing with us. He's really insane over me."

"And that's what you want?" she asked.

"Well, yeah," I said.

"Then you have my full support in your relationship."

I was stunned by her reaction. I'd been dreading the moment when I finally told her because I knew she'd somehow turn it into something that I was doing to *her*. I could almost hear the dishes smashing and the windows shaking in their frames from all the door-slamming. Instead, it turned out to be nothing. As if I told her that from now on, I wouldn't be eating refined white flour anymore.

"Have you spoken to Dr. Finch about your relationship with Bookman?" she asked.

"Yeah, he knows," I said.

"And what does *he* say?"

"Um, he's, I don't know. I guess he's okay with it. Although it seemed like he felt that I could do better. But he's not gonna try and stop it or anything. He said I should tell you and see what you thought."

"Good," she said, plucking a hair off her slacks. "I'm glad he was accepting and supportive."

When I told Dr. Finch about me and Bookman, at first he seemed angry. I'd made an appointment with Hope to see him because I thought it was sort of a big deal and I shouldn't just tell him when he was home, sitting in his underwear in front of the TV eating an old drumstick. When I walked into his office he said, "Well, young man. Take a seat and tell me what's on your mind."

It felt weird to be sitting on his psychotherapy couch, surrounded by all the boxes of psychotherapy tissues. I felt like a patient. "Bookman and I are boyfriends," I blurted out.

"Boyfriends?" he repeated.

"Yeah. It started out as friends, but now we're more than that. He's in love with me and I love him, too."

"And is this a sexual relationship?" he asked, sounding strangely professional.

I nodded.

He brought his hands up to his face and inhaled through his fingers. "I've got to tell you, young man, I went through this with my daughter Natalie."

"I know," I said. "It's sort of similar."

"While I don't believe that it's wrong for a younger person to be intimately involved with somebody older, I am concerned about your choice."

Did he mean Bookman? His adopted son? "What do you mean?"

"Well," he said heavily, "Bookman isn't a stable man. He has a lot of problems that run very, very deep."

But he was *really* good at giving head. "Yeah, but he seems okay," I said.

"Well, I'm not saying that you can't see him. Like you said, you're already involved. And I know from past experience that if a young person sets his or her mind to something, there's really nothing anybody can do to stop them. But I would like you to keep me abreast of this situation. I want you to tell me if you sense that things are taking a turn for the worse."

I felt like I was buying a used Ford Pinto and the salesman was telling me that as long as I didn't make any sudden stops in the parking lot, it probably wouldn't explode. But to keep an eye out for smoke.

"Okay," I said. "I'll be careful. But he really does seem okay now. Things are good between us."

"I'm glad to hear that," he said. Then he turned around in his chair and reached for a bottle on his bookshelf. "Would you like a few of these?" he said.

"What are they?" I asked, seeing the white bottle.

"Let me see here," he said, sliding his bifocals up his nose and examining the label. "I just got these in the mail, so I'm not sure . . . oh, yes. Okay, these are just a mild anti-anxiety medication. They might make you feel a little calmer."

I shrugged. "Sure, I'll take 'em."

He passed me the bottle and I stuck it in my shirt pocket along with my cigarettes.

Now, my mother glanced up at me and smiled. For a moment she didn't say anything, she just kept smiling, like she was proud of me or something. "You're a very independent young man," she said finally. "And I'm proud that you're my son."

"Thanks," I said, looking down at the hole in the knee of my jeans.

"Would you like to hear a poem I've been working on? It's only a first draft—very rough—but it's about my own journey inward, becoming truly connected with my creative unconscious. I think you might really find it helpful as you begin your own journey as a free and very wise young man."

Maybe my mother and Dr. F were the only people I'd told so far, but I thought there might be some suspicions. Recently, Agnes had come into the TV room.

My head was on Neil's lap.

She screamed, "What's going on in here?" and Neil told her to mind her own business. "Not a goddamn thing," he told her. He was so angry he was shaking. And when she left, we both stood up and he pressed against me. He pressed so hard, I came in my pants.

I was in the hospital for two weeks. When I left, Dr. Finch contacted the Amherst school board and explained that I'd attempted suicide and that I would be out of school for six months, under his intensive care.

It seemed to work because they stopped calling.

Three days after my return, my mother came into the kitchen where I was smoking and cooking a package of bacon in her cast-iron skillet.

"You've been spending a lot of time at the Finches' house," she said.

"Mmm hmm," I said, not feeling the need to remind her that *she* was the reason I was spending so much time at the Finch house.

"I think it's good for you to be around a lot of people like that."

This was true, I supposed. I did like that there was always someone awake at that house; there was always somebody hanging around who was ready for fun.

"And I'm just so emotionally drained right now. Struggling in my own battle to truly find myself, once and for all."

"Yeah," I said, flipping the bacon strips with a fork.

"And of course, my relationship with Fern is very stressful and consuming."

"Can you hand me some paper towels?"

"It's just very difficult for me to be the parent you need," she said, handing me a wad of paper towels.

"Mmm hmm."

"So after discussing this with the doctor, we both feel that this is really the best option." She flashed a document in front of my face.

"What's that?"

"It's good news. The doctor has agreed to become your legal guardian."

I froze. Then I looked at her. "My *what?*"

"It's really the best option right now. He and his family can give you the attention that you need. And he really wants to do this." She placed her hand on my arm. "Augusten, the doctor is very fond of you. He thinks you have a tremendous passion for life. When we were discussing this he told me, 'Augusten has a very strong sense of self. He can be anything in life that he chooses.'"

"So basically, you're giving me away to your shrink," I said.

"No," she said lovingly. "I'm doing what I think is best for you, best for us. I love you very, very much. And I will always be your parent. And you will always be my son."

A couple of signatures later and Dr. Finch was no longer just my mother's psychiatrist.

He was my father.

THE SEVEN-AND-A-HALF-INCH
DISASTER

THE KITCHEN CEILING WAS TOO LOW. IT WAS CRUSHING US. It was the source of our misery in life. "I hate it," said Natalie.

"What?" I said, wondering if she meant the ceiling, if she was feeling it too.

"My life," she said flatly. Not the way teenagers say they hate their lives, their lives suck, they want different lives. She said this with flatness far beyond her fifteen years. The kind of flatness that happens when people, usually much older, shut down. The palm of a hand, open, pills pouring into it. That kind of flat.

I exhaled, blowing Marlboro Light smoke into the air, an opaque cloud that was the only moving thing in the room. It seemed to drift toward the ceiling, moth to bulb. We sat perfectly still, like we were listening for something.

Outside it was dark. Because I was sitting at an angle to the window, I couldn't see my reflection, just the rest of the kitchen, and this made me feel like a vampire. I was invisible, I was riding in Wonder Woman's plane.

"Why do you hate your life?" Although I already knew. I knew the answer would be Terrance Maxwell.

"Oh." This came out soft and drifty, like a small note sung. "Terrance." Her shoulders slumped when she sighed.

I thought, *Here we go again.*

Last year, Natalie and Terrance *broke up*, to borrow a phrase from mainstream society. It was only after they broke up that I learned the full and complete story about Natalie and Terrance, about what their relationship *really* was. I knew he was forty-one, a former semi-professional tennis player and a patient of the doctor's. But I never knew *why* he had sought treatment in the first place: his alcoholic mother burned to death in her easy chair. She was drunk and dropped her cigarette. Oh, and they were lovers, Terrance and his mother. According to Natalie, Terrance could never accept the fact that he wasn't *quite* good enough to be a professional tennis player, and his mom was the only person who could console him.

When Doc found out Terrance was a millionaire he put two and two together: his rebellious daughter and the millionaire fuck-up who always ran around in tennis shorts, even in winter.

Natalie and Terrance were lovers from the first week they met. He was forty-one and she was thirteen. Soon after, she moved into his house.

Terrance became Natalie's legal guardian. So as far as everyone was concerned, they were father and daughter. And everyone believed this. Or at least acted like they did.

Except the doctor. He knew they were lovers. He, of course, believed that at thirteen, a person was free.

But when Terrance gave Natalie a black eye and she came running home at sixteen, people asked questions. And it all came out. All the black eyes, all the drunken brawls, all the smacking Natalie around and calling her horrible names.

In a whirlwind of family peer pressure, Natalie pressed charges.

Natalie and Terrance went to court.

Terrance lost.

Natalie had won. But what had she won? Aside from seventy-five thousand dollars in a civil case, which went straight to her father, what had Natalie won? Freedom from her abuser, I guess.

"I miss him," she said now, raking crumbs off the table with the edge of her hand, spilling them onto the floor and then dusting her hands across her jeans. "I know it's sick, but I really loved him."

"I know."

"It's hard," she said. "Sometimes it's just really hard. I wonder what he's doing?"

I knew she was picturing her old life in her head. The old life that included the Bang & Olufson stereo, the 1965 Rothschild wine, the burnt-orange Saab, the Martin guitar. Conveniently absent from her memory was the fact that she was his dirty little secret.

"You're so dirty," he used to tell her. "Filthy. Those disgusting bare feet. Can't you clean yourself up?"

But she did love him. I believe it. I know exactly how that is. To love somebody who doesn't deserve it. Because they are all you have. Because *any* attention is better than no attention.

For exactly the same reason, it is sometimes satisfying to cut yourself and bleed. On those gray days where eight in the morning looks no different from noon and nothing has happened and nothing is going to happen and you are washing a glass in the sink and it breaks—accidentally—and punctures your skin. And then there is this shocking red, the brightest thing in the day, so vibrant it buzzes, this blood of yours. That is okay sometimes because at least you know you're alive.

I was probably thinking this way because of all the foreign films I was seeing at the Pleasant Street Theater. Instead of going to school and drawing happy faces in my notebook or hunkering over a joint on the soccer field, I was seeing black-and-white films by Lina Wertmuller, French movies where first cousins fall in love and then stab each other as a weeping clown appears, representing the loss of innocence. These esoteric and maybe very bad films were highly inspiring to me.

So there is a love like that and that's what Natalie had with Terrance and that's what I had with Bookman.

This is what bonds us, Natalie and me. We are living in the same madhouse and have gone through the same mad thing and have our bad, ugly loves.

The difference, one difference between us, is that this is her home, her family, whereas I am only borrowing them.

I don't know which of us is at an advantage.

Somehow, my cigarette had burned down. I lit another and Natalie said, "Pass me that pack," and I did. I slid it across the table, and crumbs stuck to the cellophane.

Our lives were so small then that we both noticed them,

the crumbs on the cellophane wrapper of my cigarettes. Natalie had nails, so she picked them off. She flicked them off. Crumb by crumb.

I had used the last match.

Natalie stuck her fingers out and as if psychic, I knew exactly what she needed. I slipped my cigarette into her fingers and she used it to light her own. She held the smoke in her lungs and glanced at me as if to say thanks. *Thanks for knowing exactly what I needed. Thanks for not making me get up to light it on the stove.*

Her hair could have caught fire if she'd tried to light her cigarette on the stove. It'd happened before. She lost her bangs once, half of them anyway. She'd dipped her head down low over the blue flame, cigarette protruding, cheeks puffing, smoke rising. And then her bangs caught fire. She'd leapt back and laughed, smashing at her forehead with her hand, dropping the cigarette on the floor. "My fucking hair, oh my God," but she was laughing, it was hysterical. It broke up the day. Before Natalie lit her hair on fire. After Natalie lit her hair on fire. After was better. Before was only there so After could happen.

"I hate my life," Natalie said again.

"I hate the ceiling," I said.

The ceiling was low, much too low for the room, much too low for the old Victorian house. The ceiling wasn't smooth either; it was bumpy, like the backs of a woman's legs. The ceiling had cellulite.

"It's old," Natalie said, as if this meant I should forgive it.

"It's horribly depressing."

The yellow light against the yellow walls against the old

wood floor, itself a shade of yellow mixed with brown. The total effect was not cheery. It was crushing. It was yellow coming down on you. It was . . .

"Let's get rid of it then," Natalie said suddenly, looking around.

"Rid of what?"

"Let's take down the ceiling."

I smirked at the idea. "What would we put in its place?"

And it was as if fresh air passed through the insides of Natalie's eyes because her whole face changed. "Let's knock down the ceiling. Let's open it up to the roof. Let's have a cathedral ceiling in the kitchen."

I snuffed my cigarette out on a plate. "You think it'd work?" I said. It was true that from the outside the roof was pretty high and it peaked. Something must be up there. Between this low ceiling and that high roof. But what?

And that's how it happened that an hour later, sometime after midnight, Natalie and I were beating at the ceiling with rocks we'd pulled from Agnes's old flower/discarded-kitchen-appliance garden. We stood there with our rocks raised up over our heads and we smacked them against the ceiling and it came down in great chunks. Hairy chunks.

"Horsehair plaster," Natalie said. "They don't use this anymore."

For the next few hours, we worked without speaking, heaving the rocks over our heads, blinking when the plaster rained down on us. There was no need for ladders, because the ceiling itself was low enough to reach with the rocks. To free the debris between the rafters, we threw skillets and small stones. It was exhilarating to breathe the plaster dust; to cough productively and spit on the floor; to look down at our hands and see them covered in white. It was so extraordinarily out of the ordinary.

One minute we were sitting at the lowly kitchen table moaning about the sorry state of our lives and the next we were liberating the architecture with heavy projectiles. This was pure, freedom. Better than sniffing glue.

It didn't take long to remove the entire ceiling. One firm ka-boom with the rock and the plaster fell not in chips but in broken sheets, large chunks. The insulation tumbled out or was extracted by our powdery hands. It looked like hair, the insulation. In fact, the whole ceiling seemed to be made of organic materials; horsehair, human hair, bits of bone. It was like some mummified, mutant creature.

By dawn we were knee-deep in debris. The kitchen table, the top of the refrigerator, the stove, the sink—everything—was covered.

People would be surprised when they woke up and sleepily walked into the kitchen for a glass of water or some orange juice.

"Hope is just going to die," Natalie said. "And Dad. He'll absolutely freak when he sees this. Then he'll be forced to give us cash to finish it."

"Yeah. That'll be good." I was excited, thinking we could use the cash for McDonald's and beer along with the drywall. And it would be hilarious to see everyone's horror.

Or so we thought.

In the morning, the doctor came downstairs in his underwear as usual. He walked into the kitchen as usual. He made his way to the refrigerator for the orange juice as usual. What was not usual was the amount of rubble he had to step over to get there. Also highly unusual was the fact that both Natalie and I were not only awake at 7 A.M., but also quite busy. Yet he seemed unfazed.

"Good morning," he said in his deep, morning voice.

"Hey, Dad."

"Hi," I said.

"You two have quite the project going on in here," he said casually, as if Natalie and I were in the middle of an especially ambitious macramé project.

"What do you think?" Natalie asked, as she used the broken legs of Agnes's ironing board to swat the last bits of plaster away near the door to the barn.

"I think it's a spectacular mess," he said. He carried the orange juice over to the cupboard and pulled down a glass. He inspected it for signs of life before filling it with juice.

"That's all?" Natalie was disappointed. She'd had her heart set on a scene. One that could possibly end with cash.

"Well," he said, "I would hope that whenever you're through doing whatever you're doing that you'll clean up like adults."

Natalie said, "We need some money to finish. We're putting in a new cathedral ceiling and we need money."

He wanted to know how much. Money was tight then because two patients had quit treatment.

"A couple hundred."

"A couple hundred dollars!" he bellowed. He added his now empty glass to the mound of plates, pans and empty milk cartons that had been in the sink all week.

Natalie played favorite daughter. "Oh, c'mon, Dad. You'll love the new kitchen. Please? Won't you give your youngest, most favorite, most beautiful daughter two hundred dollars?" She fluttered her eyelashes playfully.

This always worked.

He promised us the cash and then went back upstairs to get dressed. Natalie pulled a chair out from the table, shoved the crap off, and sat heavily.

We were filthy and exhausted but not bored.

"That was good," she said, like we'd just had sex.

"Yeah. But what do we do now?"

There was the problem of the mess. The ceiling and its insulation were now three feet deep on the floor and on top of everything. It would take at least as long to get rid of it as it did to take it down.

She peeled a scab off her knee, revealing a small pink gash. "We'll shovel it outside, throw it behind the barn."

"When?"

"Later."

"What do we do now?"

"Take a nap."

I woke up that afternoon at about four and groggily walked out of my room, down the hall into the kitchen. Agnes was rinsing a plate under the faucet. She dried it on her apron and placed it in the cupboard. Then she shuffled through the debris to the refrigerator. She opened the door and hunched over to inspect the labels of the condiments. "We never have any relish in this house," she said. "Who's eating all the relish?

I couldn't remember ever seeing relish in the refrigerator. "Maybe Hope ate it."

"That Hope," she said. "She should know better." Agnes took her pocketbook from its position at the top of the mound of plates on the kitchen table. "I'm going to run to the store and pick up a fresh bottle. If anybody needs a clean plate there's one in the cupboard." She left through the back door.

I walked upstairs to Natalie's room and pounded on her door. "Wake up, wake up, wake up."

She answered the door wearing a sheet toga. "What time is it?" She yawned.

"Late."

"What's the kitchen like?"

"Agnes washed a plate," I said.

She yawned again. "Oh."

"I guess we should get to work on it," I said.

"Yeah," she said. Then she turned around, holding the sheet against her chest and began hunting through the mounds of clothes on her floor for her skirt. Natalie wore the same skirt every day. It was red with golden feathers on it. She'd sewn it herself. The edges were beginning to fray from so many washings. Somehow she was able to slip into both the skirt and a black tank top without ever removing the sheet.

We spent the rest of the day shoveling debris out of the kitchen and carrying it outside behind the barn. It took dozens of trips. But by evening, the kitchen was free from rubbish.

"Let's get these dishes washed," Natalie said.

So we created our own assembly line of two. Natalie washing, me drying. All the commotion had caused the roaches to retreat deep into the walls so Natalie hardly screamed at all.

When we were finished, standing in the now clean kitchen, Natalie commented on the new ceiling. "It's weird how it seems even darker in here now."

It was true. Although there was no longer a low ceiling

hanging over our heads, the blackness that stretched up was even more depressing.

What we needed was a skylight.

Natalie phoned her dad at the office and he told us he'd give us a hundred dollars to install a skylight. Natalie told him a hundred dollars wasn't enough; that we'd need at least a hundred and fifty. After ten minutes of pleading, he finally agreed to give us a hundred and twenty-five.

"So we can use a hundred for the window," she said, "and the rest we can spend on beer."

This seemed like a good plan to me. "But are you sure we can buy a window for a hundred dollars?"

"We don't need to buy a window," she said. "We can take the window out of the pantry and use that. Then we can just block that up with wood. Nobody looks out that window anyway."

Over the next few days, we worked with uncommon focus on our project. It proved challenging to remove the window from the pantry. It had been installed with surprising accuracy. But by using an axe we found in the barn as well as a hammer and a rock, we were able to free the window from the wall. The hole that remained created a refreshing cross-ventilation that made it easier to breathe in the dusty kitchen.

Far more difficult, however, than removing the window in the pantry was creating the hole in the roof for the new skylight.

"You wouldn't think it would be so hard," Natalie said, as she tried to gnaw her way through the shingles with a hacksaw.

We were sitting on top of the roof. The sun was high in the sky and we were both wet with perspiration. I'd applied Hennaluscent conditioner to my hair and combed it straight back. I'd also talked Natalie into letting me henna her hair. I'd applied the pasty mud and then piled her hair on top of her head, securing it with a tight wrapping of aluminum foil. And now she was starting to complain.

"My head is so fucking hot," she said.

"Well, just try not to think about it. The sun will really help your hair take the color." The color we'd chosen was red.

"Well, this fucking foil is driving me nuts." The foil was sliding down her forehead and she was constantly pushing it back up.

"So take it off," I said.

She slid the foil off her head, balled it up and threw it off the roof. Her hair was mud-caked and slapped against her shoulders. With the motion of the hacksaw, her hair moved as one thick sheet.

Eventually, we were able to saw a nice hole in the roof, between the rafters.

"Hi, Agnes," I said, sticking my hand down through the hole and waving into the kitchen.

"What in God's name?" she said, looking up.

Natalie poked her face into the hole. "Can you go to the store and get us some food?" she said.

"What do you want?" Agnes asked.

"I don't know. Something."

"You two better fix that," Agnes said. "We can't live in a house with a hole."

As it turned out, we *could* live in a house with a hole.

Because our measurements were approximate and our precision was nonexistent, the window from the pantry was a rough fit into the hole in the roof. We nailed it into place, using scraps of wood to seal around it. Then we added fresh shingles.

But there remained a gap. It was about seven-and-a-half inches between the roof and the top side of the window. We knew the figure, because it was the only thing we measured.

Eight months out of the year, rain fell through this gap and collected in a pot that was permanently placed on the kitchen table. The other four months, the pot collected snow. During the holidays, we took to wearing stocking caps and mittens while we prepared our feasts.

But the skylight, no matter how crude, did flood the kitchen with light.

"I really like it," Hope commented, emptying the rain-filled pot into the sink. "It's worth the trouble."

Dr. F agreed. "It brings a sense of humor to the kitchen."

Agnes didn't agree. "It's a disaster," she said. Of course, she'd said this after leaving her purse on the kitchen table in the spot where the rain-pan should have been.

QUEEN HELENE CHOLESTEROL

KATE WASN'T LIKE THE OTHER FINCHES. SHE WAS SLIM, so-phisticated and listened to Laura Nyro and fusion jazz. She dated handsome black men and her spotless apartment was decorated with Oriental rugs and African fertility icons. She sent her daughter Brenda to ballet school. And when she divorced, she kept his name. Kate was the closest thing the Finches had to a royal family member.

Oh, the others didn't think so. "Snob," they called her. "Stuck-up cunt." But I was in awe of her and was thrilled when—between boyfriends—she would ask me to wash her car or take down her storm windows.

When Kate stopped by the house, I changed my clothes as if going on a date. I was as charming and well behaved as possible. I pretended not to know the other members of the family.

My awe of her was based on the fact that she had exactly what I wanted in life. She was a professional licensed cosmetologist. Or, to use a name I loathed, *hairdresser*.

Kate was planning to someday open her own shop and I felt this was a bond between us, because I was planning to open my own *chain* of shops around the world and also have my own line of haircare products. I even wanted to have a line of products marketed exclusively to the trade because I was convinced that the perms on the market were too damaging to the hair shaft. I didn't know how to make them any *less* damaging, but I did have some packaging ideas that would give the impression of harmlessness.

Kate had been generous enough to give me her old cosmetology school textbook. It was a hardcover with no jacket and the catchy title was printed across the pink front in swashy script: HANDBOOK OF COSMETOLOGY. Inside were black-and-white line illustrations of the many procedures that the cosmetology students had to master before earning their license to practice. It was all in there—from pin curls to permanent waves—and I was determined to memorize the book before I attended beauty school. I could not take the chance that I would flunk, so I felt my best option was to already know everything in the book. Even if some of the procedures were no longer practiced or perhaps even illegal. For example, a "cold wave" appeared to involve wires attached to the head, electricity and water.

"Working with hair" was the only thing I could think of to do with myself professionally. Becoming a doctor seemed unlikely to me now. I had nearly outgrown my desire to be a talk-show host. And even though I spent many hours each day hunched over a notebook writing in my journal because I felt that if I didn't write at least four hours a day I might as well not exist, the idea of being a writer never entered my mind. My mother was *a writer* but she was also crazy. And the only people who read her poems were the depressed women in the writing classes she held at her house in the summers or friends she called on the phone. She had had one book of poems published many years before and nothing since. I knew then that I could never live like that: no money and even less fame. I craved fan letters and expensive watches. "I'll be able to get a great boyfriend," I reasoned, "once I'm the next Vidal Sassoon." I even thought I might end up with a hair model in the end.

As preparation for my future as a world-class cosmetologist, I tricked members of the house and certain patients into letting me cut their hair. As it turned out, I had an actual knack for it.

But there was a problem. And the problem was finger waves.

No matter how many times I tried, I could not comb a successful finger wave into straight or even moderately wavy hair.

"Do they really make you learn this? Do they actually test you on this?" I asked Kate.

"They really do, yeah," she laughed. "I know it's really old fashioned, I mean nobody does finger waves anymore. But that's hairdressing school for you. It goes by the book. Unfortunately, the book was written thirty years ago."

My fingers were too large to make finger waves, I worried.

Or I lacked the ability to contort my fingers in the required way.

This one thing, seemingly small, signaled to me the possible destruction of my dream. And I obsessed about it constantly. In the middle of the night when the rest of the house was asleep and couldn't bother me, I lay in bed with my journal and wrote feverishly about it until my hand cramped and I fell asleep from emotional exhaustion.

One night I was particularly upset. The finger wave issue was becoming larger for me ever since I had asked Fern's friend Julian Christopher, who owned The Kindest Cut Salon in Amherst, about it. He told me the same thing Kate did, that I'd have to master them. It was an especially sweltering summer night and all the fans in the house were already hogged by other people, so I applied an Alberto VO5 Hot Oil Treatment to my hair, wrapped my head in Saran wrap and lay on my bed to try and write my anxiety away:

3:00 A.M. Can't sleep. Am worried about this finger wave business. If I can't get these down, there's no way IN HELL they're going to let me graduate. And no graduation means no certification. And no certification means NO HAIR EMPIRE FOR ME. I asked Kate and she said they have an instructor who stands over you and watches. This will make it even worse as far as I'm concerned. Because if I do somehow manage to finally do a good finger wave here on one of these Finches, the chances are just so close to nothing that I'll be able to do it again in a testing environment with an instructor leaning over my shoulder and judging me. I hate to be judged. I hate school to begin with and tests which I cannot take, so this combination just seems like it's completely ready to explode. Already I feel doomed. I feel like I am going to end up a busboy at the Hunan Hut in Amherst and then maybe someday graduate to dishwasher. And I don't know how any of this has happened to me. How come I'm not getting ready for college? I'm fourteen and should be sitting at the kitchen table with my father, saying, "But Dad, Princeton has the better football team. I don't care that Grandpa went to Harvard. Can't I just do it my way? Like Sinatra?" Instead, I'm laying on a used twin bed with somebody else's pee stains. I'm in my mother's psychiatrist's house for god sakes, eating candy canes for breakfast. Just this morning, Crazy Dr. F went into the bathroom for his daily 5 A.M. bath. He didn't know that Poo had put the fish he won at the mall in the tub. So when he walked into the bathroom and saw the tub filled with water, he thought Agnes had suddenly decided to be a good wife and filled the tub for him. So he climbed into the tub of FREEZING cold water filled with like twenty-five fish (which I can't imagine how he missed) and then the entire house was filled with his HOWL. How did my life take such a dismal turn? What did I do wrong along the way? Oh God, I just heard a noise. I hope it's not a serial killer. Ever since I saw that movie Halloween I am paranoid about serial killers. Any of Finch's patients could be one. Especially that crazy woman who owns the Blue Moon Grill in Easthampton. I just look at her and she creeps me out. She looks like she would eat a baby. Not that she's fat. She just looks hungry in some dangerous way that can't be explained. She's always so nice and friendly. Exactly the disposition of a baby killer.

There was a soft knock at my door. A knock followed by the tickle of fingernails playing against the wood. It was Neil.

"Come in."

He opened the door and stepped into my room. "Hi, Jocko," he said, sitting on my bed, near my head.

"No, dog. You sit at the bottom near my feet or you sit on the floor," I told him.

His shoulders slumped and his eyes softened. "Please don't be like that to me tonight. Not tonight. I need you."

"You do?" I said, closing my pen into my notebook and setting it beside me on the bed. "Good. Then that's exactly what you won't have. You deserve to need me, not to have me." Ours had become a seesaw relationship, and right now it was all saw.

He winced, as if I'd just flicked water in his face.

Good.

"Come on, man. I just can't stop thinking about you. You've got this fucking power over me. It's like there's nothing else in my life. Like it's a stage, all blackened out with only one light in the center. You."

I did like the idea that he associated me with a stage and professional lighting, but I still wanted to torture him. "Well, that's too bad for you because I think you're completely pathetic. You sicken me."

I'd heard Natalie use the word *sicken* recently when describing something Agnes had done with a pound of ground hamburger. I'd made a mental note to add that word to my very sparse vocabulary. Right next to *panthenol* and *back-comb*.

Neil began to cry. He hunched over and brought his hands up to his face, cupping it, as if he was drinking water from a stream.

"Good, you cry. You deserve to be miserable and suffer.

You're a pathetic failure of a man. I know that I certainly don't love you anymore." I hoped I sounded cold and nonchalant.

He turned to me. "Please?"

"No."

"*Please?*" He tried to take my hand in his. It was his attempt at begging.

I knew what he was asking. I exhaled with effort. "Fine." I said. "This one last time."

"Can we do it up the ass?" he asked, suddenly brighter. "I won't use spit like last time. We'll use something. It won't hurt."

"Use what?" I was suspicious of him. He'd fucked me up the ass a few months ago, and it hurt like hell. I'd told him to stop but he just kept on going saying, "Don't worry, the pain goes away, it feels good after a while." I wasn't about to get into that trap again.

He scanned my bookshelves and pointed. "That," he said.

I craned my neck around to see what he had pointed to. It was the yellow tub of Queen Helen's Cholesterol. I was very fond of this product, which was absorbed almost instantly into the hair. Unlike KMS Repair, which tended to weigh hair down, the old-fashioned Queen Helen's Cholesterol was light and very effective. I tended to use it at night, while I slept, when a deeper level of conditioning could be achieved.

I yanked off my sweatpants and pulled my T-shirt over my head. Now, because of the hanging basket lamp over my bed, I was lit from above, the most unflattering light, like a hamburger at a fast food restaurant.

His cock was already hard and he began stroking it to make it even stiffer.

I, on the other hand, was completely turned off as I looked at my body under the glaring white light. Not only did I look skinny, but also almost hairless. It was disgusting. If by fourteen I still didn't have any chest hair or hair on my legs, I figured I could pretty much forget about ever getting any. My brother had hair, but my father didn't. He was smooth. I hated that you couldn't choose which genes you got and which ones skipped you.

"Lie back and put your legs in the air," he said.

I did like he said and he crouched down in front of me between my legs. He reached up for the tub of Queen Helen's and carelessly tossed the lid on the floor.

"Pick that back up," I said. I didn't want pubic hair in it.

He leaned over and grabbed the lid. "Sorry," he said. Then he dipped his fingers into the cream and rubbed it onto his cock. He dipped his fingers in again and this he used to moisturize my asshole.

My hands and feet immediately started to feel cold, like somebody had wrapped belts around them. Even though it was summer, even though it was so hot you couldn't sleep unless you laid a wet towel across your chest, I was shaking like I was freezing cold.

"It's okay," he said. "You'll like this."

He put his hands under my ass and then he plunged his cock into my asshole.

It was not fun and I didn't like it at all. "It hurts." This came out in almost a whimper and I felt ashamed that I sounded like that. I didn't even know I could make that noise.

"It's okay," he said again. Then he started moaning and closed his eyes. "Jesus fucking Christ you're tight."

The more he thrusted, the less I felt. It hurt less but it didn't feel good.

"Oh, Jesus," he cried.

"Shhhhhh," I said. "Shut the fuck up. Do you want to wake the whole fucking house, you idiot?"

I wanted to get up and turn the radio on so that the sounds of this, his moaning and carrying on and the slurping noise that was coming from my ass would be muffled. But the radio was across the room.

So I closed my eyes and imagined getting up and going over to it. My imagination was vivid. I could completely visualize how it would feel to rise from the bed and step onto the sisal carpet I had taken from my mother. I could feel the scratchiness of it on the bottoms of my feet and I could feel the radio knob in my hand.

And then it was over. He pulled out of me and I was surprised by the sudden feeling of emptiness. This was followed by a wave of sadness. On the one hand, I had gotten used to the sensation of him up there, even if it made me feel really full and like I needed to take a big shit. But on the other hand I didn't like doing it because I didn't like him anymore and I didn't like being on my back like that and it just seemed so weird.

He got up and walked over to the door, unlocking it and walking across the hall into the bathroom. He returned a moment later carrying one of Agnes's pale yellow hand towels.

"You can't use that."

"Why not?"

"Because you just can't. Use something else. Paper towels or something." The feeling between my legs was repulsive. Just lying there I could feel the slickness and the very distinct sensation of his sperm leaking out of my asshole and onto my sheets, which needed washing really bad anyway.

He ended up cleaning his dick off and then my ass with my Wacky 102-FM T-shirt. It was red and tight and I hated it anyway so I didn't care. Instead of washing it, I'd just throw it away. I'd tuck it deep into the bottom of the kitchen trash.

"You want me to suck you off?"

Instantly, my cock sprang to life. Neil had this way of sucking my cock that had addicted me to him. I'd watched him do it. It was like he slid it into his mouth between his gums and cheeks, which sounds like it would hurt, except he had really wide gums and very elastic cheeks so the feeling was incredible. I'd gotten to the point where I could come faster this way than by jerking off. In fact, with him around I almost never had to jerk off. "Yeah," I said.

When my cock was in his mouth, he used a sideways motion with his head. So it didn't go deep into his throat, but the part of it that was the most sensitive, the underside toward the top, this part got massaged really hard inside his mouth.

I exploded, coming in five deep spurts.

I wondered how far that would have shot if I'd been jerking off. Most of the time I would hit my chest. Sometimes my neck. And sometimes, if I were really horny, I'd shoot behind my head and hit the wall. I had a feeling now that this one would have hit the wall.

My entire body sank into the bed. I could understand why people said things like "He made me melt" on TV because that's exactly how I felt; like I'd melted.

After feeling this for about thirty seconds I opened my eyes and he was still there, standing over me smiling. He licked his lips like he'd just eaten ice cream and he said, "That was delicious."

He repulsed me and I wanted him to leave immediately. "Go away, dog," I said.

His face fell again. His eyelids had this way of sort of sinking over his eyes exactly like a basset hound when he was hurt. It was a look I saw a lot because I felt I had mastered the art of hurting him. Next to obsessing over hairdressing school, hurting Neil Bookman was my favorite thing to do. I never asked myself why this was. I never thought that it was wrong of me. Instead I liked the sense of control. He made me feel powerful.

But sometimes he could get angry. Like now. His eyes blazed with anger. "You are a monster," he said. "You are a fucking evil monster. You're no innocent fourteen-year-old. You're a fucking psychopath. The way you treat people," he spat, "is so fucking sick I can't even believe that you're allowed to live."

I smiled. "That's good, Neil. Keep going. You poor, pathetic loser of a man. Express all that anger, you big boy. And another thing?" I narrowed my eyes, hoping that I looked menacing. "If you ever get out of line, I'll go straight to the police and you will be arrested for statutory rape. You'll spend the rest of your life rotting behind bars."

I let that sink in.

"Now get the hell out of here."

He turned. And he left.

After I listened to him walk down the hall, after I was sure he'd really left, I put my sweatpants and a fresh T-shirt on, flopped back on my bed and picked up my journal.

Bookman just left. He came down for one of his little visits and this time he fucked me. At least I didn't have to suck on his penis. I hate the way he always forces my head down on it and no matter how much I choke or tell him not to he keeps shoving. So at least that didn't happen. We had the Anal Sex and I didn't like it. I don't like Anal Sex and don't know why people would want to have it. It's another thing about Being Gay that I don't like. I don't like that I'm going to be a hair cutter and this is considered by people to be something that is a "Gay Thing." But what people don't understand is that I want to do it in a different way. In a bigger way. God, if I thought I'd be some nelly faggot working in a beauty salon in Springfield doing purple rinses on old ladies I'd kill myself. I would kill myself tonight this minute. And just as I write this now I feel this wall of sickness coming over me, I am feeling it RIGHT THIS MINUTE about the finger wave thing. When Shitvile was plugging me up with his fat-headed penis I was thinking about the finger waves again and I decided that maybe I should get a wig to practice on. I could use my allowance and get a cheap one. This way, I won't have to keep bugging these Finches for their heads. What else. There was something else I was going to tell you that I was thinking. Oh yeah now I remember. At the end when Neil was leaving there was something in his eyes that scared me and I thought, he could be a serial killer even more than that Blue Moon Grill lady. He really and truly could do it. I think if he had had a butcher knife with him he could have used it to stab me. It freaked me out, seeing him like that. Sometimes I don't know if I even know him at all. And I don't know why I hate him so much. Probably because he is such a weak and pathetic person. But also there is something more about him that I don't like and it's always been there right from the beginning. I think it has to do with back when I was talking to him about being gay two summers ago and he was all nice and all, "it's okay to be gay, I'll be your friend," and then he made me have that sex with him and then I fell in love with him only he turned out to not be worth loving, I think I'm angry with him about that. I wonder if I should talk to Finch about this? He's always saying that if you don't get your anger out it can kill you. Now I'm worried that my anger will kill me. But the thing is, I do try and get it out. I think of good mean names to call him but maybe these aren't enough. Maybe I need to scream at him or something. Tonight I told him I'd go to the police if he didn't act right and I think this scared him a little bit because his eyes went back to normal and he sort of folded up into himself and then he left. So that's good. I have a new thing I can use on him. I would never do that of course, really go to the police. And if he ever reads this journal he will know I will never do it and then I won't have that tool anymore so I better hide this one. I need to think of a new place. God, I have all these things to worry about on top of hair school. It's a wonder I'm even alive. Sometimes I think that. I think that I can't believe I haven't killed myself. But there's something in me that just keeps going on. I think it has something to do with tomorrow, that there is always one, and that everything can change when it comes. The one thing I did learn tonight though, is that Queen Helen's Cholesterol is more than just a hair conditioner.

TOILET BOWL READINGS

MAYBE IT WAS A PATTY HEARST THING. STOCKHOLM SYN-drome or whatever it's called when you're being held against your will but then you become sucked in and fall in love. Or if not exactly love, you fall into something you can't see out of. *I can't shoot a machine gun* becomes, *Hey, this hardly has any kick-back!*

Maybe this explains why it didn't horrify me at the time. Why I just held my Pat Benatar T-shirt up to my nose to block out the smell and stared with mild curiosity at the contents of the toilet bowl.

Hope was so moved, she was on the verge of tears. "Oh my God, this is incredible," she whispered through her clasped fingers.

Natalie stood back against the wall, arms folded across her

chest. She wanted to go to Smith College in two years and this was just not something a Smith girl should be exposed to.

"See?" Finch bellowed, pointing into the bowl at his bowel movement. "Look at the size of that coil!"

Hope leaned in closer, as if inspecting an engagement ring in a jewelry display case.

I peered over Hope's shoulder.

Agnes came shuffling down the hallway. "What's all the fuss about? Why are you all crowded into the bathroom?" She shouldered her way into the room and looked at all of us looking into the toilet bowl. Her mouth fell open. "What is this?"

Finch's face reddened as his excitement grew. "See? See the way the tip of the coil breaks up out of the surface of the water? Holy Father!"

"Yeah, Dad. I see it. It's pointing straight up out of the bowl," Hope said, ever the good daughter.

"Exactly," Finch boomed. "Exactly. The tip is pointing up." He stood up straight. "Do you know what this means?"

Agnes went to his side and pulled at his arm. "Doctor, please," she said. "Please calm down."

"Agnes, go get a spatula," he ordered.

"Doctor, please," Agnes said, pulling him harder.

He jerked his arm away and gave her a shove out of the room. "A spatula, Agnes!" he screamed.

She scurried out of the room like Edith Bunker.

"What does it mean, Dad?" Hope asked.

Natalie and I looked at each other, but then looked away because we knew we'd crack up and Finch would yell at us.

"It means our financial situation is turning around, that's

what it means. It means things are looking up. The shit is pointing out of the pot and up toward heaven, to God."

As if she'd just won the Publisher's Clearinghouse Sweepstakes, Hope screamed. She screamed and clapped and kissed her father's cheek.

"There, there, Hope," Finch said. "That's my girl." He looked at me and Natalie. "Can you see how important this is? God has a tremendous sense of humor. He is the funniest man in the universe. And this is His way of saying that things are going to turn around for us now."

I was mortified but fascinated. Natalie hid her face in her hands and moaned.

When Agnes returned with a spatula, Finch snatched it from her hands before she could even say a word. He immediately handed it to Hope. "I want you to carefully remove this from the water and take it outside to dry. Put it in the sun on the picnic table."

Hope took the spatula without hesitation.

"Okay, I'm outta here," Natalie said.

"No wait," I said, grabbing her arm. "Let's watch."

"I am not gonna watch my sister scoop my dad's shit out of the toilet so she can put it outside to dry," she said, laughing.

Finch roared with glee. "That's exactly why Hope is my *best* daughter."

"See, Natalie?" Hope teased. She stuck out her tongue.

"Good for you, Hope. You're Dad's favorite. Scoop away."

I watched as Hope carefully hoisted the coiled turd out of the toilet and brought it up out of the bowl, dripping. Sitting on the spatula like that, it looked not unlike various food items cooked in the house. I also wondered if maybe it was true. If God really was a comedian and this was his way of saying things would soon improve. The thought was extremely comforting. Maybe I'd be able to attend beauty school after all.

Hope walked out of the bathroom and down the hall, careful of her precious cargo. Zoo had heard the commotion and was standing in the hallway, wagging her tail. She licked up the drops of water as they fell onto the floor. "Natalie or Augusten, one of you get the door," Hope shouted as she made the turn past the jackets and into the kitchen. "Now!"

I ran ahead and got the door for her.

"Thanks."

Natalie and I stood in the doorway watching her pad across the lawn with the spatula and then gently ease the turd onto the weathered picnic table.

"My family is so fucking insane," Natalie said. "How will I ever get into Smith?"

"You will," I said, though I didn't know how. Not without changing her last name and undergoing a complete brainwashing.

Natalie turned to me. "At least you understand."

"Can you imagine if the neighbors knew what went on in this house?" I said.

She laughed darkly. "Oh my God, they'd throw my father in an insane asylum and burn the house to the ground. It would be exactly like *Frankenstein*."

I looked at all the houses on the block, the other old Victorians. Only they had lace curtains in the windows, manicured bushes out front, actual flowers in bloom. We only had plastic tulips stuck into the dirt, blossom-first, and there wasn't a curtain or shade in the place. It wasn't hard to imagine that one of the neighbors—a Smith Admissions Coordinator perhaps—was peering out her curtain at this exact moment.

Natalie absently fingered a long strand of her hair.

I couldn't help but think it would look so much better platinum. "We should bleach you," I said.

"Huh?"

"It'd be fun. It would look really good. Bring out your eyes."

She shrugged. "Maybe later."

Outside, Hope gave the turd a nudge with the spatula, making sure the coil was tight.

Agnes began mindlessly sweeping the carpet in the living room. This was always her first response to stress. It was not uncommon to be awakened in the middle of the night to the fshhh, fshhh, fshhh sound of Agnes sweeping the hallway runner, the living room rug or the walls themselves. The sweeping had the effect of spreading the animal hairs out thinner and moving crumbs and toenail clippings into the corners.

"Knock it off, Agnes," Natalie shouted.

"You mind your own beeswax," Agnes shouted back. As she continued to sweep, she leaned heavily on the broom. Without it, I doubted she could remain standing. She would just sag onto the floor and stay there like a load of laundry.

Finch came into the room, drying his hands on his shirttails. He peered outside. "Excellent," he commented. Then he shouted to Hope. "Good work."

Hope turned back, beaming.

Finch said, "You two just wait. Things are really gonna turn around for us now. It's a sign from God."

"Can we have twenty bucks?" Natalie asked, hand outstretched.

Finch reached into his back pocket for his wallet. "I only have ten."

Natalie took that and pulled me by the arm. "Let's go for a walk."

The first sign that things were, in fact, turning around came in the form of a frozen Butterball turkey. Hope won it from a radio station by being the first caller to correctly identify a Pat Boone song. It didn't fit in the freezer, so she placed it in the bathtub to thaw. But there were only two bathrooms in the house and Hope had placed the turkey in the downstairs bathroom—the one with the shower. So instead of removing the poultry to take a shower, we all just showered with it at our feet.

When Finch received a windfall in the amount of one thousand dollars from the insurance company, he took this as a definite sign that the turd had, in fact, been a direct piece of communication from The Heavenly Father.

As a result, he scrutinized each of his bowel movements. And, because God could just as easily speak through any one of us, insisted on seeing ours before we flushed.

"No fucking way," Natalie snapped, as she flushed the toilet, despite her father's incessant pounding on the bathroom door.

"Okay, Dad," called Hope, as she sprayed Glade in the air.

After inspecting a number of Hope's turds and one of his wife's (which he deemed inferior), he decided that only his turds were acting as messengers from heaven. So each morning, he called Hope into the bathroom to remove the waste and set it outside on the picnic table with the others.

Together, he believed, the bowel movements would tell a more complete picture of our future.

Would I get into beauty school? The answer was many small, broken stools. "Chop, chop, chop, like scissors. I'd say that's a yes," the doctor said with a smile.

Would the IRS seize the house? "Diarrhea means they'll mess the records up. The house is ours!"

What about Hope; would she ever get married? "See all that corn? Hope's going to marry a farmer."

The doctor recorded these events on paper. Complete with illustrations of each turd, along with an accompanying inter-pretation. This essay went into the monthly newsletter, which he mailed to all his patients.

For weeks that summer, it seemed nothing could be done; no action taken, no decision made, unless the contents of the doctor's lower colon agreed.

"I certainly wouldn't get my hopes up about taking some job outside the house," the doctor told Agnes. "It's just not in the cards, so to speak," he said, pointing into the toilet.

The mood changed dramatically, however, when the doctor became constipated. "I haven't had a bowel movement for a day and a half," he said ominously from his seat in front of the television. "And I'm not sure what that means."

The constipation sent Hope straight to her room where she performed a barrage of bible-dips: *Will dad have a B.M.? Will the IRS take the house? Will more patients quit therapy? Have you stopped speaking to Dad through the toilet?*

To Natalie and me, it was as if everyone in the house had sipped tainted water. Except us. But instead of seeing it as a brazen form of neurological pathology, we thought it was funny. "Can you believe my father holds a medical degree from one of the most prestigious universities in America?"

"If *he* can be a doctor," I said, "*I* should be able to get into beauty school."

My fixation on beauty school intensified during times of stress. I also wrote in my journal more. Writing was the only thing that made me feel content. I could escape into the page, into the words, into the spaces between the words. Even if all I was doing was practicing signing my autograph.

"Why don't you be a writer?" Natalie suggested one afternoon. "I bet you'd be a funny writer."

My journals were not funny. They were tragic. "I don't want to be a writer," I said automatically. "Look at my mother."

Natalie laughed. "But not all writers are crazy like your mother."

"Yeah, but if I inherited the gene to write, I'm sure I got her crazy genes, too."

"Well, I just don't think you're going to be happy . . . cutting hair."

This infuriated me. I wasn't going to cut hair. I was going to own a *beauty empire*. "You don't understand the plan," I said. "You don't listen."

"I still think you'd hate it. Standing around all day long sticking your fingers in people's dirty hair. Yuck."

I had no intention of sticking my fingers in anyone's hair, just approving packaging designs from behind a glass desk. A beauty empire was my only way out. I loved the Vidal Sassoon commercials that promised, *If you don't look good, we don't look good.* That expressed, perfectly, my refined ability to put others first.

By the third day, after still no bowel movement, the doctor

instructed Agnes to give him an enema. The enema was successful, but the doctor believed the contents of his bowel had been too compressed, and then too destroyed by water, to make an accurate reading. "I'm afraid that this sudden freezing of the bowels," he said to us as we were gathered in the living room, "signals that God has chosen to no longer communicate in this way."

Hope was deeply distraught.

At that moment, the oldest Finch daughter, Kate, walked into the house, making a rare appearance. Surprised by the gathering, she said, "Hey, what's everybody doing in here?"

She smelled like perfume. Her makeup was flawless.

Natalie snickered. "Take a seat, Kate. You've missed some good stuff."

Kate smiled. "Oh, yeah? What'd I miss?" She brushed off the surface of a chair and sat on the edge.

The doctor explained the past few days to his daughter, offering to take her out back to the picnic table so she could inspect the messages from God herself.

After Kate slammed her car door and drove away, Natalie leaned forward. "You really should write all this stuff down."

I said, "Even if I did, nobody would believe it."

"That's true," she said. "Maybe it's better to just forget it."

PHLEGMED BEFORE A LIVE AUDIENCE

Although both Natalie and I lacked the ability to play piano, we were gifted at manipulating others into playing for us so we could sing. Three of Finch's patients played well enough to follow the sheet music we placed in front of them. Of these three, Karen was the best because she was tireless. Whether this quality was innate or caused by improper dosage of her medication, she would happily play the theme from *Endless Love* five times in a row and then move without fuss into a rousing rendition of "Somewhere." When Karen would begin to complain that her fingers were getting tired, Natalie would pull a Snickers bar or a joint out of the patch pocket on the front of her skirt. This would usually keep Karen playing, but sometimes she would just become very stubborn after an hour and a half of steady keyboard work. In these cases,

Natalie would resort to bribery. "You know," she would say temptingly, "I could call my dad and see if he could see you later this afternoon. I'm sure he would." Pause. "*If I asked him.*" This usually got at least another medley out of her.

It was our goal to become an international singing sensation, on a par with Peaches 'N Herb or the Captain and Tenille. When there was no patient around to play piano for us, we practiced upstairs in Natalie's room by singing along to Stevie Nicks albums. The problem was, Stevie was sometimes hard to understand and Natalie had long since lost the liner notes to the album. So I would lie on the floor with my head next to the speaker and Natalie would stand with her finger poised over the needle.

"Wait, I can't understand that—play it again," I'd say, scribbling furiously to keep up. "Is she singing 'just like a wine-ringed love' or 'white-winged dove'?"

Natalie would drop the needle on the record, causing it to screech. "Hold on, here it comes."

The verse would play and again I couldn't understand. "Fuck it, I'll just write something in."

After I finished transcribing, with dubious accuracy, the words to our favorite songs, we would sing them over and over as we watched ourselves in the mirror on Natalie's dresser.

"My arms look so fat," Natalie would comment. The problem was, she was holding a curling iron up to her mouth to simulate a microphone and this doubled the girth of her arms, which were plump to begin with.

"Well, we'll use stands," I offered. "We won't ever take the mic out of the stand."

Natalie would then toss the curling iron on the bed. "That makes sense. Good thinking."

Sometimes we would drag the fan upstairs. This would create a sort of Stevie-Nicks-in-a-wind-tunnel look that we especially loved. "I wish I had a carpetbag," Natalie would say, as her feathered hair blew back away from her face.

Our dedication to our craft was relentless.

"Knock it off you two, I'm trying to sleep," Hope would sometimes complain in the middle of the night. Of course, this just made us turn the stereo up louder.

If we happened to be in rehearsal downstairs in my room and a neighbor padded across the lawn to rap gently on the window and ask us to please be more quiet, Natalie might simply lift her skirt and mash her vagina against the window while extending her middle finger.

We had dedication. We had, we were positive, enormous talent. What we needed was a captive audience.

And what more captive an audience could one ask for than the permanent inmates of the Northampton State Hospital?

"I think it's a fantastic idea," Dr. Finch said.

"You think they'd let us?" Natalie asked. The prospect of a live audience had caused her face to flush and small bumps to rise on her forehead. She scratched madly at her face.

"I should think they'd be thrilled that two talented young performers had offered their services, free of charge."

We wanted to press him for more encouragement, but the power of the TV was too strong and he was nodding off to sleep.

"This could really turn into something," Natalie said, her eyes slightly wild.

I agreed completely. "Maybe it'll make the papers. Do you know how to write a press release?"

The bumps had spread to her upper arms and she scratched them. "No, but Hope does."

"I know it's not Broadway, but it's a beginning."

Our next step would be contacting the entertainment director for the hospital. This proved to be more difficult than we had anticipated, mainly because there was no such thing as an entertainment director at the Northampton State Hospital. There was only a depressed fat lady behind the front desk who looked at us hopelessly when we made our inquiry.

"I'm not sure I even understand what you're asking," she said.

Natalie exhaled, trying to manage her impatience. "I told you, I'm from Smith College and he's from Amherst. We're music students and we'd like to perform for your patients. As a special treat."

"Uh huh," the woman said doubtfully. "Hold on a minute and I'll see if I can find somebody." She scanned a piece of paper that was taped to the desk next to the phone and punched in an extension. She turned her head away from us and spoke softly.

"Don't worry," Natalie said. "If worst comes to worst, we can make my father call somebody. He knows people here."

The reason he knew people there was because the whole family used to live on the hospital grounds, back before Finch had his own practice. Natalie's first memory of home was of being in that very hospital, surrounded by lunatics. In fact, it had been her father's dream to someday have his *own* psychiatric hospital. When this didn't happen, he did the next best thing. He allowed his house to fall into a state of disrepair and then he invited patients to live there. I always wondered if the fact that the Finch children had been raised in a mental hospital was the reason their threshold for weirdness was so high.

"Somebody will be with you shortly. Would you . . ." she started to say something, maybe offer us a tiny paper cup of water, but changed her mind.

"Thanks," Natalie said.

We moved away from the desk and stood near the door. It seemed wise to stand near the door in case we had to make a sudden run for it. There was no telling who was on the other end of that phone.

A moment later, a robust nurse appeared. She walked with the gait of a horse wrangler and her forearms were thick and muscular, like she'd had loaves of French bread implanted under the skin. "Hi. I'm Doris. How can I help?"

Natalie repeated the lie that we were music students from Smith and Amherst and that as part of our study, we wanted to sing at the hospital.

Doris's first reaction was one of practicality. "We don't have an auditorium," she said.

Natalie said, "That's okay. We can sing right on the ward."

I was glad she spoke the lingo.

"We don't even have a piano," Doris said.

One glance around the lobby of the dilapidated building and it was easy to see that a piano wasn't all they didn't have. Running water was doubtful. This place was getting a lot of sponge-bath action, and that was about it.

Natalie cleared her throat and smiled. "That's fine. We could sing a capella."

"I don't know that song," Doris said.

"It's not a song. That's a technical term. It means we could sing without any instruments. Just our voices."

Doris placed her hands on her hips and cocked her head slightly to the side. "Let me get this straight. You wanna come here and sing for the patients and you don't need any musical instruments. Just the two of you, just singing?"

We nodded.

"For free?"

We nodded again.

Doris considered this for a moment but there was obviously something bugging her. "Can I ask why?"

I was beginning to wonder that myself.

"Because it's excellent training," Natalie answered automatically. "We need as much experience before a live audience as possible."

Doris laughed. "I don't know how live your audience is gonna be. But if you wanna come up and sing, I don't see why not."

We left feeling manic with excitement, like we'd been booked on *The Today Show*. "We are gonna blow them away," Natalie said as we trudged down the hill.

"God, what should we sing?" I said.

"Good question."

I mentally ran through our repertoire. Blondie's "Heart of Glass" might cause somebody to have a flashback. "Enough Is Enough" was good, but we really needed percussion to make it work. Plus there was always the danger that it would hit a nerve and spark a riot. "Somewhere" from *West Side Story*? No, that would just remind them that they, too, wanted to live somewhere else.

"What about 'You Light Up My Life'?" Natalie suggested.

Wow. That was a surprise. "Are you serious?" I said.

"Why not?"

That song demanded an incredible vocal range. "You think we can do that one?"

Natalie was strident with confidence. "Totally."

And that is how it came to pass that Natalie and I performed "You Light Up My Life" live, in front of a captive and highly medicated audience.

When we arrived at the hospital a week later, Doris led us onto the locked ward and into a large, open room with bars on the windows and furniture that would have remained unscathed in a typhoon.

Some of the patients were seated by their own free will. Others were strapped to their chairs or guarded by one of three orderlies. These were twenty, twenty-five of the most dismal, most tragic lost souls I had ever seen collected in a room at once.

Instantly, all stage fright vanished. I felt utterly at home.

Doris had done her best to arrange a sort of stage for us, created by moving the various wheelchairs and chairs into a half-circle. Natalie and I stood in the center of this half-circle and I looked out at the faces. Heads slumped against shoulders, mouths open with drool hanging, eyes rolled back in their sockets and tongues that seemed unnaturally long. One or two of the patients rocked steadily in their chairs. A few expressed hostility at being corralled.

"Fuck this shit," spat a nasty old man. I was relieved that he was one of the ones being guarded by an orderly because his eyes were not as dim as some of the others and I worried he was capable of some sort of outburst.

"No, no, no." This was chanted by a woman with the hairiest face I'd ever seen, except on a dog. Even her forehead was fuzzy.

Did they not allow these people mirrors? Were the mentally ill somehow infused with an extra portion of hair-growth hormones?

Natalie cleared her throat.

I looked at her and we nodded. It was time.

Our voices trembled at first, because of our nerves. Anytime you perform in front of a live audience for the first time, this is bound to happen. But by the second verse, we were both completely absorbed in the song. Natalie's voice was truly beautiful, soaring high against the perforated ceiling panels. I closed my eyes and tried to imagine a spotlight on my face, bathing me in color. I imagined a hushed audience wearing expensive earrings, tissues poised beneath their eyes.

Which is why the wet smack was such a shock to both of us.

"Fuckers." It was the hateful old man, the one without teeth, I now saw. He'd coughed deeply, productively, and spat in our direction.

Because we were standing so close together, his phlegm hit us both. In the face.

It was deeply repulsive.

And we did the only thing we could possibly do. Or at least Natalie did.

She spat right back at him.

HERE, KITTY KITTY

I WAS ASLEEP ON NATALIE'S WHITE FOTAKI RUG WHEN I WAS startled awake by a rapid knocking on the door. I reached up and slapped Natalie's stubbly calf, which was hanging over the mattress. "Someone's at the door."

"Natalie, Augusten," Hope whispered through the door. "Open up."

Natalie moaned, her feather earrings stuck to her cheek. "What *time* is it?" She reached over and turned her alarm clock around, knocking the Zippo on the floor. "Jesus Christ, it's not even five in the morning." She blinked at me with her puffy, tired eyes, then climbed out of bed, dragging the sheet with her and wrapping it around her shoulders.

I sat up and my mouth tasted horrible, like stale pot, beer and Cheetos. The exact combination of ingredients that had caused me to pass into unconsciousness on Natalie's floor.

Natalie opened the door and yawned. "What do you want?" Hope was in her nightgown clutching Freud to her chest. "What are you doing with that poor cat?"

She stepped inside the room and Natalie closed the door. "Freud's not well," Hope said. Her face was pained, deeply concerned.

Quickly, I scanned the cat for signs of a fight—dried blood on its fur, a chunk of ear missing. "She looks fine," I said.

"She's not fine," Hope snapped. "I think she's dying."

"Oh, no," Natalie said, climbing back into bed, the sheet twisted through her legs. "Hope, just take a Valium and go back to sleep. Your cat is fine."

"No, she's not. She's dying. She told me."

It seemed like I was still stoned. "What?"

"She woke me up fifteen minutes ago. I was dreaming about her, dreaming that she was eaten by a white glob. It was just awful, you guys. It was a nightmare. And then all of a sudden, I woke up and she was curled up right next to my face. Purring."

"Hope, what are you talking about?" Natalie lay a pillow over her head, covering her eyes.

"Don't you guys get it?"

"Get what?" I said. "Get that you've finally gone completely insane?"

"Freud was sending me a message through my dreams. She was telling me that she's dying."

Hope was trembling and Freud struggled to break free of her grasp. But Hope kept moving her arms in such a way that the cat was trapped.

I tried to enlighten her. "Hope, Freud wasn't talking to you through your dreams. She's just a fucking cat."

"She's not just a cat."

"Go back to bed," Natalie said. She reached for the light to turn it off.

"Wait," Hope said. "I'm serious. I really need to do something. Please."

Natalie sat up. She ran her fingers back through her hair and coughed. "Okay, what do you want us to do?"

I looked at Hope.

"Well, I don't know."

I said, "I'll go with you to the vet tomorrow so you can have her checked out."

Hope shook her head. "No, I don't want any strangers near her right now. She needs to be home. I need to comfort her."

I burped. "Well, I don't know. There's nothing you can do about it tonight. You should just take her back down to your room and go to sleep."

"But what if I have the dream again?"

"You won't," I told her. "You never dream the same thing twice."

"That's not true," Hope said. "I have a lot of dreams again and again."

"Look, Hope. There's nothing you can do tonight. Go back to bed. This is fucking insane."

The cat made a gurgling sound.

Eventually Hope did go back to bed and Natalie turned off the light. "Can you believe her? She's just so weird."

"What's the matter with her?" I said.

Natalie turned the light back on. "I need a cigarette."

I reached over and grabbed my pack, then tossed it on the bed.

Then we cracked up until Natalie had to run into the bathroom because she was going to pee in the bed.

For the next three days, Hope would not let Freud out of her sight. Or her arms.

"Hope, don't hold that cat over the stove like that," Agnes scolded. "Her tail could catch fire on one of the burners."

There was nothing Natalie or I could say that would make Hope understand that the only suffering her cat was experiencing was *her*.

"You can't hang that thing around her neck. It's too heavy."

"But Natalie, this way she can't get lost. I can hear her wherever she goes in the house."

The necklace, made of two jar lids and a length of red yarn, was secured around the cat's neck. The lids clanked together whenever the cat moved.

"What are you doing to this cat?" the doctor bellowed when it leapt up on his lap, fleeing from Hope.

"Dad, Freud's sick," Hope said, catching her breath.

"Leave this poor animal alone," was all he said before nodding off in front of the TV.

On the fourth day, the cat's condition worsened. According to Hope, Freud again contacted her during REM sleep and said that she had hung on for as long as she could, she really just needed to be left in peace so she could die now.

"Has anybody seen Hope?" I asked that afternoon. I needed a ride to the Hampshire Mall so I could fill out a job application at Chess King and Hope was the only one who could drive me there.

"I haven't seen her all day," Agnes said, scrubbing at the

dining room table with vinegar and newspaper. "Last time I saw her she was downstairs in the basement"—she used her fingernail to scrub something off the table—"with the cat."

I turned around and looked at the door to the basement. "Hope?" I called out. When I didn't hear any answer, I opened the door. It was dark. But then just as I was about to close the door, I heard something, a faint scratching sound. I flicked on the light and started down the stairs.

Hope was lying on the floor with her head next to a yellow plastic laundry basket. She appeared to be dead. "Hope, are you okay?"

"Mmmm? Who?" she mumbled sleepily.

"Hope, what are you doing down here on the floor? People have been looking for—"

That's when I saw the whiskers. They were poking out of the slats of the laundry basket, flicker, flicker, flicker.

I leaned forward and peered inside the basket. Freud was pressed against the side of it, her nose trying to poke through. "Hey cat," I said gently. Then, "Hope, what's going on in here?"

Hope slowly sat up. She brought her finger to the side of the basket and tickled Freud's whiskers. "Poor kitty."

"Why is she in the laundry basket? And why do you have this dollhouse on top of it?"

Hope looked up at me and her face told me that something dreadful had happened. It was the face you might wear if you had to tell a parent that their child had met unfavorably with a python.

"She's dying, Augusten."

The cat made a yowling sound, almost a growl.

I brushed a cobweb off my head and slapped the back of

my neck. "What you are doing down here? It's awful."

The basement was damp, with a dirt floor, stone walls and a low ceiling of exposed beams.

In a calm, tender voice Hope explained. "I'm down here with Freud to keep her company while she passes away."

My first impulse was to laugh. Except the expression on Hope's face told me she wasn't kidding. So I said, "Oh-*kay*," and I backed away, then walked slowly up the steps, turning the light off before closing the door.

Then I ran as fast as I could upstairs and burst into Natalie's room.

"Oh my God," I said. "You will *never* believe what your crazy sister is doing."

Natalie quickly let her skirt fall, covering her thighs and turned away from the mirror. "What now?"

"She's got the cat trapped in a laundry basket in the basement. She's gonna kill it."

"*What?*"

"It's true. I was just down there. She's got the thing stuck inside this laundry basket because she says it's dying and she wants to keep it company or something."

"Are you serious?" She raised her eyebrows in her trademark don't-fuck-with-me-fashion.

"Totally."

She grabbed her Canon A1.

"No, not like that. Just lean in and tilt your head up toward the lightbulb," Natalie directed, the camera gripped in her hands.

I stood by the stairs, not wanting to get more cobwebs in

my hair. I'd just taken it two shades lighter and it was very porous. I was concerned that dirt might actually stain the shafts. I wasn't sure my hair could withstand another processing.

"Yeah, that's good," Natalie said.

Hope was posed on her side, her face next to the laundry basket. Harsh light from the bulb overhead created dark, dramatic shadows under her eyes. The flashlight Natalie had aimed through the laundry basket created subtle slats across Hope's cheekbones. It looked like it would be a great photograph.

Eventually Agnes appeared at the top of the stairs, suspicious. "What are you all doing down there? You better not be smoking pot or engaging in other activities. I won't allow any of that in my house."

Natalie kept her eye on the eyepiece of the camera and shouted, "Shut up. Leave us alone."

"I'm warning you," Agnes called. "I'll speak to the doctor."

"This was a good idea, Nat," Hope said. "It's nice of you to come down here and take our picture. It's special."

Natalie laughed. "Oh, it's my pleasure."

"Cut it out down there!" Agnes screamed. She was even more annoying than usual. I wanted to walk up the stairs and close the door but since I wasn't her kid and this wasn't my house, I couldn't.

Hope said, "She is such a mothermind."

"Don't move your mouth."

A *mothermind* was a Dr. Finch-ism. It was one part busybody and one part manipulator. It was based on the principle that mothering people is unhealthy after a certain point in life. Like the age of ten. A mothermind wanted to oppress and control you. If a mothermind needed money, she might say, "Do you have ten dollars?" Dr. Finch's feeling was that it's none of your business whether or not I have ten dollars. If you need ten dollars, say, "May I have ten dollars," or "I need ten dollars."

Everyone in the house was paranoid about being seen as a mothermind. And Agnes was the biggest one of all. The Antichrist of mental health and emotional maturity.

After Natalie was satisfied with her pictures, she said, "How long are you going to stay down here?"

Hope answered gravely, "As long as I need to."

Once we were back upstairs in Natalie's room and had stopped laughing, we wondered if maybe we should call the doctor. "It seems like she's really serious," I said. "Like she's not joking."

"Your hair looks so dry," Natalie said. "Have you colored it again?"

"This isn't about my hair," I said. "But yeah, I did. I had to go a little lighter. I think it looks more natural."

"More natural than your natural color?"

Natalie would never understand, could not understand this basic concept. She barely even washed her hair. Which was one thing I really hated about her. Because she could be so beautiful if she tried, if she wasn't such a fat and sloppy thing. And as soon as I thought this, I tried to think of something else quickly. Because we were so close that I felt sometimes like she could read my mind.

"What's the matter with you?" she said.

I knew it. She heard me thinking. "I'm not thinking anything," I lied.

"What?"

"*What?*"

"What were you thinking? Your hair was fine."

Phew. "What about Hope?" I said, changing the subject.

"Let's let Dad figure it out."

That evening when the doctor was sitting in the TV room and Hope was still downstairs in the basement with the cat in the laundry hamper, we explained the situation to Finch. He listened carefully, nodding and saying, "Yes," and "I see." I have to admit, I was impressed with his professionalism. He looked and sounded exactly like a real psychiatrist. Until he opened his mouth.

"Let's ask God," he said.

Automatically, Natalie walked to the fireplace mantle and pulled down the bible. It was sitting next to a framed black-and-white photograph of a movie marquis that read, "Tonight: Velvet Tongue."

"Okay then, let's ask for guidance." The doctor closed his eyes.

Natalie fanned the pages and then opened the book.

The doctor put his finger down on the page. He opened his eyes and slid his eyeglasses down from their perch atop his head.

Natalie read the passage his finger had marked. "And in those times, there was no peace."

The doctor guffawed, causing his eyeglasses to slip down his nose. "Well, you see there. That's your answer. That's just wonderful."

"I don't get it," Natalie said. "What does it mean?" She sat down on the sofa next to her dad.

"Well," he began in his throaty baritone, "I think what God is saying is that these are very stressful times for everybody, including Hope. Maybe especially Hope. This business with the cat," he waved his hand dismissively in the air, "is just stress. I say ignore her. It'll resolve itself."

Resolution came later that week in the form of death. Opinions were mixed as to the exact cause. According to Hope, the cat died of "kitty leukemia and old age." According to me, the cat died of "being trapped in a laundry basket in the basement for four days without food or water." Part of me felt sad for the cat, but only a very small part. I was learning that if I lived slightly in the future—what will happen next?— I didn't have to feel so much about what was going on in the present.

A week later I walked into the kitchen to see Hope sitting in the chair next to the stove. She had a vacant look in her eyes and was holding a snow shovel. It was summer.

"What are you doing with that?"

She continued to stare straight ahead, oblivious to me.

"Hope," I said, waving my hand in front of her face. "What are you doing with a snow shovel?"

She started and looked up at me. "Oh, hi Augusten."

I stared at her and said, "Well?"

"Well what?"

I grabbed the handle of the shovel. "What are you doing with this?"

Tears welled in her eyes. *"Freud's alive."*

"What?!"

"It's true. I was walking home and just as I got to the back door, I heard her crying under the tree."

Hope had buried the cat under the single tree in the yard.

A week ago. "Hope, the cat is not alive. You did not hear the cat crying."

She broke into tears. "But I did. I *heard* her. Oh my God, I buried her alive." She stood suddenly. "I have to go get her."

"No," I said. "You don't." I blocked her from the door.

"But I heard her. She was calling out for me."

Hope stood trembling, clutching the handle of the shovel. That's when I noticed she was also wearing a stocking cap and a green wool coat. Something in her brain had short-circuited. She was now prepared for Christmas.

The minute she walked outside, I phoned Dr. Finch at the office. One of his patients, Suzanne, answered the phone. Finch liked her voice so much he sometimes lured her into playing receptionist when Hope was out of the office.

"I need to talk to him."

"You can't, he's with a patient," she said, pouring on thick her professional receptionist voice, even though she was really just a crazy housewife who liked to cut herself with a paring knife.

"Go get him, Suzanne. It's an emergency."

"What is it?" Suzanne thrived on drama and crisis. Which is no doubt why she ended up in the emergency room every other week.

"It's Hope. Just put him on."

"Fine," she sighed. "I'll go get him."

When Finch picked up the phone I told him that Hope was out back digging the cat up.

"Put her on the phone," he shouted.

I balanced the handset on top of the phone and went to the door to call Hope. "Your father wants to talk to you," I shouted.

She was at the tree, hunched over the shovel, digging. She turned. "Okay." She dropped the shovel and ran inside.

I don't know what he said to her. But I watched and she nodded. "Yes, Dad." She nodded some more. "Okay, Dad." A calmness overcame her face and when she hung up all she said was, "I'm going to go to my room and take a nap."

I WOULD DYE FOR YOU

Please. Hope's cunt is like Fort Knox. Nobody gets in."

"I heard that," Hope called from the kitchen. "And I don't want you talking about me when I'm not there."

Bookman yelled back at her over his shoulder, "We're not talking about you. We're talking about your cunt."

Hope walked stiffly into the room. She spoke sharply in a low voice. "I don't like you using the C-word in connection to me. It's rude and offensive."

In her hand, she held a raw hot dog.

"Take it easy, sister," Bookman said, adopting a condescending tone. "We were just discussing your love life. Or lack thereof."

"My love life is none of your beeswax," she huffed. "Besides, haven't the two of you got better things to do than sit around all afternoon talking about me?" She bit into the frankfurter.

"Seriously, Hope," Neil said, leaning back against the sofa and placing his arm around me. "Being in love is fantastic. It's the best thing there is. You should try it."

Hope sneered. "I'd hardly call you an expert."

His hands slammed down on his thighs and I could feel his muscles tense against mine. "What's *that* supposed to mean?"

She leaned against the windowsill and chewed slowly, casually. "It means I'd hardly call you an expert on love, that's all."

"Are you saying my relationship with Augusten isn't love?"

"I'm saying your 'relationship' with Augusten, who is fourteen by the way, is not a mature love, no."

"Bullshit," he screamed. "Bullshit, bullshit, bullshit."

I hated being caught in the midst of their sibling rivalry. And they weren't even real siblings.

I had been having a good time sitting on the couch next to Neil, just talking. I liked feeling his grown-up arm against my skinny one. And I liked that he didn't seem interested in anything except me. But when he got intense like this, when he got crazy, shaking like he was now, I didn't like him. It was like there were two Bookmans. The one I liked and the other one that was hidden.

"No, it's not bullshit, Neil. It's the truth. And if you're not man enough to take the truth, you have no business being with a child."

"I'm not a child, Hope," I snapped. "I'm fourteen."

"I'm sorry, Augusten. I know you're not. I didn't mean it

like that. You're very mature. I just meant that, well, it's different when you're older. Love is different. More mature."

Neil burst into a riot of malicious laughter. "And what do
you, Miss Iceberg, know about mature love? When was the
last time you had anything in your twat besides a tampon?"

"That's enough, Bookman," Hope shouted. "I'm not going
to listen to you when you're talking like a teenage boy—and
acting like one." She stormed from the room, fuming.

Neil leaned back against the couch and put on a fake smile.
"That shook her up. She's such a prude."

"Yeah, she can be," I said. "But I like her. She's pretty
normal and everything."

"You think Hope's normal?"

"Well, yeah. Pretty much."

"She's thirty. She lives at home. She works for her father.
And she hasn't had a boyfriend since she was twenty-two. You
think that's normal?"

Well, when he put it like that.

But I wasn't talking about those things. I meant, she had
a good heart and she wasn't insane. The not being insane
part, that was a lot around here. "I like her," I said.

"I like her too. She's my spiritual sister for crying out loud.
But she pisses me off. She really gets under my skin." Then
he faced me and his eyes softened, pupils dilating. "I don't
like anybody saying my love for you is anything less than
miraculous."

I liked his attention. But I also felt like there was something sick and wrong about it. Like it might make me sick
later. I thought of my grandmother, my father's mother. How
when I used to visit her in Georgia she would always let me
eat all the cookies and frozen egg rolls I wanted. "Go ahead,

sweetheart, there's more," she would say. And it seemed okay because she was a grown-up, and I wanted all the Chips Ahoy! cookies in the bag. But I always ended up feeling extremely sick afterward. I looked at Bookman, his eyes swollen with emotion. "Thanks, that's sweet."

"It's not sweet, my man. It's the truth. The love I have for you is every bit as valid and as powerful and as healthy as the love any man would feel for any other man."

"Yeah," I said, not quite believing him, but also not wanting to question him because I didn't want him to fly into a rage.

"Did you read my letter?"

He was talking about the sixteen-page letter he'd slipped under my door last night. I'd read the first page, then skipped to the end. It went on and on and on about how profound this thing between us is, how it's "blindingly intense" and "all-consuming" and how "nothing else matters so much as the fire of life behind your eyes and between your legs." I mean, I liked that he felt so strongly about me. But I worried he felt too strongly about me. I guess it scared me in some way. I was a little afraid of things when they got too intense because my mother was one of those things that got too intense and then she exploded.

"I read it, yeah. Thanks. You said a lot of great things." I hoped he didn't quiz me on specifics.

"Oh, come here, you," he said and pulled me up against him. Bookman held me so hard that sometimes I felt he'd mash my internal organs together and bruise something. It wasn't like he was holding me so much as trying to hold onto something.

* * *

That night when the house was asleep, Bookman sneaked down to my room. I was already in bed but I wasn't asleep because I knew he'd come. I liked it when we met at night, after everyone else went to sleep.

"Did that feel good?" he asked as we lay side by side, naked on my twin bed, bought secondhand from Hope. My own bed was in my mother's apartment with throw pillows on it, a place where she could sit and read over a stanza. Or where I could sleep when I was staying with her.

"Yeah, that felt great," I said. Sometimes I still couldn't get over the fact that I didn't have to use *Playgirl* magazine to jerk off with anymore. I had my own real, live, adult man pet. It felt like I was one of those lottery winners with so much money the plunger ball in the back of the toilet was made of solid gold.

It was like an extravagance.

I could say, *sit like this*, and he'd sit like that. Or, *what if we try this?* And we'd try that. He was like this fantastic, twenty-four-hour-a-day vessel available for my exploration.

"If you left me, I'd kill myself," he said.

Except when he said things like that and I hated him again.

"No you wouldn't," I tried to tell him. "Don't say that."

"But God." He broke down, crying softly. "It's so true. Don't you see, Augusten? You're everything to me."

Bookman was everything to me, too. But not in the same way. He was the only thing. Nobody else paid me attention like Bookman did. Nobody else told me I was smart and funny and sweet. Nobody else made me come three times in one day. But I knew I liked him, even loved him, despite the fact of him.

Despite his personality, I guess.

He was like *Playgirl's* Mr. October come to life. But I think I would have been happier if the only thing that came out of his mouth was the sound of a turning page.

By morning, Bookman was still in my room.

And we were still talking about how much he loved me and needed me. I wanted to kick him out; tell him he had to leave because I had to sleep. But I couldn't. I had to listen because, after all, it was all about me.

And then I got an idea. Maybe I could still spend quality time with him *and* practice for beauty school. "Can I do something to your hair?" I said.

"What do you want to do?"

I eyed the box—unopened—of Clairol Nice 'N Easy Ash Blonde that was on my bookshelf next to one of the doctor's old stuffed owls. "Just brighten it up a little."

He smiled. "You mean warmer like yours?" And he buried his face in my curls.

"Yeah," I said. "Like that, sort of."

He splayed his arms out on the bed. "I'm all yours, sir. Do with me what you may."

"Okay, good. Get up." I pulled him up by the arms and made him sit on the bed. "Now wait right here." I went into the bathroom to grab some towels and then I came back in the room.

"You sure you have enough towels there, fella?" he said.

I tossed them on the bed except for one that I draped over his neck like I'd seen in one of the illustrations in Kate's book.

I opened the box, which I had been saving for a crisis at the house, and applied the mixture to his head.

He ran his hands up and down my bare legs the entire time but I didn't mind because I'd never colored anyone before and I was very interested to see the results. The box said to leave it on for twenty minutes, but because his hair was black, I decided to leave it on for longer.

I wrapped his head in Saran wrap and then, an hour later, brought him into the bathroom to rinse his head in the sink.

Next to the sink was a free-standing plastic shelf unit. Agnes's cosmetics were on one of the shelves. I picked up one of the tubes. Max Factor mascara. Vintage. Probably from the first batch Max Factor himself ever mixed together. I tossed it back on the shelf and turned my attention back to Bookman.

"Is it out yet?" he said with his face in the sink, water running across the back of his head and his nape.

The difference was startling.

"Yeah, it's out. You can raise your head up but don't look."

He stood, his head dripping, and had a big smile on his face. The change of activity had already done him good.

I towel-dried his hair.

It was a greenish-shade of brown. And it felt exactly like steel wool, except straight.

"How does it look?" he asked.

I led him out of the bathroom. "It's a new look. It's good."

"I wanna see. Hand me a mirror."

I handed him one of my mirrors. Unfortunately, I had many. "Holy shit."

"See?" I said. "Completely different."

"It's green."

"It's not green. It's ash blonde."

"It's green," he said louder. It made his face look even paler.

"It's the lighting."

He handed the mirror back to me. "And it feels absolutely awful. Are you sure you wanna do this for a living?"

"It'll feel better when it grows out. Yes, I'm sure. What else is there for me to do? Besides, I don't care about the actual hair part. I'm only really interested in the product lines that can carry my name."

"Well you're not gonna get very far with the product lines if you don't care a little more about the hair part."

"Oh shut up. You'll get used to it."

Then he softened. "I'm just teasing. I kind of like it. And I love that you did it to me. I'm yours. You can do anything you want to me."

I thought, *There's that lotto feeling again.*

A FAMILY AFFAIR

Because the minister's wife refused to leave the minister, and because my mother required a worshipful companion, she was forced to break up with Fern and secure herself a new mate. As luck would have it, Dr. Finch had recently begun seeing a suicidal eighteen-year-old African-American girl who had taken a leave of absence from the Rhode Island School of Design.

Her name was Dorothy.

And she was destined to spend many of her early adult years as my mother's girlfriend.

Dorothy's reddish-black hair tumbled down her shoulders in kinky loops. She had large brown eyes, an expressive mouth and a nose that resembled the dorsal fin of a salmon. Instead of being called "pretty" one might have described her as having "character." I thought she looked like a young witch.

She was an excitable girl who seemed to be starved for chaos. The way other people seek comfort and security, Dorothy sought extremes. And she found this with my mother.

One of the things I liked about her was that she had long fingernails that she would carefully manicure and paint to fit her mood. If she were in a happy mood, her nails would be bright red. If she were feeling like she wanted to eviscerate her mother she would paint her nails burgundy. And when Dorothy was in one of her withdrawn, sullen moods, her nails would be neutral.

But to me, her best quality was her trust fund. It had been established by her father whom she loathed because when she was younger he showed her his penis on a rowboat. The trust fund was large enough that she was able to live off the interest alone.

And like a bottom-feeding catfish, I was able to live off the scraps.

"Here's fifty," she'd say. "Now get lost."

When I officially moved into the Finch house, I assumed my mother would keep my old room for me in Amherst. The way mothers on primetime television do. But this was not the case.

Instead, Dorothy moved from her parent's house in Buckland into my old bedroom. At least that was the arrangement at first. My mother was going to be a mentor to the troubled girl. *"I've always wanted a daughter."*

But it didn't take long before they shared the master bedroom and the other was used for storage.

Soon they were inseparable. And, I thought, extremely compatible.

If my mother was odd enough to crave a bubble bath at three in the morning, Dorothy was inventive enough to suggest adding broken glass to the tub. If my mother insisted on listening to *West Side Story* repeatedly, it was Dorothy who said, "Let's listen to it on forty-five!"

And when my mother announced that she wanted a fur wrap like Auntie Mame, Dorothy bought her an unstable Norwegian elkhound from a puppy mill.

"Damn it, Dorothy," my mother cried, "this animal is making me a nervous wreck. You've just got to take it back."

"It's not an it, it's a *she*. And she wouldn't have shit all over the stairs if you let her outside like I told you to."

"*Shat*. And I couldn't let her outside because she snaps at me whenever I set foot near her."

"She's not snapping at you. I told you, she's epileptic. You have to give her the pills." She rattled the bottle the vet had given her.

"I do not have time to be giving that damn dog pills. I have enough pills of my own to take. She has to go."

Dorothy went into the bathroom and returned with a bottle of Vicks NyQuil. "Look, we'll try this. I bet it'll settle her down." She poured a dose of the green NyQuil into the little cup and bent down.

The dog's tongue slipped into the little cup as Dorothy tipped it backward. "See? She even likes it."

The NyQuil took effect swiftly and the dog napped in the corner. "That's more like it," my mother said, stroking her hind leg with her big toe. "She's a sweet thing when she sleeps, isn't she?"

"See?" Dorothy said.

"Okay," my mother said. "As long as you can manage her."

"I can manage her. Just like I manage you."

"Oh, *you're* such a good pet," my mother said, pressing Dorothy's face between her hands and kissing her lips.

Although my mother teased that Dorothy was her *pet*, it was Dorothy who acted as if she had a trained bear for a lover. "Make that face!" she would shriek, clapping her hands like a child.

My mother would try to suppress her smile and remain dignified and composed. "I don't know what face you're talking about."

Dorothy would scream, "You know exactly which face! Make it, make it, make it!"

My mother would laugh and bare her teeth. "Grrrrrrrrrr," she would growl, holding her fingers out like bear claws.

Dorothy would bounce up and down on the sofa like a delighted little girl.

It was not uncommon to walk in the door of their home and find my mother sitting on the sofa reading over a manuscript with shampoo horns sculpted into her hair. Anne Sexton's voice would be blasting from the speakers.

A woman who writes feels too much . . .

Dorothy viewed my mother's propensity toward madness not as something to be afraid of, but rather as something to look forward to, like a movie or a newly released color of nail polish.

"Your mother is just expressing herself," Dorothy would tell me when my mother stopped sleeping, started smoking the filters of her cigarettes and began writing backward with a glitter pen.

"No, she's not," I would say. "She's going insane again."

"Don't be so mundane," she would yawn, passing my mother a shoebox filled with cat vertebrae. "She is a brilliant artist. If you want Hamburger Helper, go find some other mother."

I *did* want Hamburger Helper. And if I knew where to find a mother that could make it, I would have been there in a heartbeat.

Dorothy protected my mother, acting as a loyal guard dog who could also prepare snacks.

"Dorothy, I'm dying of thirst," my mother might call from her reclined position on the sofa. She would be fanning her face with a copy of her first book of poems, the only one she didn't have printed herself.

Dorothy would appear a moment later with a tall glass of iced tea, at the bottom of which she had placed a small plastic goat.

My mother would guzzle the tea, her eyes closed, and then succumb to a fit of coughing until she spat the plastic goat into her hand. "What in the *world?*" she would say.

Then they would both explode into a fit of laughter.

Dorothy's unpredictable nature perfectly suited my mother's unreliable brain chemistry. She was not only fun, but she acted as a buffer between my mother and me. I didn't feel that I had to keep as close an eye on my mother's mental health because Dorothy was looking after her. And when my mother did go psychotic, Dorothy went along for the ride.

On one of their rides, they brought me back a souvenir.

* * *

His name was Cesar Mendoza and he looked exactly like a cartoon lumberjack. His arms were as thick around as tree limbs. And his head was as square as an anvil. My mother had met him at the mental hospital where Dr. Finch had committed her.

"I'm not going to any goddamn mental hospital," my mother raved, her eyes looking like somebody had lit books of matches inside of them.

"It's just for observation," Finch told her calmly.

"I will not be observed!" my mother shrieked, hurling her large-framed body against the door, causing it to slam in Finch's face.

"Deirdre, you have to go," he said through the door. "Come out now or we'll have to get the police."

In the end, my mother didn't put up a fuss. She allowed herself to be taken to the Brattleboro retreat in Vermont.

She returned from the hospital still slightly mad with a six-foot-two lumberjack in tow. The lumberjack spoke only broken English. "I love you mother," he said when he met me. "And I be your new father."

I sat on her sofa, stunned by this development. Not only had my mother failed to recover in the hospital, it seemed to me she had gone even crazier.

"Where is bathroom?" he asked as he shuffled through the house, ducking under the doorjambs.

"It's in the back," I told him.

When he returned, he smelled of my mother's new Avon perfume. "You like?" he said, extending his arm. "I smell pretty now, no?"

Dorothy clung to my mother's arm, lighting her cigarettes for her and holding them between puffs. She explained the situation to me. "Your mother feels strongly that God has brought them together. And that Cesar is going to be a part of our lives from now on."

She turned to my mother and looked at her profile with admiration, as if my mother had just announced her diagnosis of cancer and her decision to fight the disease with every bit of strength she had left.

I eyed the lumberjack who was busy sniffing his perfumed arm and smiling, using his free hand to gently rub the bulge in his pants. "What do you know about this man?" I asked.

"Not much," Dorothy said. "Except that he's married, he has two kids and the police are looking for him."

Cesar grinned down at me, exposing the whitest, most perfect teeth. A surprising quality in a crazy person.

"Nice teeth," I commented.

"You like?" he said, and pulled them out of his mouth.

I winced.

Because it was my mother's first day home from the mental hospital, she was exhausted. It took all her energy to stand on her own and not use Dorothy or the wall for support. The medication had also made her movements slow and clumsy. "I'm going to bed. Dorothy, come with me." She licked her cracked lips. "My mouth is so damn dry." She turned to me. "I'll see you in the morning."

Which left me alone with my new father.

"You mother tells me you are a gay," he said, taking a seat on the couch.

I slid away from him. "Yeah."

He stretched his arms out on the back of the sofa. "I don't

think you a gay. I think you have no man in your life. No father ever. What you need is father. Good, strong father. *I* be your father. *You* be my son." His eyes had the same glossy appearance as my mother's, as if they'd both gone to the same sinister opthamologist and been fitted with identical contact lenses.

I said, "Mmm hmm."

He brought his arms forward and slapped his knees. "Now, go get your father something to drink. You have beer?"

I told him we didn't have any beer but I could get him a glass of tap water or there might be some flat Pepsi in the refrigerator. He told me to forget it, and then he popped a handful of pills into his mouth, chewed and swallowed them dry.

Although I was officially living at the Finches, I spent some nights at my mother's apartment in Amherst. Sometimes Bookman and I would stay there together or sometimes just me alone on the sofa. I told myself that I was like a bicoastal celebrity, moving between Amherst and Northampton at will, when the spirit moved me. But what I truly felt was that neither place was home. In truth, when things got too crazy at the Finches', I stayed in Amherst. When I felt like my mother and Dorothy couldn't stand me anymore, I moved back to Northampton. Usually, one night was the most I could stay in Amherst. One night every few weeks.

At just after midnight, I was awakened from a dream that a hard penis was pressing against my ass. It turned out there *was* a hard penis pressing against my ass.

"What the fuck are you doing?" I said, shoving him off.

He was completely naked, even his teeth were out of his mouth. "I only want to try," he gummed. "I love you, new son."

"Get *away* from me," I said.

I locked him out of the living room and went back to sleep on the sofa. My powers of denial were strong even then, and I was able to convince myself that it *didn't really matter because it didn't really happen.* When I heard him climbing the stairs to go find Deirdre and Dorothy, I figured he'd finally leave me alone.

Throughout the night, my mother would come downstairs and pass through the living room on her way to the kitchen. She was sweating profusely, looking extremely preoccupied. Whatever she had been doing in her bedroom, it was clear that it didn't involve sleep. When I asked her what was going on, she said, nearly out of breath, "Dorothy is still a virgin as far as men are concerned."

Later, I heard Dorothy suddenly start shrieking and then sobbing. This was followed by the muffled sounds of my mother saying something in a soothing tone of voice.

An hour later the lumberjack came downstairs. He sauntered into the living room, thumbs hooked through his belt loops, and winked at me. "She as wet as a dishrag." He motioned with his head, indicating upstairs.

The next morning, Dorothy appeared smug and pleased, but aloof toward my new father.

"Please give me the man a glass of something to drink."

"Get your own fucking drink, asshole," Dorothy replied distantly, as she brushed a fresh coat of polish over her nails. Fuchsia.

My mother, too, seemed ready to dispose of him now. Last

night he was a gift from God, a new member of the family, my lumberjack father. But today he was an insect that needed to be crushed with a shoe. The black widows had mated with him and now they needed to destroy him.

"I think it's time for you to leave, Cesar," my mother informed him as she stroked Dorothy's hair. They were sitting at the kitchen table together, with Cesar hovering over them.

"No, I just get here. I stay and be man father."

"You heard her, asshole. Scram," Dorothy said, blowing on her pinkie to dry the polish.

The elkhound slept peacefully under the table, as it had for the past six days, moving only occasionally—and then very sluggishly—for a drink from its NyQuil-spiked water bowl.

"Where I should go?" he pleaded. "Have no place?" He glanced at me, but I shrugged and looked away.

Being mentally ill, temporarily homeless and wanted by the law, the only logical place for him to go was to Dr. Finch's.

"Let me make a phone call," my mother said finally. After she hung up, she scribbled the Finches' address down on the inside cover of a book of matches. Then, instead of handing him the matches, she tore off the cover. "Here you go," she said.

Dorothy snatched up the matches and held them over the candle on the kitchen table where they burst into flames. "Pretty," she said.

At the Finch house, the lumberjack discovered and fell madly in love with Natalie.

Natalie was repulsed by him at first. "Get the fuck away

from me, you missing link," she said, slapping his hand away with the serrated edge of an aluminum foil box, one of dozens that were in the pantry, left over from the days of Joranne.

But his persistence, which came in the form of endearments like, "Shake that belly for me," and "I'll give you a hundred dollars," finally melted her resistance.

One night while Natalie and I were going for a walk at Smith she turned to me and said, "You'll never guess what I did."

I knew that I couldn't, in fact, ever guess what she had done. So I said, "What?"

"I fucked Cesar Mendoza."

"You're kidding. You fucked the lumberjack?"

"It gets worse."

"Oh, really? How does it get worse than fucking him?"

"Fucking him for cash." She held up two crisp twenty-dollar bills. "Now I can add *prostitute* to my list of life's accomplishments."

"So now what? Are you two like, dating?"

"No," she said. "I had Dad kick him out of the house. He'll be gone by the time we get back. But to make sure, we should search everywhere, even the crawl space under the barn. I don't trust that lunatic one bit."

We did search the house when we got back and we didn't find him anywhere. As suddenly as he appeared in my life, he was gone. I chalked him up to a virus my mother had caught at the hospital and then brought back and spread.

A week later, when my mother's medication had finally reached its optimum level in her bloodstream and she was back to normal, she had little memory of the father she had brought home for me.

"I'd rather not talk about that right now. This whole episode has been very intense for me and I don't have the energy to process everything right away." She was drained of energy, pale and lifeless. "But I do believe *that* may have been my last psychotic episode. I think I *finally* broke through to my creative unconscious."

I marveled at my mother's view of her mental illness. To her, going psychotic was like going to an artist's retreat.

When pressed for an explanation of their insane behavior, Dorothy would only say, "It was between your mother and me."

Actually, it wasn't. Because long after Cesar Mendoza left, his yeast infection stayed behind.

"Oh, I've got this awful itch," my mother announced one evening.

"Me too. And a cottage-cheese discharge," said Dorothy.

Natalie summed it up best. "Jesus Christ. My cunt looks like it's been brushing its teeth. It's just foaming at the mouth."

INQUIRE WITHIN

THE MOOD IN THE PINK HOUSE HAD TURNED TO CHARCOAL. A general sense of impending doom hung over our heads like one of Agnes's bad hats. Several of Dr. Finch's patients had "abandoned" treatment, meaning fewer dollars. The IRS was becoming more threatening in their move to claim the house as payment for a ten-year-old tax bill. And Finch himself was entering one of his formidable depressions.

The stress had caused the psoriasis on Hope's scalp to produce extraordinary quantities of snowy flakes. For hours, she would sit on the couch in the TV room or on her chair next to the stove and read *The Complete Poems of Emily Dickinson* while she scratched slowly and steadily. It was as if she entered some sort of trance, her fingers only leaving her head to briefly turn the page. The flakes would collect on her shoulders and scatter down the front and back of her shirt. This gave her the appearance of an actress taking a break from shooting on the set of a blizzard.

"That is so disgusting," Natalie commented one afternoon as she reached into the refrigerator.

Hope ignored her.

"I said, you are *disgusting* sitting there like that and scratching. Christ, Hope. Have you looked at yourself in the mirror?" Natalie said, waving the end of a ham in the air.

Hope ignored her. She turned the page.

Natalie bit into the ham end. She walked over to the stove where Hope was sitting. "Look at you," she said. "You're like an animal, tearing your flesh off."

Hope ignored her.

Natalie glanced over at me and rolled her eyes in disgust. I had come into the kitchen to get some water and was leaning against the sink.

"Hope the dope," Natalie said, taking a final bite from the ham. She dropped the rest of it on Hope's lap. It smacked in the center of her book.

"Goddamn it, you bitch," Hope exploded. She picked up the ham end and threw it across the room toward the phone on the wall, just missing. It landed in the hall below the coats.

Natalie laughed. "Oooh, prissy Miss Hope has a temper," she taunted. "Temper, temper, temper."

Hope took a deep breath, let it out, and blotted the book using the hem of her shirt. She began to hum "The Impossible Dream."

"That's right, you just ignore me," Natalie said. Then she

reached forward and began scratching Hope's head vigorously with both hands. A flurry of dried white skin cells rose like dust from Hope's head.

"M*mmmmmmm*," Hope moaned, felinelike. "That feels good."

Natalie stopped instantly. "You're pitiful." She stomped away and went back to the refrigerator. Opening the crisper drawer, she removed a slice of American cheese. It had been left unwrapped and even from across the room, I could see the smooth, plasticlike texture of the firm slice. Natalie bit into it, made a face and spit into her hand. "God, there's nothing to eat in this house."

"Agnes went shopping," I said.

"When?" Natalie asked.

"I don't know, maybe an hour ago. A few hours ago. I lost track."

Natalie walked over to the trash can near the sink where I was leaning. She dropped the cheese into the can and then did a double-take at my head. "What did you do to your hair?"

I shrugged. "It's semipermanent. It'll come out after ten washings." Out of boredom, I'd dyed it brown with Just For Men. I thought it made me look like a dashing young news anchor.

"It looks like a wig," Natalie said.

"It does sort of look fake," I agreed, setting my glass in the sink.

Hope glanced up from her book. "I think it looks good," she said.

"Nobody asked you, snowgirl."

"Fuck you," Hope said.

"Just try it," said Natalie, "and I'll stick a meat cleaver up your cunt."

Hope slammed her book shut. "Natalie, you are so foul-mouthed. What's the matter with you, hm? All day long you whine about wanting to go to Smith and you can't say ten words without using the F-word."

"That's right, Hope. I'm just a foul-mouthed whore. I'm your little slut sister."

"That's enough," Hope said.

"Go fuck yourself," Natalie gave her the finger. Then she turned to me. "Let's go to McDonald's. Let's get some Mc-Nuggets."

"Oh, bring me some?" Hope said sweetly.

Natalie snickered darkly. "We'll bring you a dead squirrel if we happen to see one on the side of the road."

"I don't even like the McNuggets," Natalie said. "I just get 'em for the hot mustard sauce." She licked her fingers, making a sucking noise.

We were sitting at a red plastic table in McDonalds. We'd had to scrounge around in the pockets of our dirty clothes and in the sofa just to get the measly four dollars we needed to even come here. How much lower would we sink?

"You know what we need? We need to get jobs, get the fuck out of that crazy house," Natalie said, dipping a Mc-Nugget into her sauce.

"Yeah, right. Jobs doing what? Our only skills are oral sex and restraining agitated psychotics."

She laughed. "How pathetic and true. But seriously, we

should walk around today and look for work. I'm just talking about being a clerk or something. I mean how hard is it to run a cash register?"

Considering I couldn't even do long division, the idea of running a cash register made me as anxious as running a nuclear reactor. "I don't know," I said. "It seems like you have to have experience for everything."

"Well," she said, glancing around the restaurant, "we could always start here."

"At McDonald's?" I dipped into the red barbecue sauce.

"Yeah. I mean, we could work here for a couple months, get some experience and then get a really good job at like Beyond Words bookstore or Country Comfort or something."

"I guess," I said.

"C'mon, hurry up and finish. We'll get a couple applications from the manager. And after we fill them out, we'll walk around town and look for Help Wanted signs."

I shrugged. Why not? At least it was something to do. "Okay."

We emptied our trays into the trash and asked the counter girl for a couple of applications. After filling them out we left. As we walked, Natalie kept scratching her butt.

"Stop doing that. It makes you look Down's syndrome-ish."

"I can't help it," she said.

"Well, try."

We walked into the center of town to the courthouse and sat down on the grass in front of the water fountain. Here we had an excellent view of Main Street and all the shops. Natalie pulled a joint out of her shirt pocket. "We should get a buzz first," she said.

"Yeah," I agreed.

We passed the joint back and forth. "Do you feel stoned yet?" she asked.

I exhaled. "Yeah."

"This is good stuff. *Sense.*"

"It's good," I said. It was starting already. Whereas pot either made Natalie contemplative or silly, for me it provided a kaleidoscopic view of everything that was wrong with me. I could already feel it opening all the windows in my head, giving me a panoramic view of my flaws.

"I have such skinny legs," I said, looking at them stretched out in front of me. "They're basically deformed."

Natalie stretched her own legs out and hiked up her skirt. "At least you're not fat like me." She pinched her flesh and shook. "See? Exactly like Jell-O. It's nauseating. And you know what's really depressing? It just makes me want to eat."

"When I get depressed, I don't want to eat at all." When I got depressed, all I wanted to do was sleep. Which is basically what I did for fourteen hours a day.

Natalie sighed. "Do you think I'll ever get into Smith? Or am I too fucked up?"

"I think you can still be fucked up and get into Smith. I mean, think of all the privileged girls that must be suicidal when they first get there. You know, from living this really sheltered, traditional life. All the secret shit that goes on in families. I don't know what I mean. But you know what I mean?"

"Yeah," she said vaguely. "I guess. It's just that sometimes, I worry I won't ever be undepressed."

I had the same worry that we wouldn't later be able to undo whatever it was we were doing to ourselves. "We should go. Start looking for work."

Natalie tucked the roach back into her pocket and we stood, stretching. Now all I wanted to do was sleep. The pot had made me depressed about my life. But Natalie was right, we needed jobs.

"Look," Natalie said as we crossed the street. "Sweeties needs help." She pointed to the sign in the window of the candy store.

We stepped inside and asked the guy behind the counter for two applications. He looked us up and down before saying, "Sorry, I should have taken that sign out of the window. We filled that position yesterday."

Natalie said, "Sure. No problem."

We walked up Main Street toward Smith, checking the windows for Help Wanted signs. We filled out applications at Woolworth's, Harlow Luggage and The Academy of Music, a grand old movie theater. Then we started hitting the stores without Help Wanted signs, asking if we could fill out applications in case something came up. After an hour and a half, we'd filled out nine applications each.

"Well, that's enough for one day. Who knows? Maybe something will come up," Natalie said with forced optimism.

"Yeah," I said brightly. Although what I felt was that nobody would hire us, we didn't have a chance. And not just because we didn't have any experience. But because we seemed somehow off. Like Finches.

"Let's go to Smith," Natalie said. "We could use a little Smith right now."

Smith College was easily the most beautiful campus in America. I knew this from my extensive television viewing. Harvard, Yale, Columbia, Princeton, Berkeley, Northwestern, DePaul. They had all been featured in one made-for-TV movie or another. I seemed to remember Lynn Redgrave in a wrap dress running from a stalker on the grounds of Mt. Holyoke. But I could have this confused with Ali McGraw weeping at Harvard.

The Smith campus consisted of a hundred and fifty acres of brick and ivy and rolling green hills, dressed for the occasion with hardwood trees and thoughtfully placed benches. There was even a tree swing that overlooked Paradise Pond and the expansive soccer field that lay beyond. Merely being in this glorious environment soothed any personal problems one might be struggling with. I found it more effective than Ativan though not as soothing as Valium.

Who's Afraid of Virginia Woolf? was filmed in a small white house on campus, just down from the boathouse next to the waterfall. I had seen that movie at the Amherst Cinema and loved it completely because Elizabeth Taylor and Richard Burton reminded me so much of my parents. It was the closest thing I had to a home movie.

"Listen to the roar," Natalie said as we stood next to the falls.

It reminded me of the sound New York City makes. When I was small my mother had taken me with her to Manhattan a few times to see the museums. And what I loved most about that city was the sound it made.

"I wish I could just vanish into that sound," Natalie said, leaning over the railing.

And then I had an idea. "We could."

"Could what?"

"We could vanish into it. We could walk under it, across. See that ledge?" I pointed to a ledge just behind the curtain of falling water. It ran the entire length of the waterfall and was easily wide enough to walk on. If we were careful.

Natalie looked at me with her mouth open in disbelief. "You've got to be kidding, right?"

"Well, I don't know. We're bored and it's something to do. At least it's different."

"True," she said.

And this is how we found ourselves hand-in-hand, crossing under the waterfall at Smith College at six in the evening. My hypothesis that we would remain dry due to the fact that the ledge was *behind* the water proved to be wrong. The water was astonishingly powerful and cold. But Natalie's hand in mine was still the most powerful thing I felt with my body. If we fell, we would fall together.

The sound was deafening. Looking at an ordinary glass of water, you'd never even imagine that water was capable of making so much noise, no matter how much of it there was. The sound filled my entire body, not just my ears. I could feel my cells vibrating with it.

Natalie screamed the whole way across. Primal, guttural screams and hysterical laughter. And I could barely hear her.

When we got to the other side, we collapsed on the soccer field, completely exhausted and drenched.

"Oh my God," she said.

I lay back with my arms stretched out and stared at the sky.

I had never felt so free in my entire life.

We made a point to *not* take the side streets on the walk home. We strolled through the center of town, stopping in any store that was open. We even walked into stores where just an hour ago we had filled out job applications.

"A brownie and a Diet Pepsi," Natalie told the counter girl at Woolworth's. Her hair was still plastered to the sides of her face, dripping down her back.

My hair, because of the heavy chemical processing it had endured, was completely dry.

We enjoyed the stares we received on the streets of Northampton. We liked to imagine what the young Jennifers and Mehgans might think when they saw us. "Oh my Gahd, mother. You cannot imagine the creatures I saw in town tonight while I was at the store for a watch battery. They were positively *ghastly*," they might say, protracted jaws pressed against the dormitory phone.

When we finally made it back to Sixty-seven, Dr. F was on the sofa snoring as usual and Agnes was in the chair next to him stitching the toe of one of his fifteen-year-old socks. She glanced up when she saw us, then looked back down at her sewing. Then looked back up. "Good Lord, what happened to you two?"

"We walked under the waterfall at Smith," Natalie said casually, as if we'd gone to the store for milk.

"That's insane," she laughed.

We dripped our way down the hall and into the kitchen. Hope was jealous. "Aw, you guys," she whined. "You never do anything fun like that with me."

"You wouldn't have done it anyway," Natalie said.

Hope closed her bible indignantly. "Yes I would."

"What is this?" Natalie frowned, lifting the lid off a boiling pot on the stove.

"That's my special soup."

I walked over and peered into Hope's cauldron. I thought

I caught a quick glimpse of an unfamiliar-shaped bone and backed away.

"God, it smells awful. What did you put in it?" Natalie said.

Hope smiled secretively and rolled her eyes up toward the ceiling. "Things," she said.

"What *things?*" I asked.

She made the gesture of buttoning her lip and tossing aside the key. She shrugged her shoulders.

"*Ick.* Well, I'm not having any of it," Natalie said.

"That's too bad for you then," she said. "You won't get to appreciate my secret ingredient."

Natalie slid her eyes toward Hope. "What secret ingredient?" She fanned her shirt out from her skin to shake off some of the water.

"Well, I went outside and dug Freud up. So she's in there."

Natalie shrieked and recoiled instantly from the stove. She slapped her hands across her legs, her arms and her chest as if trying to brush away a swarm of locusts. "Oh my God, you *fucking* lunatic, I knew you were fucking insane," she screamed.

Hope smiled triumphantly. "*I'm only kidding, jerks!* Ha, ha, got you back."

When Natalie regained her composure and stopped laughing, she said, "Got me back for what?"

"I got you back for not getting me anything at McDonald's when you guys went there today."

"I'm sorry about that," Natalie said. "We really should have brought you back something."

"Yeah, Hope. I'm sorry too."

"That's okay," Hope said. "At least we all got some anger out." She smiled warmly at both of us and extended her arms. *"Group hug."*

And as easy as that, we were one big, happy family again.

LIFE IN THE GREAT OUTDOORS

NATALIE STOOD AT THE COUNTER SCOOPING FRIENDLY'S mint chocolate chip ice cream into the blender and Hope sat at the kitchen table leafing through her bible. She'd book-marked earlier bible-dips and was now going back over them. Glancing up at Natalie she said, "Sure looks good."

Natalie hit the puree button. "There's not going to be enough for you."

"Oh come on," Hope complained. "Why not? Why can't you make me one, too?"

Natalie stopped the blender and added some chocolate syrup. "Because you haven't been behaving," she said.

Agnes looked up from the television, which was on a cart next to the love seat. "Now don't you two get into another fight."

"Hear that, Natalie?" Hope said.

"Maybe you can have a little," Natalie teased.

"Oh, wow!" Hope cried. "Listen to this." She turned her bible sideways and read from a note in the margin. "Last fall I asked, 'Will the IRS get the house?' and my finger landed on the word *defeated*. Isn't that great? It was right."

"That's fantastic, Hope. You've got your own little Magic Eight Ball there."

"Well, I think it's pretty incredible."

"Where are the glasses?" Natalie said.

I remembered seeing them just recently. "They're in that suitcase," I said, pointing next to the old clothes dryer.

"Oh, okay," Natalie said.

The wind picked up and Hope closed her eyes. "Mmmmm, that feels so good."

Agnes reached forward to change the channel. "It is rather pleasant out here."

"The best part," said Natalie, plucking a blade of grass from the lip of the coffee mug, "is that cleanup is so easy." She filled four mugs with milkshake and then leaned over and rinsed the blender out with the garden hose.

We'd been living outdoors now for almost a week. Although we didn't sleep outside, we certainly napped.

It had started as a simple tag sale. Hope had suggested we make some extra money by laying a few things out on the lawn and sticking prices on them. At first, Natalie didn't think it was such a good idea. "Who the hell's gonna buy Dad's old electroshock therapy machine?" But when somebody paid ten dollars for Agnes's ratty old sealskin coat, she changed her tune.

Little by little, we added more things. The old love seat

from the barn, the washing machine that didn't have a spin cycle anymore. We brought out the spare kitchen table that had been hogging so much room next to the piano in the living room. And the extra TV in Hope's room that she never watched. There was even an old kitchen counter in the basement. And we dragged it all out onto the front lawn.

Once we got it out there, we saw that we had enough major furnishings to create a sort of room. The love seat in front of the TV, the kitchen table in the middle, the cabinet next to the washer. And although the old stove didn't work, it did help create a homey feeling.

We all liked the setup so much, we decided to remove all the price tags and move outside for the summer.

The appliances—including the blender, the toaster oven, the electric knife and the crock pot—were all powered by an extension cord we ran from inside the living room, through the window and onto the lawn.

The large Oriental carpet we'd placed on the grass kept our feet clean and dry, thereby reducing the risk of death by electrocution.

Cars that drove past the house tended to slow to a crawl. Sometimes, a window would slide down and a camera would be raised. The flashing made us feel like celebrities.

"I feel just like the Queen Mother," Agnes blushed, bringing her hand to her hair, which had been freshly permed.

Even the doctor took to life in the great outdoors. Now after work, he would walk down Perry Street and instead of pulling his keys out of his pocket, unlocking the door and going inside, he would simply cut across the lawn and sit in his barcalounger. "This is a hell of a lot more comfortable than that sofa inside," he said. "Don't accept any offer less than five hundred dollars."

He even saw a couple of patients outdoors, shielding them from the prying eyes of the passing cars with Agnes's old needlepoint folding screen. He kept his prescription pad in the drawer of Vickie's old nightstand, which was arranged conveniently next to the love seat.

Only the rains drove us inside.

Meanwhile in Amherst, my mother was having her own experiment with outdoor living. But hers would end with a police cruiser and heavy medication.

All summer I'd taken the PVTA bus back and forth between my mother's house in Amherst and my room in Northampton. I liked being able to freely move between the two locations. When I was annoyed with my mother and her girlfriend, Dorothy, I would stay in Northampton. When Neil and I wanted to spend quality time together, we'd both go to Amherst. My mother was more accepting of my relationship than any of the Finches. Agnes, especially, did not approve of what was going on between me and Neil.

So for weeks, I'd been hanging out at my mother's, sometimes sitting in on the writing workshop she held for lesbians in her living room. I liked sitting on the shag carpeting, drinking Celestial Seasonings and hearing overweight women with crew cuts read poems about wounds that never stop bleeding, fertility and full moons.

My mother, meanwhile, was working feverishly on a new poem. It was entitled, "I Dreamed I Saw the Figure Five in

Gold." At first she worked on the poem during the day and spent the evening with her girlfriend eating cucumber sandwiches on Roman meal bread and gossiping about various Finches or patients.

But then I began to notice a change in my mother's eyes. The pupils seemed to dilate, making them appear darker.

I had even gone so far as to warn the doctor. "I think my mother's going to have another psychotic break." But he'd told me I was being overly sensitive, that he did not think my mother was going psychotic again.

Like a sheep or a dog that can predict an earthquake, I had always been able to sense when my mother was about to go crazy. Her speech quickened, she stopped sleeping and she developed a craving for peculiar foods, like candle wax.

My first clue that summer that she was losing her grip was when she started listening to the same song over and over again on the record player. It was Frankie Lane's "You're Breaking My Heart 'Cause You're Leaving." This coincided with her sudden need to decoupage the kitchen table with magazine clippings. "I want my home to be a creative outlet," she said, her red-ringed eyes wild. "Hand me that *Atlantic Monthly*."

I tried to get her to sleep but she only slapped me away. "I need to do this," she said. "These are the images I need to be surrounded by for my writing."

"But it's just a bunch of cigarette ads," I said.

She clipped a picture of Merit Ultra Light Menthols from the page. "Cigarettes hold a great significance for me. They are symbolic."

"Of what?"

"Shhhhh," she said. "I need to listen to my heart." She ran

her fingers across the table, lifting magazines, looking for something. "Are you sitting on my glue stick?"

Dorothy had brought excellent albums into her relationship with my mother and I liked to go to Amherst and listen to Karla Bonoff while I chain-smoked.

But this night, I knew something was wrong the instant I turned onto Dickinson Street. Every light in the house was on and the blinds were up. The street in front of my mother's house was illuminated like it was noon.

Slowly, feeling a sense of impending doom, I approached the door. It was wide open.

Leonard Cohen was playing loudly from the stereo and I walked through the house to find Dorothy in the kitchen laughing as she squirted mustard on Wheat Thins. "Hi!" she said excitedly, unable to contain her hysterical state of mind. "I'm making a sna—" She was so intoxicated with the hilarity of the mustard/cracker combination that she couldn't get the words out.

The back door was wide open.

"Where's my mother?"

"I'm in here," she sang from the tub in the back bathroom.

Carefully, I slid past Dorothy, who was doubled over in laughter, and peered into the bathroom.

My mother was reclined in the bathtub, which was filled with pink bubbles.

Dorothy came up beside me. "Your mom had a little accident," she laughed. "She broke a glass in the tub."

My mother's laugh was deeper, more sinister. It terrified me.

"I'm bleeding," she said. "But I didn't break the glass. Dorothy did."

Calgon, take me away . . .

I walked out of the bathroom to stand in the kitchen. And then I caught a glimpse of something on the lawn. I walked around the corner into the dining room where I noticed the door to the china cabinet was ajar. The cabinet itself was empty. I walked to the open door.

In the light of the porch, I could see a debris field. All the dishes, the television, chairs, books, dishes, forks, spread out over the backyard and glistening in the moonlight.

"What the fuck have you two been up to?" I shouted. I was seized by a feeling of panic. *This can't be happening. Again.*

Dorothy came up beside me, still laughing. "We were having some fun."

Her eyes looked wild, too. And I realized that not only had my mother gone completely mad again, she had taken Dorothy with her.

"You two are out of control," I said. My heart raced and I wanted to flee. And then I didn't want to flee, I wanted to kill my mother. My face became like the heating coil on the stove, and I trembled with hatred. And then just as suddenly, I felt absolutely nothing. It was like a door quickly opened, showing me what horrible feelings I had inside, and then slammed shut again so I wouldn't have to actually face them. In many ways I felt I was living the life of a doctor in the ER. I was learning to block out all emotions in order to deal with the situation. Whether that situation involved a mother who was constantly having nervous breakdowns or the death of the family cat by laundry hamper.

My mother appeared in her robe, dripping with pink bubbles. "Dorothy did it," she said, lighting a cigarette, and motioning toward the backyard.

Dorothy spun around and slapped my mother on the arm. "I did not, you liar."

My mother laughed and said in a wise-woman tone of voice, "Oh yes, you did."

"Liar!" Dorothy squealed gleefully.

I said, "I'm going upstairs. I have to get something."

"Get what?" Dorothy wanted to know.

"Just *something*," I said angrily, as I stormed from the room and up the stairs. Immediately, I phoned Hope. "My mother's gone crazy again and Dorothy seems crazy too."

Hope was always excellent in a crisis, like the rest of the Finches. She wasted no time. "I'll phone Dad. You keep her safe."

I hung up the phone and went back downstairs. My mother and Dorothy were sitting in the front room of the house, the living room. Dorothy was burning a fifty-dollar bill over the flame of a candle.

"What are you doing?" I said.

My mother answered, "She is using her money in the way that she wishes. As if it's any business of yours."

I sat on the opposite end of the couch from Dorothy. My mother sat in a chair across from us. The African mask on the wall behind her head bared its yellow teeth.

Not only did my mother look stark raving mad, but she looked smug in her madness. Like she was pleased to take this mental vacation. She glared at me from across the room, smoking deeply, exhaling with purpose.

"You don't seem normal," I said.

She cocked her head in an arrogant fashion. "And have I

ever seemed normal to you? Have I ever been the mother you wanted?"

It seemed important not to get her riled up. "You've been a good mother," I lied. "I'm just worried about you. You look slightly manic."

Dorothy jumped down my throat. "You are so fucking judgmental. It's people like you that are the reason your mother has to fight so hard. I mean, you might not mean it, I don't think you do it on purpose, but you're oppressive." She turned the fifty-dollar bill against the flame, igniting the edge.

My mother continued to stare at me, studying me it seemed.

Dorothy was like a little girl with her marbles, focused entirely on the candle's flame, the burning bill and her long red fingernails. Her nails were a sharp contrast to my mother's, which were always chewed down to nubs.

After twenty minutes, Hope arrived. She came into the room, winded. "Hi," she said, cautiously, easing her rainbow bag to the floor. She set her PBS bag on a chair. "What's up?"

"Well, what an unexpected surprise. Welcome, Hope," my mother said, although she quickly glared at me.

Hope came and sat on the sofa next to me. Because of all her years working for her dad, Hope's manner was smooth, calm and professional. She was like a paramedic for the psychologically collapsed.

"I just came by to see how you're doing, Deirdre," Hope said. Her voice was friendly, tinged with concern.

"I'm doing fine, thank you very much," my mother said. Her voice dripped with condescension. She picked a small basket up off the table next to her chair. "Do you know what is in this basket, Hope?"

Hope leaned forward, smiling. "No, Deirdre. What?"

"Dorothy," my mother said, "would you come over and get this basket, then hand it to Hope?"

Dorothy smirked. "Sure." She got up, took the small basket from my mother and then handed it to Hope.

Hope opened the basket and screamed, recoiling. She slammed the basket on the coffee table. "Oh my God, what are those?"

My mother roared with laughter and Dorothy sat on the floor next to her, stroking her leg. "Those are dried locust husks. My friend Sonja sent them to me from Texas. You don't like them?"

Hope made a face. "They're disgusting. They give me the creeps."

My mother was fond of such things. She had a cow skull hanging in her bedroom and a rattlesnake skin stretched across the wall above the bookshelf in the dining room. She had bowls of seashells and driftwood and jars filled with bits of fur and feathers. She used many of these things in her writing workshops. "What memory does the bone bring?" she might direct. Or, "Hold the hair between your fingers and describe the sensation."

Hope leaned forward to peer again into the basket. "I wouldn't want something like that around the house, they look like roaches."

"Yes, they certainly do," my mother agreed with controlled poise.

Hope sat back on the sofa and wore a pleasant expression while Dorothy stayed by my mother's side on the floor, like a royal subject. My mother stared directly ahead at me.

I didn't like her eyes at all. They were fierce. I didn't like that they were trained on me.

Hope said, "Deirdre, are you feeling okay?"

My mother's head snapped toward Hope. "Of course. How are you, Hope?"

I sat there thinking about all the times I had seen this very show before. For years, since I was nine or ten, my mother had gone mad in the fall. I would start to see that look in her eyes, smell that odd aroma wafting off her skin. And I would know. I would always know before anyone else. I had been born with some kind of sonar that detected mental illness.

The plate nearly hit me in the forehead. Because I ducked to reach my matches, it smashed on the wall behind me instead.

Hope shrieked and leapt from the sofa.

My mother screamed at me, "You are the goddamn Devil," and she hurled the cup that matched the saucer.

I ducked again and jumped up from the couch. "What the fuck is wrong with you?" I screamed. I was furious and terrified. She was an animal.

My mother rose from her chair, eyes wild. "I didn't give birth to you," she growled. "You are a Nazi."

I ran up the stairs to the bedroom and Hope followed behind me, panting. "Dad couldn't come. He said for me to check her out and see how she is. Obviously, she's nuts."

"We have to do something," I said.

"We need to—" Hope froze, hearing my mother on the stairs.

"Shit," I said.

"Goddamn you both to hell," she screamed.

"Deirdre, calm down," Dorothy said after her. "Take it easy."

This got her. My mother stopped and turned around to go back into the living room. "Dorothy, don't you dare tell me what to do. Not ever. Do you understand me? I will not be stifled by you in my own home."

Hope picked up the phone next to the bed and punched 9-1-1. "We need help," she said. "I'm a psychiatrist's daughter and we have a psychiatric emergency."

I loved this side of Hope. The side that could, if necessary, give you an intramuscular injection or restart your heart.

Within minutes, police officers were at the door. Hope and I were crouched in my mother's bedroom looking out the window, and when they arrived, we went downstairs.

My mother was not pleased by the uninvited guests.

"What the hell are you doing here?" she demanded.

Dorothy cried, "Hey, let go of her."

This was in response to one of the officers restraining my mother when she tried to bite him.

Hope said, "This is Deirdre. She's a patient of my father and she's having a psychotic episode." I knew from reading crime novels that Hope was trying to humanize my mother. The subtext was, *This could be your mother, officer. So treat her with respect.*

It didn't matter to the cops. What mattered was that the handcuffs were securely fastened and that she didn't bite them as they dragged her from the house into the waiting cruiser. My mother's heels bounced off the steps as they pulled her and I felt a horrific sadness watching her stripped of her dignity and her will. I also thought, *Whatever happened to Christina Crawford? I wonder if she's okay.*

Inside, Dorothy sobbed on the couch and Hope sat down to console her.

I went out the back door into the yard. The crystal stemware was shattered, and glittered in the grass. Light from the kitchen glinted off the sterling forks, knives and spoons that were scattered everywhere. It gave the yard the magical look of a set. And I would not have been at all surprised to see Marie Osmond rise from the ground in a white sequined dress, singing "Paper Roses."

YOU ARE NOTHING BUT A
SEX OBJECT

THERE WAS A NOTE ON THE BACK OF THE NESTLE'S CRUNCH bar wrapper. It read: *You are nothing but a sex object.* I bought the candy bar from the vending machine downstairs next to the ice. I bought it for Bookman. He ate half, slipped me the rest and then scrawled the note, passing it to me while my mother lay on the bed in front of us, unconscious in her curly black poodle sweater and covered in Johnson's baby powder.

I was nearly fifteen, Bookman was thirty-four and we were in the midst of our tumultuous love affair.

We were staying at the Treadway Inn motorlodge in Newport, Rhode Island. Me, Bookman, Hope, Dorothy, and the doctor.

And, of course, my mother.

She was the reason we were all there. She'd gone crazy again. And this time it was really bad.

Instead of committing her to the Brattleboro retreat, Dr. Finch decided to take her to a motel in Newport, where he could treat her around the clock himself. Her therapy involved scrawling the numeral 5 with her lipstick on every smooth surface, raging at everyone who came within sight, and recycling the motel furnishings into kindling. She even scraped some of the popcorn-textured ceiling down with her stubby fingernails and ate it.

We took turns watching her. Hope and the doctor had already spent hours with her and they were asleep in one of the three rooms the doctor had rented. Neil and I were on guard.

Because of the medication the doctor had given her, my mother slept soundly. I was grateful for this because her hysterics terrified me. I'd been awake for three days straight. I just wanted to go to sleep, but I knew that she could hurt herself if we didn't watch her. So we watched her. And Bookman passed me the note.

I stuck my tongue out at him after I read it.

He smiled. Then he scribbled another note on the rest of the wrapper. *You have the most beautiful eyes I've ever seen.*

I had my mother's eyes. Everybody always told me this. And it scared me that I had her eyes because I worried that it meant I had whatever else she had back there that made her believe she could not only speak to the dead, but smoke cigarettes in the bathroom with them.

As I sat there, I thought about what would have happened if I hadn't decided to go to the mental hospital; if I had decided to just go to school instead. I'd be expected in school the next day. How would that have happened? Even if I had wanted to be in school, there just wasn't room for it in my world. I wondered what the Cosby bitch would do in my situation, if it were her father on this bed in a poodle sweater. "No, Daddy, Fat Albert isn't hiding in the corner with an axe. You're Fat Albert, don't you understand?"

I'd tried calling my father collect to tell him what had happened to my mother. I was hoping that maybe he would feel bad and come get me, take me somewhere. On a trip, maybe. But, as usual, he refused to accept the charges. I decided that when we returned, I would send him a dildo in the mail, C.O.D. "What's this?" he would say in front of the mailman. And then he'd open the box. I would make it a nine-inch black dildo.

I sat on the stiff vinyl chair, Bookman sat on the other and I wondered how anything would ever be normal again. What if my mother didn't get better? What if she couldn't be pulled back from wherever she was? And more importantly, what would the cheap motel soap do to my hair?

The first time my mother was hospitalized, I was eight. She was gone so long, I forgot what her face looked like. I worried she would never return from the hospital and when she did, it was like not all of her came back. She returned flat, sad. As though an important part of her personality had been surgically removed.

Since she started seeing Finch, she'd gone crazy every fall. It was like her brain went on a Winter Clearance Sale. Sometimes the doctor would take her to a motel room where they would stay for four or five days. They would "work through" the psychotic episode together. Other times, she would be hospitalized. That would usually last for two weeks. It made me sad to visit her in the hospital. Not because she didn't fit in there with the crazy people, but because she did.

Each time my mother went psychotic, I hoped it would be the last time. Afterward, she would tell me, "I think that was the final episode. I think I had a breakthrough." And I would believe—for a few months—that it was true. That she was back to stay. Maybe it was like having a rock star mother who was always on the road. Were there Benatar children? Did they sit around and wonder if their mom's *Hell Is for Children* tour was going to be her *last* tour?

Eventually, I dozed off. And Bookman must have carried me, because when I woke up, I was in bed, under the sheets. I was wearing my shirt, but my pants had been stripped off.

"You feeling better?" he asked, sitting on the other bed smoking a cigarette.

I felt heavy, like I had slept for months. "I don't know. How long was I asleep?"

"An hour maybe," he said.

"Oh. How's my mother?"

"Still asleep."

I wanted to go back to sleep. But I couldn't stop replaying the conversation I had with her before she went to bed.

"Are you alright?" she asked me.

"Yes."

"Are you sure?"

"Yes."

"How do you know?"

"Because I am."

"I don't think you're alright."

It went on for twenty minutes. If she'd just asked once, it might have made me feel better, like she was still my mother and that she cared. But because she was like a broken record, because she couldn't stop asking, it made me feel she was truly insane.

Finch said the reason my mother went psychotic was because she was in love with him and afraid to admit it. He said her repressed emotions for him made her sick.

"I need to talk to you," Neil said.

I realized I was staring blindly at the floor and looked up at him. "Yeah?"

"I'm going through my own crisis here," he said. "Over you."

I didn't want to hear anything he said. I wanted him to go away; to go back to Rhode Island and wait for me. "What do you mean?"

"I mean that my feelings for you are so huge, I don't think I can contain them. Sometimes I want to hold you so tight it scares me. Like I want to hold you until the life is gone, so you can't ever vanish."

This sounded alarmingly like something you'd hear on an episode of *Charlie's Angels*; a final episode where the Angels are taken to a warehouse and doused with gasoline, firecrackers stuffed in their pockets. "You're not going crazy too, are you?" I said. Was everybody going to go insane now? Was it contagious, like the flu?

"I may very well be going insane," Bookman said. He was trembling. His lit cigarette making a zigzag of light in the darkened room.

"Can we talk about this later? I just can't deal with anything else right now."

"But I can't deal with my emotions, with what you've done to me. You have a power over me."

I hated it when he talked about the power I had over him. He was like one of those people who sit in the hallway and bang their head against the wall over and over. He just wouldn't stop. "Later," I snapped.

He reclined on the bed, staring straight ahead.

I'd pissed him off. I went over to him, put my arms around him. "I'm sorry," I said. "I just feel like I'm gonna explode."

"Don't you see," he said, "that's exactly how I feel."

For two days my mother was like a grizzly bear. In fact, she seemed to increase in mass and sprout fur. Her body gave off a repulsive odor that was both sweet and metallic. And no matter how much medication the doctor gave her, she didn't seem to be getting any better. I began wishing she would throw herself out the window so that life could go back to normal. Nothing, it seemed, would fix her.

Until Winnie Pye came along.

Winnie was a sassy waitress at a coffee shop down the street. My mother had insisted that she wanted a grilled cheese and tomato sandwich and when the doctor said he'd send Hope or me off to get it, she screamed, "I will go and get my own goddamned sandwich." Finch had told her she wasn't well enough to be out in public. And she'd taken his Brill Cream and sprayed him in the face with it. "If I'm well enough to aim, I'm well enough to get my own damn sandwich."

So Finch had gone with her to the little diner on the corner. Like a bodyguard, I followed, lagging slightly behind.

Winnie had been their waitress.

She had tall, teased blonde hair and tan, leathery skin with tiny wrinkles surrounding her mouth. Bright pink lipstick bled into the corners. Her eyelids were painted sky blue and she wore gold heart earrings that were the size of onion rings.

My mother loved her instantly.

"I'm being held hostage by this crazy man," my wild-eyed mother said when they sat at the counter.

"Are you now, honey. You two lovebirds having a little fun with the baby powder?" she teased with a wink.

"You don't understand." My mother leaned in. "*He's* the crazy one, not me."

"Hey, sugar. I don't make no judgments about no one. To each his own. Now, what can I getcha?" She licked the tip of her pencil and poised it over her order pad.

My mother ordered her sandwich, the doctor ordered a slice of Boston cream pie.

I sat at the far end of the counter and watched. When Winnie came to take my order she said, "What's a little man like you sitting here all by your lonesome?"

"I'm with them," I said, nodding toward the far end of the counter.

"Oh," she said. Then she leaned in. "What's the matter, sourpuss, you don't like your momma's new friend?"

I rolled my eyes. "He's her shrink."

Winnie opened her mouth. "Her shrink? Your momma's gone and shacked up with her shrink? Boy, she must be one crazy lady."

"They're not shacked up. My mother's crazy and he's taking care of her."

"Your momma's crazy?" Winnie said, sliding her eyes sideways.

My mother was talking to her spoon.

"Yeah," I said. "She's out of it. Her doctor took her to that motel across the street to try and get her better."

Winnie frowned. "That don't make no sense. Why would a shrink take his crazy patient to a motel?"

"Well," I said, "he's sort of an unusual shrink."

"Unusual my ass," Winnie said. "Somethin's fishy. I better go have me a look." And she walked back down to the other end of the counter.

I watched as Winnie approached my mother and Finch, smiling. Then she reached across the counter, put her hand on the doctor's shoulder and said something that caused him to laugh and blush. She pointed to the rest rooms at the far end of the room. Finch got up from the counter and walked back to the bathroom. Then Winnie came around from behind the counter and took the stool next to my mother. She turned sideways so they were face to face, and they had a chat. A moment later when the doctor reappeared, Winnie got up, went back behind the counter and came walking back to me.

"Sugar, somethin' funny's goin' on," she said.

"Yeah," I said. "My mother's stark raving mad."

She shook her head. "I don't know, sugar. I got an instinct about this one." She leaned forward and whispered. "I seen a lot of crazy people come in here. Folks madder than hatters. But your momma's different. She says that doctor of hers, he's trying to get him a little action, if you know what I mean." She gave me a knowing wink.

"Don't listen to her," I said. "She doesn't know what she's saying. This morning she said her dead grandfather was standing next to her holding out a basket of pecans."

"I love pecans," Winnie said. Then, "Hey, we got us some

pretty good pecan pie. Would you like a slice?" She added, "On the house."

"No, thanks."

She shrugged. "Suit yourself. But it's good pie. Not too sweet."

"I don't like pie," I told her. "I don't have much of a sweet tooth."

Her face fell. "You don't have much of a sweet tooth? Everybody has a sweet tooth, sugar."

"Not me."

"Well, you must got other things on your mind."

I glanced over at my mother and Finch and saw that he was gripping her arm, firmly. Great. Now she was gonna have a fit in public, right here in the restaurant.

"I told your momma I'll come and visit her later at the motel."

"You did?"

"I did. Your momma could use a friend," Winnie said. "That shrink of hers." She shook her head. "I don't know. He may be a shrink, but he's still a man."

I could not imagine what my mother said to get this perfect stranger to visit her in her motel room. I could not imagine the kind of person that would, upon seeing a crazy talcum-powder-covered Southern lady think to herself, *Hmmmm, she might make a great new friend.* The line between normal and crazy seemed impossibly thin. A person would have to be an expert tightrope walker in order not to fall.

That evening, Winnie came to the motel. She came wearing white denim jeans with rhinestone roses on the back pockets. She wore a red-and-white checkered shirt that she had knotted just below her large breasts.

Finch was lying on top of my mother on the bed, struggling to pin her arms against the mattress. I was standing by the TV wishing my mother would stop thrashing. When I heard the knock, I was sure it was the motel manager, coming to throw us out. Instead, it was Winnie.

"What the hell is going on in this room," she demanded.

Finch turned and my mother slipped out from under him.

Winnie ran to my mother's side. "You ain't like no doctor I ever seen before. You're the one that looks crazy."

My mother was panting. "He is, Winnie. He's the crazy one."

Winnie turned to my mother. "We've got to get you all cleaned up, sugar. What's that man gone and done to you?"

My mother began to sob.

Winnie turned to me. "Sweetums, you go and get yourself a Coke from the vending machine. You got quarters? Reach in my bag over there and pull out my wallet. I got some change in there."

"That's okay," I said.

"Well, alright then. But scram."

Then Winnie eyed Finch, who was standing at the foot of the bed, utterly bewildered. "And you," she said, hugging my mother tight, "you take those hands of yours and leave us alone."

Finch cleared his throat. "Look, Miss," Finch said. "You do not understand this situation. This woman is in a state of crisis and she needs—"

Winnie released my mother and walked over to Finch. In her high-heeled red boots she was at least four inches taller than he. She lowered her voice and looked him straight in the eyes. "You notice all those rigs in the parkin' lot?" she said. "Those are my boys. I know every one of 'em. There's Fred from Alabama, he's up here makin' a peanut delivery. And Stew? He's out here all the way from Nevada. Now," she said, placing her hand on her hip, "I don't think my boys would take too kindly if I was to tell 'em that some shrink was in this here motel room holding a lady in crisis down on the bed like I seen when I walked in. As a matter a fact, I think that just might ruffle their feathers. Now you go on and you leave us ladies alone."

Finch said nothing. He simply turned and walked out of the room.

Winnie went back over to my mother and cupped her face in her hands. "It's okay," she said. "Winnie's here."

The door did not open again for three days, except to receive deliveries from a few of Winnie's friends.

When my mother finally exited that motel room, she was transformed.

"Oh my God," Hope said when she finally saw her.

"Deirdre?" Bookman asked.

I didn't recognize her myself.

My mother was wearing one of Winnie's colorful Hawaiian muumuus. Winnie had also treated her to a makeover, painting her face so heavily she looked like a former Vegas lap dancer. Her eyelids were like two cabochons of turquoise and when she blinked, her new plastic eyelashes touched her brow.

My mother loved her new look and her new friend.

I scrutinized Winnie for visible signs of mental illness. I wondered if my mother had somehow captured her mind, made her crazy, too.

"There we are," Winnie said, presenting my new mother. "She just needed a little talking to and a little makeover. A lady's got to feel like a lady."

"Shall we go?" my mother said.

Nobody said a word.

"Winnie's coming with us," my mother said. "She's decided to take a leave of absence from her job. To make sure I get back on my feet."

Winnie smiled and fluttered her polyester eyelashes.

All the way home in the car, I stared at my mother's new face. Every few miles she would comment, "What a lovely tree," or "That is a beautiful lawn." To the untrained eye, my mother might have appeared to be normal. But I knew better. I could see the wildness behind the eyes, crouching, hiding. I could see the tiny hint of a smile at the corners of her mouth that said, *I'll fool you all.*

I flopped my head against Bookman's shoulder and he moved his hand carefully to my crotch, checking the rearview mirror to make sure that Hope wasn't watching.

He tried jerking me off through my jeans, but I couldn't get hard.

THIN AIR

ONE NIGHT NOT LONG AFTER MY FIFTEENTH BIRTHDAY
while I was lying on my bed writing in my journal about how
much I hoped to someday meet Brooke Shields, there was a
knock at the door. I knew it was Bookman. Nobody else would
knock on my door at two in the morning; they would just
waltz right in. I wasn't about to give him a blowjob, that much
I knew.

I opened the door. "What?" I was angry with him for being
distant recently. Everybody had noticed it—my mother, Dorothy, Natalie, Hope. Everybody was mad at him for with-
drawing.

"I'm going out for some film," he said.

I thought it was odd that he would tell me this. And why

did he need film at two in the morning? "Okay," I said. "See you later then."

For a beat, he looked at me with an expression of sadness so complete, I mistook it for calm.

He turned and walked down the hall and I went back to my bed and continued writing. I wrote about how I imagined Brooke and I would be excellent friends because I truly thought she was a gifted actor, though I didn't believe she'd yet had the right role, with the exception of *Pretty Baby*.

A few hours later I went upstairs to his room looking for him. He wasn't there.

I don't know how I knew, but I knew.

I immediately went into the kitchen, grabbed the phone book and looked up the number for Amtrak. It only took a five-minute call to discover that a one-way ticket to New York City from Springfield, Massachusetts, had been purchased in the name of Neil Bookman.

I ran straight to Hope's room and pounded on the door. "Bookman ran away," I shouted. "Hope, wake up, Bookman's gone."

The door flew open. "What? What's going on?"

I told her what had happened, then about my hunch and how I called Amtrak and it turned out he was on that train.

If there was one thing I could count on from Hope it was that she never minimized.

"This is not good," she said. "I'll go wake Dad."

I ran back into the kitchen and paced frantically around the table. I grabbed a dried, raw hot dog off the counter and drummed it against my chest. "What should I do? What should I do? What should I do?" I was like an autistic sitting against a wall.

A moment later, Hope reappeared. "Dad said to call Amtrak and see if they can stop the train."

"Okay," I said. "I've got the number right here."

"Wait," Hope said, pausing my arm. "How do we get them to stop the train, what do we say?"

"Okay, lemme think, lemme think," I said. "Let's tell them that—here." I handed her the phone. "Say you're his psychiatrist's daughter, that he's run away from treatment and that he has a bomb."

"That's smart," she said and dialed the number.

But it was too late. The train had already arrived in Manhattan.

An hour later, Hope and I were in the Buick, on our way to New York. We'd thrown a change of clothes into a paper bag, taken all the money out of her father's wallet and filled the car with gas. "Jesus, Hope, why is he doing this?"

"Because, Augusten," she said, "He doesn't know what he's doing. He's been very angry with Dad lately. Dad's been worried about him." She glanced at me. "I'm sorry I didn't tell you, but it's true. Dad's been worried."

I thought back to one night last week. Bookman and I were lying upstairs on the floor in his room, side by side. He was telling me that it had all become too much. "What?" I had asked.

"You, your mother, Hope, and especially Doctor." He spoke slowly, his teeth clenched, eyes focused straight up at the ceiling. When I pressed him for more he said, "I'm afraid I'll end up killing myself or Finch or you or all of us." At the time it had given me shivers, a clammy feeling that ran throughout my body. But then I talked myself out of it, saying he was only being dramatic because he wanted attention. I thought it was another ploy to make me admit that I was still madly in love with him.

"What if we can't find him?" I said to Hope.

"We'll find him, Augusten. Don't you worry."

I had reason to believe her. When I was eleven and still living in Leverett my dog ran away from home. It was Hope who showed up at my house with five hundred fliers that read LOST DOG. And it was Hope who drove me around Leverett all night long sticking the fliers in mailboxes. My father had called it a "tremendous waste of time and energy" but the next day I got a phone call and my dog was returned.

"We've got to find him, Hope," I said.

We arrived in New York City five hours later and Hope drove straight to Greenwich Village. "It's the gay section of the city. It's where he'd most likely go." We parked in a twenty-four-hour garage and set about on foot.

The problem was, there were too many bars. We'd never be able to hit them all. My eyes burned from exhaustion; it was as if I could feel the blood vessels in them vibrating. I didn't know what to do.

But Hope did. "We'll take his picture and show it to the bartenders, see if any of them have seen him."

One by one, we hit the gay bars of New York. And one by one, the bartenders shook their heads. "Are you sure?" Hope asked every time.

When it became clear to us that we would never find him by going door-to-door, we decided our best bet was to go back to Northampton and wait by the phone. Eventually, he'd call. And if we were there, we'd have a better chance of talking him home than anyone else who answered the phone.

We drove straight back to Northampton, stopping once for gas but not for food.

And for the next three nights, I did not sleep. I stayed awake, sitting in a chair beneath the phone in the kitchen.

Hope called his parents, who hadn't heard from him in years. She called his former roommate, who said she hadn't heard from him since he moved out. And that, as far as Bookman's social life was concerned, was the end of the line.

I waited by the phone for a week. Then a month. Then two months. Then a year.

At night, I dreamed he returned and I would ask him, "Where did you go?" and "Why?"

After a year, the few belongings in his room were packed into boxes and placed in the upstairs hall closet.

At night, I imagined him sneaking around outside the house, coming over to my window and tapping it gently with his finger to wake me. But he wouldn't need to wake me because I would already be awake, waiting.

This didn't happen. He didn't come back.

Leaving the most awful and curious itch inside me that I couldn't scratch.

ALL-STAR RUNNING BACK

Brenda danced on the pink porch in the twilight wearing skin-tight Gloria Vanderbilt jeans. Deborah Harry threatened at full volume through the speaker propped in the open window, *I'm gonna getcha, getcha, getcha, getcha.*

Brenda ran her hands across her burgundy Danskin and down her thighs. She licked her lips and tossed her head back. At eleven, she was stunningly beautiful. There was a grace about her that made me think she would grow up to be a famous dancer in New York City.

Years later, she would move to Memphis and become an unlicensed massage therapist who gave hand jobs, but this evening, with the pale orange sunlight glancing off her jet-black hair, Brenda looked poised for Lincoln Center.

"That's great, B," Natalie said. She was leaning back against the railing on the porch, smoking.

Brenda expertly fingered the swan that was stitched into her hip pocket. "You're so good with your hands," I told her. Of course, this comment would prove to be prophetic.

Brenda's mother, Kate, had finally given in to her constant whining and woven Brenda's hair into dozens of slim braids. Once her hair was dry, Brenda unbraided it and pranced around the house with her new kinky hair.

In the fading light, her kinky mane created a sort of dark halo around her head. When she tossed her head to the side and swung out her hip, it was easy to picture her on stage.

"She reminds me of me when I was her age," Natalie said of her niece. I thought I caught a melancholy look in her eyes as she glanced away into the street. "Hey, I could really go for a beer."

"Mmmm," Brenda said, "me *too*."

Natalie laughed. "You bad girl. You're too young to drink."

Brenda stopped dancing. "I am not." Her lips plumped out in a frown.

"You are too," Natalie said. "No beer for you."

"Then how 'bout a joint?"

Natalie rolled her eyes and smiled. "No, bad girl. How about some milk?"

"Whatever," Brenda said. Then she opened the door and stomped inside. A moment later, the record came to an abrupt, scratchy stop.

Natalie leaned over to crush her cigarette on the porch. "I really was just like her. She's such a free spirit."

*　*　*

Freedom was what we had. Nobody told us when to go to bed. Nobody told us to do our homework. Nobody told us we couldn't drink two six-packs of Budweiser and then throw up in the Maytag.

So why did we feel so trapped? Why did I feel like I had no options in my life when it seemed that options were the only thing I *did* have?

I could paint my room black. I could bleach my hair blond. Or use Krazy Kolor to dye it blue. When Natalie pierced my ear one night with a hypodermic needle nobody complained. My mother didn't gasp and say, "What have you done to your ear?" She didn't even notice.

Nobody ever told me what to do. When I was living with my mother and father, I could raise my mother's blood pressure just by moving one of the cork coasters on the side table an inch. "Please," she would say, "I have everything arranged the way I like it." But at the Finch house, I could hack a hole through the ceiling in my closet to connect to Hope's room upstairs and nobody cared. "You're a free person with a free will," Finch would say.

So why did I always feel so trapped?

I worried that my feeling of being belted into an electric chair was due to some sort of mental illness.

More than anything, I wanted to break free. But free from what? That was the problem. Because I didn't know what I wanted to break free from, I was stuck.

So I figured if I didn't have the answer, maybe somebody else did. And I decided that what I needed was a boyfriend.

A boyfriend, I decided, would be my key to freedom. My ticket out. Of whatever it was I was in.

It had been over a year since Bookman vanished. I had to move on. I was sixteen years old and single. It was pitiful.

As I sat on the midnight PVTA bus to Amherst, I scanned the male faces, looking for a potential boyfriend. My standards were high: anyone who looked back at me. Nobody did.

As I got off at Converse Hall, I walked along the Amherst Common and then made a right. This would take me past the All-Star market where I could get cigarettes. As I opened the door I knew immediately that the course of my life was about to be changed forever. He was the cutest guy I'd seen on public transportation or in any convenience store in weeks. Maybe even months.

Nonchalantly, I walked into the store and headed to the back for a Diet Coke. I felt this would give him a chance to see me in my Calvin Klein jeans. I was glad I'd worn the red sweatshirt with them. The sweatshirt made me look not quite so pale.

I grabbed a can and walked to the counter, casually pretending to be scanning the shelves. My heart was completely freaking out in my chest. It was pounding so loud, I worried he'd be able to hear it and think I had a heart condition and not consider me real long-term relationship material, but just a casual-sex fling. And that was one thing I didn't want: NO CASUAL SEX. I thought it was disgusting, the idea of just screwing around and then that's it.

I set the can on the counter and said, "And a pack of Marlboro Lights."

He gave me a friendly, sort of cocky smile out of the corner of his mouth and reached above his head for the cigarettes.

There were large wet stains under his arms and this excited me. I never sweated and this made me feel like a girl. I hated that I didn't sweat. Sometimes when Natalie and I went out for a walk in town, I would use her spray bottle to saturate the front of my shirt and under my arms.

"Nice out there tonight, huh?" he said, punching the keys on the register.

"Yeah, it's really warm."

"Too bad I'm stuck in here. And it's my birthday."

I was sure he winked when he said that. I was sure that he was thinking the same thing about me that I was thinking about him. I started to feel a small—but developing—feeling of love for him. I needed to think of how to prolong the conversation so he could ask me my name and then give me his telephone number or invite me to a movie at the Pleasant Street Theater. I hadn't seen Truffaut's last film and I wanted to. But I had too many thoughts in my head to think of anything to say and I was feeling weird standing there with my change in my hand so I said, "Okay, take care," and then I walked out the door.

I walked about twenty feet down the street and then I crossed to the other, darker, side and looked back. I could see him perfectly through the window.

And he was on the phone!

I was sure he was calling his version of Natalie, telling her that he'd just met this great guy but that he got away and now what was he going to do?

Well, I would solve that.

I raced the six blocks home and was heaving by the time I made it to the front door. I slid my key into the lock and quietly closed the door behind me.

My mother and Dorothy would be upstairs asleep. They didn't mind if I came over and spent the night without calling. But they didn't like it if I woke them up. Or if the light was on in their bedroom and the door was closed, I had to leave them alone.

I didn't turn on any lights until I made it into the kitchen. The first thing I did was open the pack and light a cigarette. I leaned with my lower back against the sink and plotted. I had an idea in my head, but I needed to polish the details. I needed to make it foolproof.

Then, as I was staring at the pilot light of the stove, I had the perfect solution. Immediately, I went into the dining room and opened the glass-front bookcase where my mother kept her pens and paper. I grabbed a pen and a small notepad, then I sat down at the kitchen table.

I wrote one draft of the note but my handwriting was awful so I wrote another. The next one was okay, except I signed my name weird, so I did it again. In the end, I wrote the note fifteen or sixteen times before I was completely satisfied.

Carefully, I folded the note in half and slipped it into the rear pocket of my jeans. Then I swiped my keys off the table and left the house again.

But now he had company. There were two girls and a guy, both around his age, in the store with him. He was throwing his head back laughing. I took a deep breath, made a face that I hoped looked casual and friendly and then I walked into the store.

At first, they all just went on talking. But because I just stood there waiting, he finally noticed me and said, "Oh, hey. You again. You forget something?"

I confidently walked up to the counter and his friends moved to the side to let me through. I handed him the note. "Happy Birthday," I said. Then I smiled and walked out of the store.

I did my crossing-the-street trick again, lurking in the shadows and watching.

I could see him turn the note over in his hand, open it and read it, then turn it over again. He passed it to his friends, who passed it between them.

Then I watched him make a shrugging gesture with his hands.

And then they were all laughing again.

My mortification was total and overpowering. I was suddenly having a very difficult time standing. I experienced a perfect note of utter and true clarity.

He was straight.

This was followed with the sound of my letter being read out loud inside my head, by my own voice:

Hi.

I know this seems pretty weird but . . . when I saw you tonight, I just got a really good vibe. I wanted to say something to you in the store, but I freaked out. I guess I'm kind of shy. But what I wanted to say is, that it was really nice to meet you and I wouldn't mind seeing you again sometime. The number at the bottom of this note is my mother's apartment. I live there part of the time and the other part in Northampton. She's cool, so don't worry about calling. I really would like to get to know you, but this is NOT a casual sex thing. I'm not into that AT ALL. I guess I've been hurt before and don't want to get involved with that stuff again. I'm 16, but pretty mature for my age. Oh, and my name is Augusten but I probably should have put that first. Anyway, that's all. Take care.

Augusten.

On the front of the card, I had written the words *Happy Birthday!* in what I now realized was a dreadfully girly script.

And then at the bottom, I had scrawled my mother's phone number. Now, as I walked back to her house, I worried that he or his friends would make crank calls. That they would call constantly and my mother would have to have her number changed. Dorothy would be furious and I would have to explain what I'd done. Once Dorothy knew that I did this, that I actually passed this creepy note to a perfect stranger, she would tell everybody and then Natalie would know and if Natalie knew, all of the rest of the Finches would know, including Brenda. Brenda would tease me constantly and I would never hear the end of this.

It was a disaster.

I reached in my back pocket for my cigarettes but had forgotten to take them.

Fuck.

Well, one thing was for sure. I would never, ever go to the All-Star market again for any reason no matter what. And if I was staying over at my mother and Dorothy's place and they needed me to run out and get something, I'd just have to walk farther, to the Cumberland Farms. Hopefully, they wouldn't need anything after midnight because All-Star was the only twenty-four-hour place in town.

But what if they did need something? What if I had to go in there?

Well, maybe he wouldn't be there that night. He probably wouldn't be. He was probably a student and had a lot of classes. He couldn't work there every night because he had to study.

But what if he was working the night I had to go there?

By the time I reached the front door, I was a wired mess. I half-expected to see my mother and Dorothy waiting for me with their arms folded across their large chests. But when I walked in, the house was quiet.

I'd never felt so trapped in my entire life. And I did it to myself. I had made myself a prisoner, unable to walk on that side of the street ever again, go into that store.

I sat on the couch in the dark. Then I got up and went into the kitchen for my cigarettes and came back. I lit one and stared at the shadows of the African masks on my mother's walls, her pen-and-ink drawings behind glass frames, the shelves and shelves of books.

The problem with not having anybody to tell you what to do, I understood, is that there was nobody to tell you what *not* to do.

PENNIES FROM HEAVEN

It was the summer that Prince Charles married Lady Diana Spencer and nobody could look at the television without thinking about Natalie.

"Jeez, you look just like her, Natalie, you really do," Agnes said as she sat back on the sofa rubbing her feet together at the bunions.

"Oh, yeah, right." Natalie lit a Marlboro Light.

"It's true, Nat. Maybe you should ask Kate to cut your hair like hers," Hope said.

"What's the matter with you people? I am not Princess fucking Diana. We look nothing alike."

Actually, they did.

Princess Diana was almost like a parallel-universe version of Natalie. A version that didn't give her first blowjob at eleven, wasn't traded for cash by her father at thirteen and didn't long for a job as a counter girl at McDonald's.

"It's in the eyes," I said. "You have the same eyes. And there's something about your face that's a lot like hers," I said.

Natalie turned to me. "You think?"

"Yeah."

She punched me on the shoulder and smiled. "You're such a liar."

"No, it's true. You really do look alike."

She stood up and raised her chin in the air. "I am Princess Natalie Finch and you shall all kiss my royal ass."

"Oh, sit down," Agnes said. "Don't get all high and mighty on us now. There's one thing that Diana girl has that you don't and that's a figure."

"Oh, Agnes, that's not nice," Hope said.

Natalie sat on the arm of the wing chair. "Are you saying I'm a fat cow?"

Agnes turned away and looked back at the TV. "I didn't call you a fat cow. You're just a bigger girl than that Diana."

"Well, I take after you," Natalie said.

Agnes shrugged and rubbed her toes together. "I'm no spring chicken, but when I was your age I had a very good figure. As a matter of fact, when your father and I first—"

"I can't believe you," Natalie said, smirking. "I can't believe you're calling your own daughter fat."

"I'm not calling you fat. I'm just saying that when I met your father—"

"Oh shut up, Agnes. Nobody wants to hear another one of your stories," Hope said.

"Don't tell me to shut up. I have every right to talk. I have every right—"

"Hope's right. We don't want to hear you ramble on and on."

"Fine," Agnes said.

Natalie crushed her cigarette out in the ashtray that was sitting on the chair. "So tell me more about how fat and disgusting I am."

Agnes pretended she didn't hear. She stared straight ahead as NBC replayed highlights of the wedding. "What a beautiful dress."

"So you're disgusted by your piggy daughter. You don't approve?" Natalie taunted.

Agnes said, "And that's a lovely tiara."

Natalie got up off the chair and went over to the TV. With her big toe, she punched it off.

"Natalie!"

"What, Agnes?"

"Turn that television set back on. I was watching."

Natalie cocked her head to the side and placed her hands on her hips. "No. Tell me more about how I disgust you."

"Leave her alone, Nat," Hope said, shifting uncomfortably on the other end of the sofa.

"You stay out of this," Natalie ordered.

"Fine, I will," said Hope. She picked up her white bible and began thumbing through the pages.

Seeing this, Natalie said, "What are you doing, Hope? Asking God if I'm a fat cow?"

Hope closed the bible and squared it on her lap. "Look, don't drag me into this, Natalie. I'm not the one who called you fat. This is between you and Agnes."

"So then, little Miss Biblethumper, stay the fuck out of it."

"Don't talk to your sister like that," Agnes scolded, still watching the TV even though it was off.

Natalie shifted her weight onto one leg. She glanced over at me and rolled her eyes.

I rolled my eyes back. "Let's go," I said.

"Yes," Agnes said. "Why don't you two go to McDonald's."

"You fucking bitch," Natalie said.

"That's enough, Natalie," Hope said.

Natalie stomped over to Agnes and snatched her purse. "Fine, we'll go to McDonald's."

"Now you put that down." Agnes grabbed the corner of her bag but Natalie pulled it away. "Give me that back, Natalie. That's mine."

"You said go to McDonald's, so we're going to go to McDonald's." Natalie reached into the purse, pulling out Agnes's wallet. She tossed the purse back on the couch and the contents spilled onto the cushions. "All you have is a twenty?" Natalie said. "Fine, then I guess that's all we'll take." She took the twenty and tucked it into the hip pocket on her jeans.

Agnes shouted, "Natalie, I need that money. You have no right to take that. I'm going to speak to the doctor about this."

Natalie stood in the doorway, ready to leave. "Fine, you talk to *the doctor* all you want." Then she looked at me. "Well?"

I got up from the sofa and followed her out of the room.

Upstairs in her room, Natalie stood in front of her full-length mirror. She pulled her shirt up just below her breasts. "I am a pig," she said, clutching her flesh in her hand.

"No you're not," I told her. "You're not fat."

She turned her back to the mirror and stretched her head around. "God, look at my ass. It's huge."

"Natalie, knock it off. You look fine. You're very pretty."

"Fuck it," she said. "Let's go get Big Macs."

We went to McDonald's and gorged ourselves on Big Macs and extra-large fries. After she sucked down the last of her milkshake, Natalie burped and said, "We only have forty cents left."

I checked my Timex. It was only two in the afternoon. We would not survive the day without additional funds. "Who can we ask for money?"

Natalie wiped her mouth on the back of her hand. "Your mother?"

"We could try," I said. "But I think all she'll do is get hysterical about my father not giving her enough child support."

Natalie chewed on the straw and went deep into thought.

I stared out the window at the cars in the parking lot. Why was everybody driving brown cars? Why not black or white or gray? Even red. But brown?

"Okay, I know what we can do," Natalie said.

"What?"

"Let's go to Amherst and hit Kimmel up."

"Oh, yeah," I said. It was such a good idea. Like finding a ten-dollar bill in the pocket of your jeans. Kimmel might give us money. He was the doctor's "spiritual brother" and also a Catholic priest, the head of his own church in Amherst.

We walked to the bus stop in front of Thorne's Market and smoked until the bus came. We sat in the back, slumped down with our knees on the seat in front of us. "You think he'll give us anything?" I said.

"Oh, yeah," Natalie said. "He'll cough something up."

When we arrived at the church, we were able to walk straight into Father Kimmel's office. It was surprising that there were no guards or even a secretary to protect a priest. It seemed like anybody could just go right up and touch one.

"Well, hello," he said from behind his desk. Sunlight glinted off his silver glasses. He motioned us into his office.

Natalie and I sat in the two chairs in front of his desk. Natalie reached for the crystal Jesus paperweight on his desk.

"That's fragile, dear," Father Kimmel said the instant Natalie's fingers touched it.

"Oops, sorry," she said. Then she sniffed her fingers. "We just went to McDonald's. Wouldn't want to get any french fry grease on Jesus."

Father Kimmel smiled and cleared his throat. "Well then, so," he said. "What is the reason for this delightful surprise today?"

Natalie pointed to the cross behind Father Kimmel's head. "Is that real gold?"

He was stiff with age and it wasn't easy for him to turn. "What's that?" he said, staring straight ahead at us, smiling.

"The cross. Behind you. Is it gold?"

Father Kimmel clasped his hands on top of his desk. "No, I think that's probably just brass. We wouldn't keep gold here. You know, because of the students down at the university."

"Oh," Natalie said.

I smiled at Father Kimmel and thought about the first time I visited him. I was maybe eleven and with my mother and Dr. Finch and we were upstairs in his private apartment in the rectory next door. The three of them went into the bedroom to discuss something, so I was alone in the living room.

Because it was there, I opened his desk drawer. And that's where I saw my first copy of *Hustler* magazine.

"We need some money," Natalie said. "Can you help?"

Again, Father Kimmel cleared his throat. He looked uncomfortable, like we'd just asked him to defend some church policy on abortion. "Ah, well, um," he stammered, "how much money do you need?"

"Whatever," Natalie said. "Enough for a movie."

He was visibly relieved and he smiled. "Oh, well, of course. A movie, I think we can manage that."

"And popcorn," Natalie added.

Father Kimmel reached across to his file cabinet and grabbed the handle of the tithing basket. He poked through the money dish, extracting dollar bills.

Natalie slid her eyes to me and grinned. *See?* she mouthed. I smiled back.

"How is fifteen dollars?" Father Kimmel said, offering us a stack of fifteen crumpled one-dollar bills.

"Can you make it twenty-five?"

He sighed. "Let me see here," he said as he routed around through the dish. "Some of it'll have to be in quarters," he said.

"That's fine." When he wasn't looking, Natalie stuck her finger on the crystal Jesus head, leaving a smudge.

"Okay, then. Twenty-five dollars with two dollars in quarters." He poured the money into Natalie's hands.

And then he asked, "Is everything alright at home?"

"Yeah," Natalie shrugged. "Same as always. Anyway, we gotta go." She stood.

Father Kimmel rose from his seat. He extended his hand

to me. "It's good to see you, Augusten. You're a fine young man."

"Thanks," I said.

"And you, dear," he said to Natalie, pursing his lips.

She leaned in so that he could kiss her cheek.

She tucked the money into her pocket and we headed for the door. As we were leaving, Father Kimmel said, "Give my best to your father, Natalie."

"I will," she said.

Once we were outside, we burst into a fit of laughter. "He's such a crooked old man," Natalie cried. "Can you believe him? Giving us money from the tithing tray so we can see a movie."

"I can't believe he's a priest," I said.

"All those poor people, forking over their precious quarters to God. Just so we can go see *On Golden Pond*."

"Oh my God," I said. "Is that out yet?"

"Yeah," Natalie said. "I think today."

"We have to go."

We attempted to hitch a ride to the Mountain Farms Mall in Hadley but nobody would pick us up so we ended up walking. Along the way Natalie said, "I think I caught him looking at my tits."

I said, "Really? Are you serious?"

"Yeah," she said. "But that's okay. As long as we get to see a movie out of it."

"Yeah," I said. "I know what you mean."

OH, CHRISTMAS TREE

NATALIE AND I ARE IN THE MANGY TV ROOM WATCHING *The Love Boat*. We've dragged the wing chairs up on either side of the Christmas tree and are reaching over to pick through its branches in pursuit of any candy canes that remain. Most of them have already been eaten. By accident, Natalie stuck a plastic one in her mouth. Why Agnes insists on mixing plastic candy canes in with the real ones is beyond both of us.

I should mention that it's May.

Most of the needles have fallen off the tree and are now carpeting the floor and have been tracked throughout the house. Everyone has brown, sharp little needles in their beds. The branches are dry and crispy and tend to snap off when you tug at them.

I absently pull at a branch until it snaps. Julie, the cruise director, suggests to a clinically depressed passenger that the aft deck is a fine place to meet new people, recover from a failed love affair, and I let the branch fall on the floor with the others.

Our lives are one endless stretch of misery punctuated by processed fast foods and the occasional crisis or amusing curiosity.

The fact that the Christmas tree is still standing five months after Christmas is extremely disturbing to everyone in the house. But we all feel someone else should be the one to remove it. It is somebody else's responsibility. And in most everyone's mind, that somebody is Agnes.

But Agnes has refused to remove the tree. "I'm not your slave," she has screamed again and again. She will straighten her Virgin Mary candles on the sideboard, sweep the carpets, wash the occasional pot, but she will not touch this tree.

"Personally, I don't give a fuck if this tree stays here forever. I'm used to it now," Natalie states as she stares straight ahead at the TV. "I hope it does stay up forever. It'll teach Agnes a lesson."

I don't really care if it stays up forever, either. It fits perfectly with the rest of the house. It's kind of like dust. There seems to be a certain amount of dust that will collect on the surface of things and then no more. The house is already such a hodgepodge of strangeness that the tree is not out of place.

Besides, I have experience with a misplaced Christmas tree in my past.

*　　*　　*

I was ten and all winter my mother and father had been screaming at each other. My brother had moved out of the house to live with members of his rock band, so I was trapped alone with my parents. There was a Christmas calendar on the refrigerator, the kind with little doors that you open one day at a time until the big day, December twenty-fifth. I would sit on the floor in front of the refrigerator opening the doors and wishing I could crawl inside one of those warm, glittering rooms.

"You goddamn son of a bitch," my mother screamed at the top of her lungs. "You want me to be your damn mother? Well I am not your damn mother. You are in love with that woman, you sick bastard."

"Jesus Christ, Deirdre. Would you please calm down. You're hysterical."

"I most certainly am *not* hysterical," my mother screamed, utterly hysterical.

It went on like this all winter. Snow piled on the deck railings outside and the house grew darker as the bows of the pine trees leaned against the windows, heavy with snow.

My father spent as much time as he could downstairs in their bedroom drinking. And my mother channeled her energy into a manic holiday frenzy.

She played one song on one album again and again: "We Need a Little Christmas" from *Mame*. When the song would end, my mother would set down the bowl of cranberries she was threading for the tree and place the needle back at the beginning.

She set red and green candles out on the teak dining table, and placed the Norwegian nutcracker in the center of a bowl of pecans from her father's orchard in Georgia. She dragged her Singer sewing machine out of the basement and began making Christmas stockings, angels and reindeer ornaments for the tree.

When I suggested cookies, she baked fourteen batches.

She read me Christmas stories, sketched a Christmas card with pen and ink and had it printed to send to family and friends, and she even let the dog sleep on the sofa during the day.

Her sudden and feverish intensity of cheer transferred onto me. And I became obsessed with decorating my room in the spirit of Christmas. Specifically, I wanted my room to look like one of the displays at the mall. While my mother was tasteful and restrained, I filled my room with multiple strands of cheap blinking lights. They hung from the ceiling and dripped from my window and walls. I wrapped thick ropes of gaudy silver garland around my desk lamp, my bookshelf and around my mirror. I spent my allowance on two blinking stars that I hung on either side of my closet door. It was as if I had become infected with a virus of bad taste.

My mother insisted on the largest tree we could find at the Christmas tree farm. It had to be removed from the ground with a chain saw and then carried to the car by two burly men. When they roped it to the top of the Aspen, the car sank.

At home, the tree nearly reached the top of our seventeen-foot ceiling. And it was nearly as wide as the sofa.

My mother had it completely decorated in a matter of hours. There were balls nestled deep in the branches, silver bells placed above gold ribbons. It had everything, including popcorn and cranberry garlands she had hand-strung while watching *The Jeffersons.*

"Isn't this festive?" she asked, sweating profusely.

I nodded.

"We're going to make this a special Christmas. Even if your goddamn sonofabitch father can't bring himself to do anything but raise a glass to his lips."

She began to sing along with Angela Lansbury's warbling about dragging out the holly and throwing up the tree before my mood crashes and I want to kill myself, or however it went.

Two days before Christmas my brother came home. He was his usual, sullen self and when my mother asked him if he planned on staying for Christmas, he grunted and replied, "I don't know."

I, myself, had my own doubts about the coming holiday. Although there were already dozens of presents beneath the tree, I had not noticed a single one in the shape of the gift I most wanted: Tony Orlando and Dawn's *Tie a Yellow Ribbon 'Round the Old Oak Tree.* If I did not get this album, I had no reason to live. And yet there was nothing flat and square under the tree. There were plenty of puffy things—sweaters, shirts with built-in vests, the bell-bottom polyester slacks I loved, maybe a pair of platform shoes—but without that record, there might as well be no Christmas.

My mother must have sensed my feelings.

Because that evening, when my father came upstairs and made a comment about all the pine needles stuck in the carpet, my mother's brain chemistry mutated.

"Well, if that's the way everybody feels," she screamed, running into the living room, her blue Marimekko caftan flowing behind her, "then we'll just call the whole damn thing off."

I was astonished by her physical strength. What had taken two large men many minutes of concentrated effort to hoist on top of our brown station wagon, my mother was able to topple in a matter of seconds.

Tinsel, shattered Christmas balls and lights were smeared across the floor as she dragged the thing through the living room, out the deck door and straight over the edge.

I'd never seen such a display of physical strength from her before and I was impressed.

My brother snickered. "What's the matter with her?"

My father was angry. "Your damn mother's crazy is what's the matter."

My mother stormed back inside the house and swiped the needle off the record. She leaned over and began rummaging through the wooden captain's trunk where she kept her albums. When she found the record she was looking for, she placed it on the stereo, turned the volume up full blast and set the needle down.

I am woman hear me roar in numbers too big to ignore . . .

Hope comes into the TV room. "There anything left?" she says, pointing to the tree, meaning food.

"No," Natalie says, stuffing the bend of a candy cane in her mouth. "This is the last one."

"It figures," she says and walks away.

"I'm depressed now," Natalie says. "And fat."

Poo comes into the room. He goes to the tree looking for a snack. The tree has become the new refrigerator. Miraculously, he finds a chocolate Santa head in the back. How did it escape? He peels away the foil and pops it in his mouth. "What's up?" he says.

"Nothing," Natalie says, staring straight ahead at the TV.

Julie cracks a joke on TV and several of the passengers laugh.

Poo says, "You guys are boring," and goes away.

Hope comes back into the room, angry. "You know," she begins, "since you guys spend the most time in here, I really think you should take care of this tree problem."

We both turn and stare at her.

"Well, I do," she says.

Natalie says, "You want the Christmas tree out of here?"

"Yes. It's May, for crying out loud."

Natalie stands and reaches for the base of the tree. In one swift motion she yanks and the tree falls. Wordlessly, she drags the tree through the doorway down the hall and crams it into Hope's bedroom.

"Don't you dare do that, Natalie," Hope shouts.

But Natalie has done it. "Now it's your fucking problem."

As Natalie heads up the stairs Hope shouts after her, "If that's how you feel, maybe we shouldn't even have a Christmas this year. Maybe we should just cancel it."

I walk into the living room and sit at the piano to play the single song I know: "The Theme from *The Exorcist*."

That evening, the tree has found its way into the dining room. It is on its side beneath the bay window. Agnes is in the dining room with her broom, hunched over sweeping. She sweeps around the tree. She sweeps for hours. She sweeps until at sometime after midnight Hope comes into the room, groggy.

"Jesus, Agnes. I'm trying to sleep. Do you have to make such a racket?"

"Somebody's got to stay on top of things in this house," she says. "I'm just trying to hold it all together."

"Well, would you mind holding it all together in the morning? I need to be at Dad's office early."

"Just go back to sleep. I'm hardly making any noise at all."

"It's all your humming," Hope says. "At least stop that."

"I'm not humming."

"Yes you are, Agnes. I can hear you clean through the wall into my room. You're humming that damn 'Jingle Bells.' Jeepers, it's not even Christmas." Hope turns and goes back to her room.

Agnes resumes sweeping. "I wasn't humming," she mutters to herself. "These crazy kids."

The next morning as I look at the discarded tree, I am reminded of a turkey carcass. For some reason, Christmas trees and poultry bones have a difficult time finding their way out of this house.

Preparation for Thanksgiving may be an intense and focused event at this house, but cleanup is not. It's interesting that Natalie will go without sleep for two days straight; she will clean the entire house with a scrub brush; she will single-handedly prepare a feast for twenty; she will do this all without a murmur of complaint. But afterward, the dishes and pots and pans will remain unwashed for weeks. The turkey itself, now just a cage of bones, will be passed from room to room. It is not uncommon to see the turkey bones sitting on top of the television set one day and in the bathroom under the sink another. But never, ever will you see it in the trash.

I have found wishbones in that house that predate the Nixon administration. And drumsticks that could quite possibly be of interest to archaeologists.

Eventually, the pans will be washed, the glasses returned to their roach-infested cabinets, and the silverware scrubbed free of debris. But Christmas trees and turkey bones tend to stay awhile.

RUNNING WITH SCISSORS

Natalie had been out of clean clothes and too dysfunctional to wash a load, saying, "Oh, why bother? They'll just get dirty again." So for the third day in a row, she was wearing her polyester McDonald's counter girl uniform.

"Are you sure it's not illegal?" I asked her. If it was a crime to impersonate a police officer, couldn't it be a crime to walk around in public as a representative from the world's favorite fast food restaurant?

"It's perfectly legal. I *do* work there. Just not today."

Today, we happened to be on a whale watch, off the coast of Cape Cod. I was in cutoff jeans and a Fruit of the Loom T-shirt and Natalie was in her uniform because it was the only thing besides her bathing suit that she packed. "Aren't you hot in that thing?"

Natalie wiped her arm across her forehead. Her hair was pasted to the sides of her face with sweat. "Yeah, it's pretty hot. But it gets hotter at the restaurant, take my word for it."

I *had* to take her word for it, because I *didn't* work at McDonald's. And it wasn't fair. We'd been applying for the same jobs together forever, and neither of us had any experience. So why, finally, would they chose one and not the other? "Maybe they didn't like your sneaky eyes," was Natalie's in-depth analysis.

As a result, I had no money as usual, except a twenty Hope loaned me, and Natalie had a hundred and seventy-five dollars because she'd just received her first paycheck. So she was footing the bill for our little trip.

"Is that a whale?" Natalie said, squinting and pointing out to sea.

"It's just a lousy old garbage bag," the lady next to us offered. "I saw that five minutes ago. Took four goddamn pictures of it too, before I realized. Four perfectly good pictures, down the toilet. What am I going to do with four pictures of a trash bag? If we keep cruising through garbage, I won't have any film left when one of those fishes finally does show up."

We slid down the railing away from her. "Crazy old bitch," Natalie muttered under her breath.

"God, I hate old people," I said. "They're so senile. Why isn't she locked away in a nursing home?"

"She should be. I hope she falls overboard."

Natalie scanned the surface of the water looking for a whale. "I wish I had sunglasses. I left them in the room with my stupid earrings. I feel naked without my earrings."

"You look fine. I mean, nobody's going to notice that you're not wearing earrings. When you're wearing a McDonald's uniform."

"You know something? I hated this uniform at first, but now I like it." She did a deep knee bend. "It's the only thing I own that fits. I'm always ragging on Agnes for wearing polyester, but I have to say"—she did another knee bend and then a kick—"there's really something to be said for being able to move. I don't think I can go back to wearing jeans."

"Yeah, but you can't just wear that uniform everywhere. I mean, people will think you're a freak."

"No they won't," she snorted. "They'll think I'm a career girl who just got off from work."

"And decided to go on a whale watch?"

"Oh, these people don't even notice. They're all looking out there trying to see whales which are never gonna show up."

I reached into my back pocket and pulled out my pack of Marlboro Lights. I tried lighting a cigarette, but the wind kept blowing the match out. "Here, stand in front of me," I said. "Block the wind."

Natalie moved sideways, and I learned in close and struck a match.

"Hey, watch it," she said. "This uniform is flammable."

There was nothing better than fresh air, sunshine and a cigarette. "It's great out here. How come we don't take trips more often?"

"Because we never have any money. Besides, there's always some crisis or something back at the house that stops us."

"Yeah."

For awhile, we stared out at the ocean, not talking, just

looking. If there were whales out there, they sure weren't coming to visit our boat.

"Do you think they'd serve us beer?" Natalie asked.

"You mean inside?"

"Yeah."

"No."

"Why not? We look eighteen. It's worth a shot. There's
nothing to do out here, that's for sure."

We walked inside and felt immediate relief to be out of
the sun. There was a line at the snack bar, so we joined it.

"I could go for a hot dog," Natalie said.

"That's a good idea. Test the limits of your uniform."

"Fuck you."

"You wish."

"May I help you?" the girl at the counter asked. Then she
took a double-take at Natalie's *Introducing Chicken McNuggets!*
button and smirked.

"Two beers, whatever you have on tap."

The girl eyed us suspiciously, then turned around and
poured our beers. "Four dollars," she said.

Natalie gave her a five and I felt consumed with envy. She
had so many more fives than I did. The balance had shifted.
She was more powerful now.

"Here," Natalie said as we walked away.

We sat on a blue plastic bench near the window, watching
the people who were looking for whales.

"Look at that old man," Natalie said, motioning with her
head. "Isn't that sad?"

"What's sad about him?"

"Well, you know, just some old man all alone. God, I hope

I don't end up alone like that. Some pathetic old woman with nobody to go on a whale watch with."

"Oh, you won't," I said, swallowing. "You'll marry some Smith professor."

"Yeah, right," Natalie said. "If I'm lucky I'll marry a Smith janitor."

The boat heaved from side to side, something I hadn't noticed when we were standing outside. But now the sea was framed by the windows and the earth outside looked like it was drunk. "Do you ever get seasick?" I said.

Natalie belched. "Oh my God, excuse me," she giggled, still capable of finding burps and farts hysterical. A charming quality in a way.

"Do you?"

"Do I what? Get seasick? No. I don't think so. Just bored."

"You're bored?"

"Kind of. There's nothing to do out here. When we get back to shore, you wanna get lobsters?"

"Yeah."

"Sea roaches. That's what lobsters are. Roaches of the sea."

"Like tuna, the chicken of the sea."

"Chicken's a biological reptile, you know," she said.

"What do you mean?"

"I mean that biologically, chicken is a reptile. Instead of scales, they have feathers. But they both come from eggs."

"That's disgusting."

"Shit. I wish I'd remembered to bring my earrings." She touched her earlobe. "I hate it when I forget something. I don't ever want to forget anything."

"Remember it all."

"Yes," she said.

* * *

The Lobster Pot was touristy. The sign was a giant plastic red lobster wearing a bib. It was our kind of place.

"You need shoes," the waitress said when we walked in the door. She had frazzled blond hair with long dark roots. Her lips were wrinkled. She looked twenty going on fifty.

"We lost them," Natalie said.

I moved behind Natalie slightly. She was better than me at pulverizing her way through normalcy.

"Look guys," the waitress said, eyes darting across the room to check her tables, "I'm not allowed to serve you without shoes. You have to wear shoes here. It's like the law or whatever."

I watched a small boy at one of the tables frown at his father and sulk into the back of the booth. The father pointed at a napkin on the table; the boy shook his head no.

"Look, we'll just sit down and nobody will notice," Natalie said. "We'll give you a big tip."

The waitress was being mentally tugged away by her tables. People wanted water and butter and extra napkins and their checks. "Okay, fine. Just sit down."

Natalie turned to me and smiled. "See?"

It was like her McUniform had given her some sort of authority. "It would have been a bummer if they didn't let us in."

"No shit," she said, straightening her shirt.

We had taken our shoes off in the motel and decided not to put them back on. They felt confining.

We took a booth near the door. I slid in first and then

Natalie slid in on the same side. "Hey," I said. "Go sit on the other side."

"I wanna sit here." She looked at me and fluttered her eyelashes. "Next to you, my honey."

I shoved her. "C'mon, Natalie, there's not enough room. Move."

She slid up against me and pressed. I hated it when she got like that. She was in her fat mood. When she gets into a fat mood, she just wants to sit on everything. I laughed so that I didn't give her the satisfaction of knowing she'd pissed me off. "C'mon, move your ass to the other side and let's order."

She sighed dramatically. "Fine. Snobby Augusten doesn't want to sit next to his best friend in the whole world, Piggy Natalie." She slid out of the booth and sat across from me and I felt relief. Then I felt depressed because she was all the way across the table. "Come back and sit over here."

She leapt up, smacking the tops of her thighs on the underside of the table, and snuggled in against me. "That's better," she said.

When the waitress came over we ordered two lobsters and two Cokes. "And a side of fries," Natalie added at the last minute.

"What's going to become of us?" I said.

"We're going to eat lobster and get fatter and go home and be depressed and wish we could throw it up and . . ."

"No, I mean in the long term, you fool."

"Ho hum," she said, pouting. "Why do you always have to drag me back down to reality?"

"We can't just go on like this forever. I mean, look at us. You're seventeen, I'm sixteen and we're barefoot at a lobster place and that's basically all that's happening in our lives."

"I know," she said. "We have to do something. What do you want to be when you grow up? Are you still going to be a hairdresser to the stars?"

Without knowing why, I answered, "I'm going to run away to New York City and become a writer."

Natalie looked at me. "You should, you know. You're the writer in your family."

I laughed. "Oh, barf. I am not going to be a writer. I'd never even get into college."

"Sure you would," Natalie said. And the look on her face told me that she believed this completely and felt slightly sad that I didn't see it and believe it, too.

"Well, thanks."

"You underestimate yourself, you know."

The waitress brought our Cokes and we both slurped them without the straws. "How?"

"Because you've always been a writer. For as long as I've known you you've had that pointy nose of yours tucked into some notebook. You've lived with my family and noticed every single thing about us. God, it's spooky how good you are at imitating people."

"I can't be a writer," I said. "I don't even write. All I do is scribble stuff in notebooks. I don't even know what a verb is or how to type. And I never read. You have to read, like, Hemingway to be a writer."

"You don't have to read Hemingway, he's just some fat old drunk man," she said. "You just have to take notes. Like you do already."

"Well, I don't know. I'll probably end up as a male prostitute."

"You can't do that," she laughed. "Your ass is too skinny."

"Ha, ha. If only I had your ass."

"If you had my ass, you could rule the world."

"So what about you? What do you want to be when you grow up?"

"Maybe a psychologist or a singer."

"A psychologist or a singer?" I said. "How similar."

"Shut up," she said, slapping me on the arm. "I'm allowed to be two things. If you get to be a writer and be all those different people, then I get to be at least two things."

"You should do it, Natalie. Smith would definitely let you in. They'd be lucky to have you, you know."

"Oh, I don't know. It's not that easy."

"That's why you have to do it," I said.

"That's why you have to do it, too."

Natalie leaned in and put her elbows on the table. "Don't you ever just feel like we're chasing something? Something bigger. I don't know, it's like something that only you and I can see. Like we're running, running, running?"

"Yeah," I said. "We're running alright. Running with scissors."

Our food arrived and we both reached for the same sea roach at once.

"They were right here and now they're gone. The fucking maid stole my earrings."

"Are you sure?"

"I'm positive," Natalie said.

She'd already turned the motel room upside down looking for them; the sheets were all off the bed and wadded into a mound on the chair; the cushions of the chair were on the floor, the TV had been moved, all the mini soaps opened.

"Maybe you lost them someplace else."

"I didn't," she said with authority. "I'm absolutely positive that I left them right here next to the phone. I remember setting them down. Right here." She stabbed at the table next to the phone.

"So what are we gonna do?"

"We're gonna call the fucking manager and make him get them back."

I felt sick from the lobster and the fries.

Natalie called the front desk. She explained the situation to the person who answered and was then placed on hold. A new person came on the line and she explained the situation all over again. Then she screamed, "No, motherfucker, I did not lose them. I left them right here. Right next to the phone. My friend and I went on a whale watch and out to dinner and we came back and the room was clean and the earrings are gone. Can you call the maid at home and tell her to bring me my earrings please?"

Then she was listening. And I watched as her face transformed from annoyance to anger to rage to complete calm. Her foot stopped tapping a rhythm on the carpet. She hung up.

"So he says his maid didn't steal them. He says I lost them."

"Fuck," I said. "Oh well."

"Oh well?" She looked at me with her eyebrows raised. "What's that supposed to mean?"

"It means, oh well. No more earrings. It sucks, but that's life."

Natalie folded her arms across her chest, bunching her uniform under the arms. "You have a very bad attitude," she told me. "Haven't you ever heard the phrase, 'when life gives you lemons, make lemonade'?"

"What are you talking about?"

"Here," she said bending over and gripping the side of the mattress. "Help me with this thing."

"Huh?"

"Help me lift this fucking mattress. We're going to turn a negative situation into a fun situation."

We were able to ease the mattress into the swimming pool out front without making so much as a splash.

The television set, the chair and both nightstands didn't make much of a splash either.

"Hey motherfucker," Natalie screamed toward the front office of the motel. "I did like you said and looked everywhere and I still didn't find my earrings."

As the manager opened the door to see what all the shouting was about, Natalie and I tore off into the cool, salty Hyannis night. I grinned as I watched her sprint ahead of me, her long hair whipping behind her. Just your everyday McDonald's counter girl, on the run.

YOU'RE GONNA MAKE IT AFTER ALL

WHEN I WAS SEVENTEEN AND NATALIE WAS EIGHTEEN, WE moved into our own small apartment in South Hadley, Massachusetts. Natalie had enrolled in Holyoke Community College and the apartment was close to school. Inspired by her, I took—and passed—my GED exam. This wasn't difficult, as the questions were things like "Spell *cat*." Then I, too, enrolled in the community college.

As a pre-med student.

To pay my way, I applied for and received a slew of student loans and a Pell grant. Most of which I spent on new clothes and a 1972 Volkswagen Fastback that I chose not for mechanical soundness but because it didn't have any scratches and was showroom-shiny.

The best part about being a pre-med student was that my

laminated student I.D. stated my major: pre-med. I carried it in the front pocket of my jeans so that I could remove it throughout the day and gaze at it, reminding myself why I was there. When overwhelmed by a tedious microbiology lecture, I would simply pull out my I.D. card, look at my picture along with the words "Pre-med" and imagine myself at a future point in time double-parking my Saab convertible.

Natalie worked very hard, studying well past midnight each night. She was taking more advanced classes than I, so we didn't study for the same courses together. This meant that I was forced to study alone. Instead, I sat in my small bedroom and typed short stories on my manual typewriter for English class.

English 101 was mostly about the technicalities of language—verbs, adverbs, what's a split infinitive, what's a double negative. I found all of this mind-numbing, so instead, believing my professor would be thrilled, I wrote ten-page essays on such topics as *My Trip to the Depressing Mountain Farms Mall*, *Why Are There So Many Brands of Hair Conditioner?* and *My Childhood Was More Screwed Up Than Yours.*

By midterms, it seemed I was going to fail English class. As well as chemistry, anatomy, physiology, microbiology and even choral.

The only bright spot was that my English professor routinely wrote notes on my essays. "*Wonderful and strange, but this was not an assignment. If you could focus on the core materials in the course, I believe it would help your creative writing. You do show a flair.*"

My anatomy professor also took pity on me and called me into her office one afternoon after an exam.

"Close the door," she said, sliding off her faux tortoiseshell bifocals and resting them on top of her desk. She was a man-nish woman—handsome, with a fierce intelligence. In fact, she wrote the published textbook from which the class was taught.

I was certain she was going to inform me that I had a gift for science unlike any she'd ever seen. Perhaps she would tell me that I could skip community college and go straight to Harvard Medical School.

Instead, she picked up my exam from the pile of papers in front of her and read from it. "Augusten. On the test a ques-tion was asked: Identify the structure A. And you wrote, 'I believe this is a tibial tuberocity. But it could also be one of the foramans that I failed to memorize. Thank God for mal-practice insurance, huh?'"

I smiled at my witty answer.

She said, "Do you really want to be a doctor? Or do you want to play a doctor on a soap opera?"

At first, I thought this was a terrible insult. But then I saw her face, saw that she was not being nasty, merely asking an honest question. I said, "I really want the respect of a doctor. And I want the white jacket. And I want the title. *But . . .* I guess I really would like to have my own time slot opposite a game show."

"You seem to me," she said, leaning back in her swivel chair, "to have a very creative side. Why not *major* in some-thing creative? English? Or maybe theater?"

My shoulders slumped and my throat went dry. I felt de-feated. I explained that I was failing English. "I *would* like the writing part of English, but there's no writing in it. Except for the stuff I do on my own. It's all things I don't need. Like memorizing prepositional phrases. I don't need to memorize prepositional phrases. You'd think English would be about writing. But it's not."

"You have to learn a lot of things you may not want to learn, may not feel you need to know. Before English Composition there is English 101. It's a building process, you establish a foundation and then you build and build and build."

"I guess," I said. I knew she was right. And I knew that I was not cut out for school, even college. Ironically, I had been excited to go to college, but in order to be able to do it, I really needed study habits and knowledge I would have learned in high school.

Oops.

So I withdrew from school before the semester was out.

And a week after I withdrew, one evening when Natalie and I were in our little apartment, my mother called.

She said she needed to see me. That she would be over in an hour to pick me up.

"What? What's this about?" I asked.

"I'll tell you in person when I see you."

In the same way that a tornado rips the roof off a double-wide trailer, leaving the occupants dazed and staring at the clouds from the splinters of what used to be their living room, it was over.

"I am no longer going to have anything to do with Dr. Finch or any member of the Finch family." We were sitting in her car, the old brown Aspen station wagon. She was smoking a More and I was smoking a Marlboro Light. She looked calm, almost flat. And she didn't seem crazy.

"What are you talking about?" I noticed a suitcase on the

backseat and next to it her straw wide-brim hat.

"This has been building for many years, Augusten. There's much you don't know or understand about my relationship with Dr. Finch. But for years, he has been medicating me in a way that I have come to see as unhealthy and, well, very wrong."

"What?"

"And years ago, when I had that psychotic episode in New-port, do you remember?"

I nodded slowly, as if underwater. This was moving too fast and everything she was saying was a complete blur.

"He raped me in that motel room."

"*What!?*"

"The doctor has been controlling me, manipulating me emotionally and with drugs. He's a very sick man and I'm just now seeing this." She tossed her burned-down cigarette out the window and lit another. "I know this must come as a shock to you, but it's been building. I need to go away now, on my own, to do some thinking. He's very, very angry with me. I need to get away for awhile."

I felt deeply tricked. Stunned. And furious. I also felt my default emotion: numbness. "You know, I have to go back inside. I don't know what to make of any of this." I climbed out of the car but my mother reached for me.

"Please. Wait. I'm sorry, this must be extremely upsetting to you. It is to me. But I'm right about this, Augusten. He's a very dangerous man and I don't know why it's taken me so long to see that. I wish you'd—"

I pulled away, slammed the door and ran back upstairs to my apartment. When I came in the door, Natalie was standing in the center of the kitchen, looking at me. "I just got off the

phone with my father," she said. "Your mother has finally completely lost it."

I told Natalie what my mother told me. "Bullshit," she said.
"Augusten, your mother is a complete mental case. Look at
you. She just abandoned you when you were twelve, sent you
to live with my family. And you're going to believe *her?*"

"I don't know what to believe," I said.

"Believe *me*," she said. "I know my dad. I know he's a little
weird. Okay, a lot weird. But he's not sick or crazy. He'd never
rape your mother or drug her. That's absolute fucking
bullshit."

But I believed what my mother said. I believed it in my
guts. After all, more than once when I'd gone to his office
complaining of my general misery, he'd reached behind his
head and handed me the first sample bottle his fingers landed
on. Mellaril, Ativan, Valium, Librium, Lithium, Thorazine. I'd
taken them all as if they were candy corn. As for the rape,
well, Dr. Finch did seem like a pretty horny old fat man. I
thought back to his masturbatorium, his many "wives."

Natalie knew in which direction I was leaning. She could
sense it because she knew me so well. "Don't let her warp
your mind," she said.

"This is just so . . . shocking," I said.

"Yeah," she agreed sadly. "It's shocking alright."

The rest of that evening, we barely spoke. Something had
happened between us. Sides had been formed. Natalie wanted
me on her side. She wanted me to drive to her dad's house
in the morning, declare my loyalty, disown my crazy mother.
And my mother wanted . . . what? She wanted to be left

alone, I guess. She certainly didn't want me involved with the Finches anymore.

But Natalie was a Finch. And she was my best friend.

"It's going to be difficult for us," Natalie said just before we went to bed. "We're caught in the middle of this. It's going to be very hard to remain friends. This is big, Augusten. You're going to have to decide."

So it came to this: Was I a turd-reading Finch? Or was I my crazy mother's son?

In the end, I decided that I was neither.

In the middle of the night, without saying good-bye, without packing my things, I moved out of our apartment feeling like a spy, or rather an actor from daytime television *playing* a spy. I took my backpack and drove to Motel 6 where I spent the night.

I didn't call Natalie the next day. Or the day after that. I swam in the urine-tainted indoor pool and ate Cheese Nips from the vending machine. Natalie and I, we needed a little time apart, I figured, until this thing was sorted out. When I finally called her, she was very upset. "Where the fuck are you?" she said, furious.

"I'm staying at a motel. I needed to get away."

"My father is very upset with you. He feels that you're taking your mother's side in this. And he needs your support because he wants to have her committed to a hospital."

A creepy feeling spread over my arms. Like watching a horror movie and suddenly knowing the killer is upstairs hiding in the closet, has been there all along. "I don't think she needs to be committed to a hospital," I said.

"What motel are you at? We'll come and get you."

I hung up the phone.

That week, I found an affordable apartment located in a slum in Holyoke, Massachusetts. The top floor of the building was without windows, but at least I had hot water. And because I was accustomed to living with vermin, the mice didn't bother me.

I also found a job as a waiter at a Ground Round restaurant in Northampton that had just opened up.

"Hi, my name is Augusten and I'll be your server," was the only thing I needed to keep in my mind. I entered a period of sleepwalking. A low-intensity time where the worst thing that could happen to me was that I spilled French onion soup on my apron. I felt safe, even though the restaurant was in Northampton, because none of the Finches would go there. It wasn't within walking distance of the house.

In secret, my mother rented her own apartment in rural Sunderland, miles from the Finches. "Dorothy is under Dr. Finch's spell and there's nothing I can do to get her out of it," she told me in a phone call. Her girlfriend believed my mother was having a complete mental collapse and she was so upset, she was staying at the Finches' house. My mother arranged for a mover to clear all her things out of the apartment. When Dorothy returned to the house in Amherst, it was empty and my mother was gone.

I took an inventory of my life: I was seventeen, I had no formal education, no job training, no money, no furniture, no friends. "It could be worse," I told myself. "I could be going to a prom."

But there, glittering in the distance of my mind, was New York City. It seemed to me that New York was the place where misfits could fit.

Maybe Bookman had known this.

So I served patty melts and chicken salads and potato skins and whiskey sours. And I walked around in a trance, day-dreaming about Manhattan. Trying to see if I could picture myself there among the skyscrapers and hot dog vendors.

And I could see it.

I had no idea how I would ever get to New York or what exactly I would do once I arrived, but I knew that if I could save enough money to make it there for a week, somehow I'd figure out a way to stay.

And as I cleared Thousand Island dressing from the table with my rag, noticing that yet again I'd received only a fifty-cent tip, I understood one thing more clearly than I had ever understood anything before.

Of course I can make it in New York City. There's no way New York could be crazier than my life had been at the Finches' house in Northampton, Massachusetts. And I survived that. Unwittingly, I had earned a Ph.D. in *survival.*

I had a vision of Liza Minnelli in a black leotard singing, *"If I can make it there, I'll make it anywhere . . ."* and then tossing me a black top hat that I expertly catch and place on top of my head, astonishing all of Broadway with my debut in the stage version of *New York, New York.*

Running parallel to this vision was another in which I am crouched down in the back of a police cruiser parked on a side street in Greenwich Village. I am giving a blowjob to a fat cop on the verge of retirement. He waves ten dollars in my face and gasps, "Fifteen if you swallow."

Who knows?

In the opening sequence to *The Mary Tyler Moore Show*, Mary's in a supermarket, hurrying through the aisles. She pauses at the meat case, picks up a steak and checks the price. Then she rolls her eyes, shrugs and tosses it in the cart.

That's kind of how I felt. Sure, I would have liked for things to have been different. But, *roll of the eyes*, what can you do? *Shrug.*

I threw the meat in my cart. And moved on.

EPILOGUE

D<small>r.</small> **Finch** lost his license to practice medicine after the American Medical Association found him guilty on charges of insurance fraud. Despite this, many of his patients remained in treatment. He died from heart disease in 2000.

Agnes lives in a nursing home.

Natalie graduated from Holyoke Community College and applied to Smith. Not only was she accepted, she was accepted with a full scholarship. She graduated magna cum laude with a double major: psychology and voice. She later earned a post-graduate degree and works in the field of public health.

Hope continued to live at home and work for her father until the time of his death. She has since left the Northeast.

Fern, the minister's wife, is divorced and now lives in Sonoma,

California, where she runs a bookstore geared toward the recovery community.

Dorothy, my mother's former girlfriend, is married and has children. It is my understanding that her husband does not know of her past relationship.

Poo Bear sells RVs in Western Massachusetts. He is married and has children.

My mother lives alone in a small apartment on a river near the Massachusetts and New Hampshire border. Because of a major stroke, she is paralyzed on one side of her body and is dependant on aides. She continues to write poetry and has been published in a number of small disability and women's journals. We are estranged.

In 1998, **my father** was involved in a serious accident, rolling his Range Rover and breaking his neck. Although mobile, he retired from his position at the University of Massachusetts. Sober for more than twenty years, he leads a quiet life in the same town as my mother, though he lives there with his second wife of nearly twenty years.

My brother is divorced, lives with his longtime girlfriend and has a son. He owns a successful exotic car dealership in Springfield, Massachusetts. A few years ago, I sent him a Nikon as a gift. I had a hunch that he would enjoy taking pictures, safe behind the lens. This turned out to be true, and my brother is now enjoying a blossoming second career as a professional photographer.

Neil Bookman was never seen nor heard from again.

Read on for an excerpt from Augusten Burroughs's

Dry

Now available in paperback from Picador

JUST DO IT

Sometimes when you work in advertising you'll get a product that's really garbage and you have to make it seem fantastic, something that is essential to the continued quality of life. Like once, I had to do an ad for hair conditioner. The strategy was: *Adds softness you can feel, body you can see.* But the thing is, this was a lousy product. It made your hair sticky and in focus groups, women hated it. Also, it reeked. It made your hair smell like a combination of bubble gum and Lysol. But somehow, I had to make people feel that it was the best hair conditioner ever created. I had to give it an image that was both beautiful and sexy. Approachable and yet aspirational.

Advertising makes everything seem better than it actually is. And that's why it's such a perfect career for me. It's an industry based on giving people false expectations. Few people know how to do that as well as I do, because I've been applying those basic advertising principles to my life for years.

When I was thirteen, my crazy mother gave me away to her lunatic psychiatrist, who adopted me. I then lived a life of squalor, pedophiles, no school and free pills. When I finally escaped, I presented myself to advertising agencies as a self-educated, slightly eccentric youth, filled with passion, bursting with ideas. I left out the fact that I didn't know how to spell or that I had been giving blowjobs since I was thirteen.

Not many people get into advertising when they're nineteen, with no education beyond elementary school and no connections. Not just anybody can walk in off the street and become a copywriter and get to sit around the glossy black table saying things like, "Maybe we can get Molly Ringwald to do the voice-over," and "It'll be really hip and MTV-ish." But when I was nineteen, that's exactly what I wanted. And exactly what I got, which made me feel that I could control the world with my mind.

I could not believe that I had landed a job as a junior copywriter on the National Potato Board account at the age of nineteen. For seventeen thousand dollars a year, which was an astonishing fortune compared to the nine thousand I had made two years before as a waiter at a Ground Round.

That's the great thing about advertising. Ad people don't care where you came from, who your parents were. It doesn't matter. You could have a crawl space under your kitchen floor filled with little girls' bones and as long as you can dream up a better Chuck Wagon commercial, you're in.

And now I'm twenty-four years old, and I try not to think about my past. It seems important to think only of my job and my future. Especially since advertising dictates that you're only as good as your last ad. This theme of forward momentum runs through many ad campaigns.

A body in motion tends to stay in motion. (Reebok, Chiat/Day.)

Just do it. (Nike, Weiden and Kennedy.)

Damn it, something isn't right. (Me, to my bathroom mirror at four-thirty in the morning, when I'm really, really plastered.)

It's Tuesday evening and I'm home. I've been home for twenty minutes and am going through the mail. When I open a bill, it freaks me out. For some reason, I have trouble writing checks. I postpone this act until the last possible moment, usually once my account has gone into collection. It's not that I can't afford the bills—I can—it's that I panic when faced with responsibility. I am not used to rules and structure and so I have a hard time keeping the phone connected and the electricity turned on. I place all my bills in a box, which I keep next to the stove. Personal letters and cards get slipped into the space between the computer on my desk and the printer.

My phone rings. I let the machine pick up.

"Hey, it's Jim . . . just wanted to know if you wanna go out for a quick drink. Gimme a call, but try and get back—"

As I pick up the machine screeches like a strangled cat. "Yes, definitely," I tell him. "My blood alcohol level is dangerously low."

"Cedar Tavern at nine," he says.

Cedar Tavern is on University and Twelfth and I'm on

Tenth and Third, just a few blocks away. Jim's over on Twelfth and Second. So it's a fulcrum between us. That's one reason I like it. The other reason is because their martinis are enormous; great bowls of vodka soup. "See you there," I say and hang up.

Jim is great. He's an undertaker. Actually, I suppose he's technically not an undertaker anymore. He's graduated to coffin salesman, or as he puts it, "pre-arrangements." The funeral business is rife with euphemisms. In the funeral business, nobody actually "dies." They simply "move on," as if traveling to a different time zone.

He wears vintage Hawaiian shirts, even in winter. Looking at him, you'd think he was just a normal, blue-collar Italian guy. Like maybe he's a cop or owns a pizza place. But he's an undertaker, through and through. Last year for my birthday, he gave me two bottles. One was filled with pretty pink lotion, the other with an amber fluid. Permaglow and Restorative: embalming fluids. This is the sort of conversation piece you simply can't find at Pottery Barn. I'm not so shallow as to pick my friends based on what they do for a living, but in this case I have to say it was a major selling point.

A few hours later, I walk into Cedar Tavern and feel immediately at ease. There's a huge old bar to my right, carved by hand a century ago from several ancient oak trees. It's like this great big middle finger aimed at nature conservationists. Behind the bar, the wall is paneled in this same wood, inlaid with tall etched mirrors. Next to the mirrors are dull brass light fixtures with stained-glass shades. No bulb in the place is above twenty-five watts. In the rear, there are nice tall wooden booths and oil paintings of English bird dogs and anonymous grandfathers posed in burgundy leather wing chairs. They serve a kind of food here: chicken-fried steak, fish and chips, cheeseburgers and a very lame salad that features iceberg lettuce and croutons from a box. I could live here. As if I didn't already.

Even though I'm five minutes early, Jim's sitting at the bar and already halfway through a martini.

"What a fucking lush," I say. "How long have you been here?"

"I was thirsty. About a minute."

He appears to be eyeing a woman who is sitting alone at a table near the jukebox. She wears khaki slacks, a pink-and-white striped oxford cloth shirt and white Reeboks. I instantly peg her as an off-duty nurse. "She's not your type," I say.

He gives me this *how-the-hell-do-you-know* look. "And why not?"

"Look at what she's drinking. Coffee."

He grimaces, looks away from her and takes another sip of his drink.

"Look, I can't stay out late tonight because I have to be at the Met tomorrow morning at nine."

"The Met?" he asks incredulously. "Why the Met?"

I roll my eyes, wag my finger in the air to get the bartender's attention. "My client Fabergé is creating a new perfume and they want the ad agency to join them tomorrow morning and see the Fabergé egg exhibit as inspiration." I order a Ketel One martini, straight up with an olive. They use the tiny green olives here; I like that. I despise the big fat olives. They take up too much space in the glass.

"So I have to be there in a suit and look at those fucking eggs all morning. Then we're all going to get together the day after tomorrow at the agency and have a horrific meeting with their senior management. Some global vision thing. One of those awful meetings you dread for weeks in advance." I take the first sip of my martini. It feels exactly right, like part of my own physiology. "God, I hate my job."

"You should get a real job," Jim tells me. "This advertising stuff is putrid. You spend your days waltzing around the Met looking at Fabergé eggs. You make wads of cash and all you do is complain. Jesus, and you're not even twenty-five yet." He sticks his thumb and index finger in the glass and pinches the olive, which he then pops in his mouth.

I watch him do this and can't help but think, *The places those fingers have been.*

"Why don't you try selling a seventy-eight-year-old widow in the Bronx her own coffin?"

We've had this conversation before, many times. The undertaker feels superior to me, and actually is. He is society's Janitor in a Drum. He provides a service. I, on the other hand, try to trick and manipulate people into parting with their money, a disservice.

"Yeah, yeah, order us another round. I gotta take a leak." I walk off to the men's room, leaving him at the bar.

We have four more drinks at Cedar Tavern. Maybe five. Just enough so that I feel loose and comfortable in my own skin, like a gymnast. Jim suggests we hit another bar. I check my watch: almost ten-thirty. I *should* head home now and go to sleep so I'm fresh in the morning. But then I think, *Okay, what's the latest I can get to sleep and still be okay? If I have to be there at nine, I should be up by seven-thirty, so that means I should get to bed no later than*—I begin to count on my fingers because I cannot do math, let alone in my head—*twelve-thirty.* "Where you wanna go?" I ask him.

"I don't know, let's just walk."

I say, "Okay," and we head outside. As soon as I step into the fresh air, something in my brain oxidizes and I feel just the slightest bit tipsy. Not drunk, not even close. Though I certainly wouldn't attempt to operate a cotton gin.

We end up walking down the street for two blocks and heading into this place on the corner that sometimes plays live jazz. Jim's telling me that the absolute worst thing you can encounter as an undertaker is "a jumper."

"Two Ketel One martinis, straight up with olives," I tell the bartender and then turn to Jim. "What's so bad about jumpers? What?" I love this man.

"Because when you move their limbs, the bones are all broken and they slide around loose inside the skin and they make this sort of . . ." Our drinks arrive. He takes a sip and continues, ". . . this sort of rumbling sound."

"That's so fucking horrifying," I say, delighted. "What else?"

He takes another sip, creases his forehead in thought. "Okay, I know—you'll love this. If it's a guy, we tie a string around the end of his dick so that it won't leak piss."

"Jesus," I say. We both take a sip from our drinks. I notice that my sip is more of a gulp and I will need another drink soon. The martinis here are shamefully meager. "Okay, give me more horrible," I tell him.

He tells me how once he had a female body with a decapitated head and the family insisted on an open casket service. "Can you imagine?" So he broke a broomstick in half and jammed it down through the neck and into the meat of the torso. Then he stuck the head on the other end of the stick and kind of pushed.

"Wow," I say. He's done things that only people on death row have done.

He smiles with what I think might be pride. "I put her in a white cashmere turtleneck and she actually ended up looking pretty good." He winks at me and plucks the olive from my drink. I do not take another sip from this particular glass.

We have maybe five more drinks before I check my watch again. Now it's a quarter of one. And I really need to go, I'll already be a mess as it is. But that's not what happens. What happens is, Jim orders us a nightcap.

"Just one shot of Cuervo . . . for luck."

The very last thing I remember is standing on a stage at a karaoke bar somewhere in the West Village. The spotlights are shining in my face and I'm trying to read the video monitor in front of me, which is scrolling the words to the theme from *The Brady Bunch*. I see double unless I close one eye, but when I do this I lose my balance and stagger. Jim's laughing like a madman in the front row, pounding the table with his hands.

The floor trips me and I fall. The bartender walks from behind the bar and escorts me offstage. His arm feels good around my shoulders and I want to give him a friendly nuzzle or perhaps a kiss on the mouth. Fortunately, I don't do this.

Outside the bar, I look at my watch and slur, "This can't be right." I lean against Jim's shoulder so I don't fall over on the tricky sidewalk.

"What?" he says, grinning. He has a thin plastic drink straw behind each ear. The straws are red, the ends chewed.

I raise my arm up so my watch is almost pressed against his nose. "Look," I say.

He pushes my arm back so he can read the dial. "Yikes! How'd that happen? You sure it's right?"

The watch reads 4:15 A.M. Impossible. I wonder aloud why it is displaying the time in Europe instead of Manhattan.